IDEAS OF THE GREAT PSYCHOLOGISTS

About the Author

Samuel Smith received the degrees of A.M. and Ph.D. from New York University. He has held positions as research associate and director of research for state and federal programs of psychological testing and adult education, as research director and co-author of the National Achievement Tests, and as editor of the Dryden Press handbooks of psychology, educational psychology, sociology, and physics. He was formerly head of the Editorial Department of Barnes & Noble, Inc.

Dr. Smith is the author of *Best Methods of Study* (with Louis Shores and Robert Brittain) and of the text for *An Atlas of Human Anatomy* in the Barnes & Noble College Outline Series; a contributor to *Educational Psychology* and *Principles of Sociology,* also in the College Outline series; and author of *Read It Right and Remember What You Read* and *Ideas of the Great Educators,* two volumes in the Barnes & Noble Everyday Handbook Series. He is the education editor of Twayne Publishers' World Leaders series.

IDEAS OF
THE GREAT
PSYCHOLOGISTS

SAMUEL SMITH

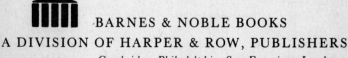

BARNES & NOBLE BOOKS

A DIVISION OF HARPER & ROW, PUBLISHERS

Cambridge, Philadelphia, San Francisco, London
Mexico City, São Paulo, Sydney

FIRST EDITION

Library of Congress Cataloging in Publication Data

Smith, Samuel, 1904–
   Ideas of the great psychologists.

   Includes index.
   1. Psychology—History. 2. Psychologists—History.
I. Title. [DNLM: 1. Psychology—History. 2. Psychology—Biography. BF 81
S659i]
BF81.S56 1983   150   82-48135
ISBN 0-06-015087-4   83 84 85 86 87 10 9 8 7 6 5 4 3 2 1
ISBN 0-06-463561-9 (pbk.)   83 84 85 86 87 10 9 8 7 6 5 4 3 2 1

CONTENTS

Preface   *xi*

1. PHYSICAL STRUCTURE   1

1 Hippocrates
4 Aristotle
5 Herophilus and Other Scientists
7 Galen
9 Early Modern Scientists
13 Müller
15 Cajal and von Waldeyer
15 Sherrington
17 The Phrenologists
17 Bain and Flourens
18 Broca
18 Fritsch, Hitzig, and Ferrier
19 James and McDougall
20 Freud
20 Cannon
21 Woodworth, Thorndike
22 Pavlov
   Pavlov and the Behaviorists
   Pavlov and the Gestalt Psychologists
   Pavlov vs. Lashley and Other Critics
26 Schools of Psychology

2. SENSATION, ATTENTION, PERCEPTION   28

29 Weber and Fechner
31 Helmholtz

Contributions to Physics
Researches on Vision and Hearing
Helmholtz and Hering
The Resonance Theory
Factors in Perception
37 Wundt
Wundt's Point of View
Experiments and Theories of Perception
Wundt's Analysis of Temperament
43 Titchener
46 Pillsbury
49 Dewey, Koffka, Watson
John Dewey
Koffka
Watson

3. HEREDITY AND ENVIRONMENT   54

54 Empedocles and Aristotle
55 Theophrastus and Lucretius
56 Early Modern Scientists
57 Nineteenth-Century Biologists
60 Galton, Pearson, Dugdale, Goddard
62 Twentieth-Century Scientists
65 Studies of Twins
Thorndike
Newman et al.
Wingfield
Kraepelin and Kallmann
Bouchard
69 Environmental Studies
Itard
Davis
Terman et al.
Eleanor and Sheldon Glueck
Jean Piaget
Other Recent Investigators

4. GROWTH AND DEVELOPMENT   79

80 Froebel, Preyer, Cooley, and Bühler
81 Comenius, Rousseau, and Piaget
82 Granville Stanley Hall
85 Thorndike, Dewey, Watson, and Judd
90 Freud and Fromm
90 Rank, Allport, and Erikson
92 Adler, Mowrer, Kluckhohn, Horney, Sullivan
93 Gesell and Other Child Psychologists

5. INDIVIDUAL DIFFERENCES, TESTS, AND
MEASUREMENTS   100

101 Galton, Pearson, Stern, Cattell, and Farrand
104 Ebbinghaus, Binet, and Terman
108 Kuhlmann, Pintner, Arthur, and Goodenough
110 Porteus, Marie, Graham, and Kendal
111 Wechsler
112 Group Tests by Yerkes, Otis, Terman, Pintner
115 Spearman, Thorndike, and Thurstone
118 Tests of Aptitudes and Interests
122 Personality Tests
128 Achievement Tests
130 Achievement Test Series

6. ACTION, MOTIVATION, AND ADJUSTMENT   133

133 Wundt
134 Titchener
135 Thorndike
136 Kraepelin
138 James
141 McDougall, Woodworth, Dewey, Freud
145 Adler, Lewin, Cannon, Jung, Pillsbury, et al.

7. EMOTIONS   152

153 Herbart, Henle, Fechner, Ribot
155 Darwinian Scientists
157 McDougall

157 James, Lange
159 Cannon, Dana, Bard, Crile, Carlson
161 Psychosomatic Disorders
163 Wundt and Titchener
164 Woodworth, Carr, Dewey
166 Watson and Coghill
168 Janet, Breuer, Freud, Rank, Erikson, Fromm
170 Adler, Jung, Pillsbury, and Others

8. MEMORY, IMAGINATION, AND DREAMS   173

173 Plato and Aristotle
175 Quintilian, Saint Augustine, Maimonides, Aquinas
175 British Associationists
179 Ebbinghaus
182 George Elias Müller
183 McGeoch
184 James, Dewey, Angell, Seashore, Woodrow
186 Woodworth and Thorndike
188 Pillsbury
190 Titchener
191 Pavlov
192 Watson and Skinner
194 Gestalt Psychologists
195 Piaget
196 Bartlett, Zeigarnik, Ballard, John, Hubel, et al.
198 Freud et al.

9. LEARNING AND REASONING   201

201 Socrates, Plato, Aristotle
202 Cicero, Lucretius, Quintilian
203 Christian Church Leaders
204 Humanists
204 Loyola, Mulcaster, Bacon, Locke
207 Wundt, Judd, James, McDougall
208 Thorndike
212 Pavlov, Watson, Skinner
216 Dewey

217 Gestalt Psychologists
218 Piaget

10. PERSONALITY AND CHARACTER   220

220 Hippocrates, Plato, Aristotle, Theophrastus
223 Bacon, Locke, Rousseau, Fourier, Owen, Kant
226 Müller, Henle, Meumann, Fouillée
226 John Stuart Mill, Bain, McDougall
227 Stern, Scheler
228 James
229 Lombroso, Kretschmer, Sheldon
231 Jaensch, Spranger, G. W. Allport, Goldstein
234 Behaviorists
235 Psychoanalysts
236 Existentialists
237 Pillsbury

11. MENTAL ILLNESS   240

240 Hippocrates, Plato, Asclepiades, Celsus, Aretaeus, Galen
242 Alexander of Tralles, Avicenna, Averrhoës
243 Paracelsus, Agrippa, Weier, Scott, Saint Vincent
     De Paul, Sydenham
246 Tuke, Conolly, Pinel, Esquirol, Seguin
248 Muller, Chiarugi, Rush, Beers
250 Mesmer, Braid, Charcot, Liébeault, Bernheim, Janet
254 Von Haller, Griesinger, Meynert, Morel, Magnan
255 Kraepelin, Bleuler, Wagner-Jauregg
259 Trotter, Kretschmer, Schilder, Alzheimer, Bender
260 Meyer
262 Cameron, Malinowski, Benedict, Faris, Horney
263 Rogers, Thorne, Moreno, Klein, Anna Freud
265 Watson, Skinner, Rolf, Perls, Beck
266 Sigmund Freud
268 Jung
269 Berger, Moniz, Freeman, Watts, Poole
270 Sakel, Von Meduna, Cerletti, Bini

12. PSYCHOLOGY IN MODERN SOCIETY   272

272 Spencer, Spranger, McDougall, Freud
276 Dewey, Mead, Parsons, Weber, Watson, Skinner
278 Bernheim, Le Bon, Tarde, Dewey, Sidis, Thorndike, Piaget
281 Bekhterev, Cooley, Simmel, Durkheim, Lewin, Riesman
284 Blumer, Boas, Benedict, Mead, Klineberg, Clark, et al.
286 Doob, Thurstone, Miller, A. M. Lee, E. B. Lee
291 Taylor, Mayo, Münsterberg, Burtt, Dichter
294 Park, McKenzie, Barker, et al.

Index 297

PREFACE

This handbook is designed as a brief introduction to the principal fields of psychology from a historical perspective. It describes the contributions of great psychologists to the study of human behavior from the earliest times to the present stage of research and experimentation. The presentation of important discoveries and theories is chronological in order to illuminate the progress of psychology and its status today as an experimental science.

Frequently as I was engaged in the task of writing this volume from an eclectic point of view, I felt deeply grateful to the leading psychologists, philosophers, and educators with whom it was my privilege to be associated as student, coauthor, and editor during more than a half century of professional activity, especially William McDougall, William Ernest Hocking, Walter Bowers Pillsbury, Rudolf Pintner, Paul Rankov Radosavljevich, Douglas Fryer, Herman Harrel Horne, Charles E. Skinner, Paul V. West, Robert E. Park, and Walter J. Coville. Some of their diverse views have found an echo in this volume.

I wish to thank the Department of Manuscripts and University Archives of Cornell University for biographical information about Edward Bradford Titchener, and the Bentley Historical Library of the University of Michigan for informative autobiographical notes of Walter Bowers Pillsbury.

I am indebted to Nancy Cone and Jeanne Flagg, editors at Barnes & Noble Books, for indispensable suggestions concerning the organization and contents of the handbook and for expert editorial emendations; and to Peggy Fagin, who patiently evaluated the text and recommended alterations that improved the presentation.

1 PHYSICAL STRUCTURE

Mental and emotional experiences can be explained only with reference to the physical mechanisms that make them possible. For this reason, psychologists during their researches must take into account the facts provided by biological sciences concerning those bodily structures and functions that affect the mental and emotional life of the individual.

Significant conclusions about the relationships between physical structures and psychological experiences were formulated in ancient times by great thinkers, such as Hippocrates, Plato, Aristotle, and Galen, and in modern times by pioneering scientists, such as Johannes Peter Müller, Sir Charles Scott Sherrington, and Ivan Petrovich Pavlov. The ideas and findings of these and many other philosophers and scientists concerning physical structures and psychological functions enabled modern experimental psychologists to carry out important studies of sensation, attention, perception, growth and development, motivation, and other aspects of human behavior.

HIPPOCRATES

Hippocrates, often called the father of medicine, introduced a new method of inquiry (careful observation and the collection and interpretation of facts) into the physical, mental, and emotional reactions of individuals. His point of view represented a revolutionary advance over the faith of ancient peoples in magic, superstition, and supernatural powers as the determinants of human nature, conduct, and destiny. The early Greeks and Romans, who rejected the animistic beliefs of primitive man, still adhered to polytheistic doctrines of ancient Babylonians and

1

Egyptians, but Greek philosophers and mathematicians—such as Thales, Pythagoras, and Anaxagoras—developed rational nonreligious theories about natural phenomena. Only Hippocrates, however, pioneered in applying systematic observation of facts to the study of human nature and experience.

Hippocrates was born on the Greek island of Cos (southwest of Asia Minor) in a family of priests and physicians (ca. 460–377 B.C.). He was educated at a famous school in Cos and later received training in medical skills from his father and another leading practitioner, Herodius of Selymbria. He studied under two of the foremost philosophers of antiquity: the Sophist Gorgias of Leontini in Sicily, a nihilist and skeptic who declared that no such thing as truth exists; and Democritus of Abdera (in southwestern Thrace), who formulated an atomic theory based on the unique concepts of his predecessor Leucippus of Abdera.

Practicing medicine in Athens and in other Greek centers, Hippocrates acquired remarkable proficiency in the diagnosis, prognosis, and treatment of diseases. He kept detailed records, which describe cases of arthritis, hysteria and epilepsy, mumps, tuberculosis, and other ailments. From his observations and records, he concluded that physical, mental, and emotional disorders are caused by such factors as organic injury, inherited susceptibility, and an imbalance of secretions and fluids in the body. He cited case studies to prove his theory that good health and good personality depend on the proper proportions of four body fluids or "humors": blood, phlegm, black bile, and yellow bile. He attributed an overly enthusiastic or sanguine temperament to excessive blood; an indifferent, phlegmatic temperament to phlegm; a depressed, melancholy temperament to black bile; and an aggressive, choleric temperament to yellow bile. He declared that it was the duty of the physician to restore and maintain the normal balance of the four body fluids. For the diagnosis of emotional disorders, he suggested (just as Sigmund Freud did in the twentieth century) that the patient's dreams should be analyzed to identify the roots of the difficulty. His famous Hippocratic oath set forth high standards of professional conduct applicable to the work of modern psychiatrists and clinical psychologists, including the obligation to keep information about patients confidential, to protect their interests, to devote every possible effort to cure them, and to be generous, honest, and compassionate in relationships with them.

The observations and conclusions of Hippocrates had immense influence on innumerable philosophers, scholars, and scientists throughout ancient, medieval, and modern times. During the Middle Ages, however, orthodox Christian Fathers, including Saint Augustine (A.D. 354–430), condemned physicians and anatomists, especially those who, unlike Hippocrates, practiced dissection of the dead, for their attempts to pry into secrets of the human body. Saint Augustine declared that knowledge of God and the soul was the only worthy goal of mankind, a dictum that weakened the progress of science in medieval times. However, he advocated the use of introspection (the method of attending to and recalling mental experiences) as the best means to discover causes of psychological disturbances, thus making a contribution to the study of emotions and personality. Hippocrates had depended mainly on his observation of patients, not on their introspective impressions. His conclusions about the contralateral results of brain injuries, his analyses of brachial palsy, facial neuralgia, hysteria (which most Greeks attributed to disease in the womb), sepsis, and spinal injuries resulting in paralysis, and his ideas about man's affective life found their way into the principal medical textbooks of medieval times and, notwithstanding numerous errors, retain a measure of validity or utility even today.

Eminent scholars and scientists in modern times acknowledged their indebtedness to Hippocrates. René Théophile Hyacinthe Laënnec, the French physician who invented the stethoscope in 1819, stated that he owed the basic idea to Hippocratic works. The theory of the four humors, though modified or rejected by psychologists, has consistently had repercussions upon language and literature, as seen, for example, in Burton's *Anatomy of Melancholy* (1621) and Shakespeare's plays. The French scholar Nicolas de Malebranche in the seventeenth century, the German anatomist Friedrich Gustav Jacob Henle in the nineteenth century, and the American psychologist William James in the twentieth century associated temperaments and the emotions with glandular secretions or similar causes. The psychologists Sir Charles Scott Sherrington, Ernest Kretschmer, and William H. Sheldon likewise formulated classifications of personality based on the physical characteristics of individuals.

ARISTOTLE

The idealist Greek philosopher Plato (427–347 B.C.), disciple of Socrates and teacher of Aristotle, made a sharp distinction between mind and body, a distinction accepted ever since by many psychologists. Plato concluded, moreover, that physical entities are only fleeting appearances, whereas ideas in the mind are everlasting, universal, and real. He regarded both mental and physical reactions as functions of the soul and attributed thought processes to the brain, will and courage to the heart, and appetite to the liver. He anticipated some aspects of Freudian psychology, as in formulating an interpretation of dreams and discussing, but unlike Sigmund Freud condemning, catharsis as a method of working off excessively strong emotions or passions.

Aristotle (384–322 B.C.) noted regretfully that Plato, seemingly ignoring the reality of concrete things, had turned away from the atomic theories of Democritus. Aristotle criticized Democritus, however, for his exclusive emphasis on physical structure and declared that living things have souls, which give them power to move, reproduce, and fulfill their desires and purposes. His *De Anima* was the first systematic treatise on psychology.

The divergent ideas of ancient philosophers persisted throughout medieval and later times in a controversy still evident in the conflicting views of two groups of modern experimental psychologists: (1) those who, like Pavlov, John Broadus Watson, and Burrhus Frederic Skinner, believe that physical structure controls human behavior entirely, and (2) those who, like William McDougall and Wolfgang Köhler, insist that purposive action, desire, and ideas are just as potent as physical structure.

Aristotle noted the emotional consequences of desires and ideas, but in the main accepted the view of Hippocrates—similar in some respects to the modern concepts of William James and Carl Georg Lange—that bodily conditions or changes create or constitute the emotions. Thus he declared that anger may be attended by little or no mental action and must therefore be attributed chiefly to the overheating of the blood around the heart. (Note our references today to hot-blooded anger.) He agreed with Hippocrates that mental illnesses stem from physical causes, a statement considered true throughout the Middle Ages. Among Aristotle's numerous errors in biology and psychology, one that prevailed for fifteen hundred years in the history of Western civilization was his conclusion that the heart, not the brain, was the main organ of sense experience. The primary function of the brain, he said, was to reduce excessive heat in the body. He rejected Plato's view of the brain as the seat of perception, with the heart as the center of will and spirit. (Aristotle's erroneous conclusion was accepted universally until late in the thirteenth century, when the anatomist Peter of Albano of the University of Padua and other Italian scientists identified the brain as the central organ of the nervous system, and the heart as the central organ of blood circulation.)

Aristotle mistakenly attributed fetal growth in part to connections between the blood cells of the mother and those of the fetus. On the other hand, he dissected numerous animals, and his remarkably correct observations about their physical structure were praised by the French naturalist Baron Cuvier, founder of modern comparative anatomy, and by the British naturalist Charles Darwin, famous for his theory of evolution.

HEROPHILUS AND OTHER SCIENTISTS

Following the deaths of Hippocrates and Aristotle, several renowned medical scientists in Greece and Egypt made significant contributions to the investigation of physical structure and human behavior.

The Greek surgeon and experimental physiologist Herophilus (b. 344 B.C.) conducted a school of anatomy at Alexandria that corrected serious errors in the conclusions of Hippocrates and Aristotle. On the basis of post-mortem examinations, Herophilus asserted that the brain, not the heart, is the main organ of neural reactions and even traced the actions of muscles to motor nerves in the brain and spinal cord. Another famous Alexandrian anatomist, Erasistratus (ca. 300–250 B.C.), is credited with similar discoveries about the veins, arteries, membranes, heart valves, cranial nerves, sensory and motor nerves (between which he clearly differentiated), and numerous features of the brain and other bodily structures. Erasistratus, however, accepted the popular erroneous notion that the arteries contained air.

The work of these and other Alexandrian medical scientists was facilitated by liberal Egyptian governments that permitted them to dissect the human body and describe its parts, relationships, and functions. The first three Ptolemies, rulers of Egypt for a century (from 323 to 221 B.C.), encouraged anatomical and medical research and wide dissemination of scientific information. But for one thousand years thereafter, both in Egypt and in Greece, only occasional advances in the study of physical structures were achieved, while myths, factual errors, and gross misconceptions gained credence and prevailed. For a millennium there were but few noteworthy contributors to medical science, the most prominent being Celsus; Aretaeus of Cappadocia; Dioscorides of Anazarbus, Asia Minor; Rufus of Ephesus; and Galen of Pergamum.

In the first century A.D., the Roman author Aulus Cornelius Celsus wrote a multivolume work on medicine, *De Medicina,* that reflected his considerable knowledge of anatomy and discussed in great detail health and hygiene, symptoms and treatment of mental illnesses, diseases of internal organs, and surgical procedures. He wrote about paralysis (resulting from fractures of the spinal cord), epilepsy, apoplexy, migraine, and facial neuralgia. His comments on the auditory apparatus indicate acquaintance with the semicircular canals of the ear. His manuscript, after being lost for many centuries, was found and printed in the fifteenth century, when it contributed substantially to the revitalization of the biological sciences.

Like Celsus, the Greek physician Aretaeus (first or second century A.D.) wrote descriptions of hysteria, epilepsy, paralysis, migraine, and other common diseases, evincing extensive knowledge about physical structures. He associated various mental illnesses with hereditary susceptibility, maladjustments in the brain, and disorders of internal organs—a point of view adopted by twentieth-century adherents to psychosomatic medicine who believe that every psychic experience seeks bodily expression. He regarded insanity as an exaggeration of normal tendencies and reactions.

The Greek surgeon Pedanius Dioscorides (ca. A.D. 40–80) was famous for his five-volume guide to medicines derived from plants, *De Materia Medica,* which contained information accepted widely by physicians for over one thousand years. Although perhaps one hundred of the botanical medications he described are still regarded as useful, hundreds of others possess little or no curative value. Nevertheless, his writings established a precedent for modern medical and pharmaceutical reference works. Dioscorides traveled extensively and gathered from many European countries botanical specimens reported to have been used successfully by physicians. His works helped to sustain interest in biological and medical studies throughout medieval and early modern times.

Another noted Greek physician, Rufus of Ephesus (ca. A.D. 100), described the human brain, discussing its large size, gray areas, and extensions, including connections from the cerebellum to other parts of the brain and to the eyes. He discriminated between sensory and motor nerves, and he reported on his experiment of producing loss of consciousness through compression of the carotid arteries.

GALEN

The most prolific and influential medical author following the death of Hippocrates was the Greek physician Claudius Galen (ca. A.D. 129–199), who merits high praise for his experimental investigations and summaries of contemporary knowledge but has been severely criticized for the perpetuation of erroneous conclusions and metaphysical theories about physical structure and its relation to human behavior. His extensive writings became dominant, authoritative sources of information in biology, psychology, and medicine throughout the Middle Ages.

Galen, a native of Pergamum (in Asia Minor), was educated

by his father, an erudite mathematician and scientist who tutored him in major fields of learning, emphasizing especially the philosophical and scientific works of Aristotle. Beginning in his late teens and for a decade thereafter, Galen concentrated on the study of anatomy and physiology, traveling widely to receive instruction in these subjects from eminent teachers in cities of Asia Minor and in Alexandria. He returned to Pergamum and served as a physician to injured gladiators, in which capacity he earned a high reputation for extraordinary skill. Later he settled in Rome and enjoyed immense prestige as personal physician to the Roman emperors Marcus Aurelius (r. A.D. 161–180.) and Commodus (r. A.D. 180–192).

In his authoritative treatises, Galen recapitulated the principal discoveries and ideas of Hippocrates. He experimented on animals such as monkeys, carefully delineating their physical structures. He described correctly muscles of the eyes, jaw, head, neck, larynx, and extremities, but concluded incorrectly that the heart is not a muscle, being misled by its hardness and continuous movement. He assigned the origins of sensory nerves to the brain and the origins of motor nerves to the spinal cord. He described in detail the parts of the animal brain, noting the membranes, blood vessels, cranial nerves, and ventricles; the internal organs, including the kidneys, liver, and digestive, urinary, and reproductive organs; and, with considerable accuracy, the bones of the cranium and thorax, the ribs and vertebrae, and the bones and joints of the extremities. He asserted that the arteries were filled with blood, contradicting the dogma that they contained only air. He declared that the brain was the main repository of the intelligent spirit or soul.

As Hippocrates had done, Galen diagnosed cases of tuberculosis, gout, and other major diseases; and, like Dioscorides, he treated patients by prescribing diverse botanical medications, such as opium. He tracked down the effects of spinal injuries and severed nerves upon sensory and motor reactions, noting, for example, the loss of sensation, the impairment of movement, and the contralateral paralysis of limbs. He attributed mental illness to both physical and psychological factors, citing as causes the excessive ingestion of alcohol, brain injuries, and shocking life experiences. But his metaphysical ideas (which were adopted widely in medieval times) about divine influences on body organs and illnesses retarded progress in biology for centuries.

Galen's assumption that physical structures and functions of animals are identical with those of human beings also led him astray and saddled medieval medical disciplines with a great deal of misinformation. His psychology of the passions, based on the erroneous Hippocratic theory of the four humors, became popular in European countries during the Renaissance as a mechanistic explanation of human emotions and behavior. Nevertheless, his numerous writings, of which about one hundred treatises have survived, represented the peak achievements of the ancient Greeks and Romans in biology and the medical sciences.

EARLY MODERN SCIENTISTS

Scientific investigation of physical structure and human behavior was revitalized during the sixteenth and seventeenth centuries. Beginnings had been made, however, in the thirteenth, fourteenth, and fifteenth centuries, particularly by Italian medical scientists such as Peter of Albano (ca. 1250–1316) in Padua, Mondino de' Luzzi (1275–1326) in Bologna, and Achillini (1463–1512) in Bologna. Italian physicians dissected the human body and, despite errors in some analyses, carefully described the structures of the heart, noting the phenomenon of blood circulation; the various digestive organs; the dura mater and ventricles of the brain; the bones of the ear; and the optic and ocular nerves.

Early in the sixteenth century, the Swiss physician Paracelsus (Theophrastus Bombastus von Hohenheim, 1493–1541) of Basel and Salzburg rejected the concept of the four humors as well as many other conclusions of Hippocrates and Galen. He asserted that the human body and its ills were chemical in nature, that mental disorders had definite natural causes, and that magnetic forces within the body had potent effects on its structures and functions, a theory akin to that of modern hypnotism. Because of his insistence on lecturing in German instead of Latin, his novel theories, and his candid criticisms of medical and public authorities, Paracelsus was forced to give up his teaching at the University of Basel. However, his spectacular career and his extraordinary success in treating apparently incurable patients stimulated wide interest in new experimental investigations and in chemical means of therapy.

Among other notables during the sixteenth century, the great Italian anatomist Berenger (Berengario) of Carpi and Bologna wrote treatises reporting significant findings based on his dissections of scores of bodies. He described epithelial, connective, muscle, and nerve tissues; arteries and veins; the pituitary and pineal glands; the parts of the inner eye; and other structural features in a well-organized, systematic presentation comparable with the reports of twentieth-century specialists.

The famous Flemish scientist Andreas Vesalius (1514–1564) taught anatomy at the universities of Padua, Bologna, and Pisa. He insisted on the necessity for post-mortem dissections in research (a practice for which he was condemned by the Church), vastly improved upon the discoveries of preceding investigators, and developed an inclusive anatomical description of the entire human organism. The surgeon Costanzo Varoli (ca. 1543–1575) of Bologna traced the fibers of what was named after him the pons Varolii in the brain and the role of the optic nerves. The surgeon Hieronymus Fabricius (1537–1619) achieved fame for describing the valves in veins as well as for teaching the English physician William Harvey, who is credited with discovering the system of blood circulation. (Harvey analyzed the system as one of circular movement whereby blood flows away from one side of the heart through the aorta and other arteries, then flows to body tissues, and finally returns to the other side of the heart through the veins.)

Another English physician, Thomas Willis (1621–1675), personal physician to King Charles II and founder of the British Royal Society, described an interconnecting group of arteries (known as the circle of Willis) located at the base of the brain; he also described structural details of the lungs, glands, and intestines. Willis performed numerous operations on animals, the results of which led him to conclude that perception and other psychological functions are localized in specific parts of the brain.

The invention of the compound microscope by Zacharias Jensen in 1591 greatly facilitated progress in the study of physical structure. The British experimentalist Robert Hooke (1635–1703) used his own improved microscope in 1667 to observe the cellular nature of organic tissue. Italian anatomist Marcello Malpighi (1628–1694) discovered, with the aid of the microscope, that blood flows through capillaries from arteries to veins, a phenomenon that Harvey had failed to notice. In 1671 Malpighi described the cells and physiology of plants, the capillaries, skin, and kidneys, the tissues of the lungs, and structures and nerves in the spinal cord and brain.

The eighteenth-century Swiss anatomist, surgeon, and poet Albert Haller (Albrecht von Haller, 1708–1777), professor of medicine at the University of Göttingen, stated correctly that the conduction of neural impulses results in muscular reactions exhibiting irritability and contractility. Italian anatomist Antonio Scarpa (1747–1832), professor of anatomy at the universities of Modena and Padua, contributed information about the ear, nerve ganglia, and nerve plexuses. German anatomist Samuel Thomas von Sömmering (1755–1830) delineated the cranial nerves and wrote pioneering volumes on various aspects of human anatomy, including a remarkable comprehensive summary volume edited by F. G. J. Henle (1809–1885), who himself investigated the kidney tubules; skin derivatives such as the mammary glands, hair, and nails; and physical causes of numerous common diseases. British physician Thomas Young (1773–1829) investigated the mechanism of the eyes and pioneered in the analysis of astigmatism, color perception, and the wave nature of light; by using a botanical microscope, he discovered that accommodation of the eye to the distances of objects depends on changes in the curvature of its crystalline lens resulting from contractions of the ciliary muscles. The foremost physiologist of the nineteenth century, Johannes Peter Müller, laid the foundations of the modern science of physiology and taught several pioneers in this field, including Helmholtz and Emil Du Bois-Reymond.

German anatomist Theodor Schwann (1810–1882), the discoverer of pepsin (the catalytic enzyme that aids the digestion of proteins), corroborated Heller's conclusions about the irritability

and contractility of muscle tissues. In 1839, about 170 years after Robert Hooke had described cells in living organisms,
Schwann and the German botanist Matthias Jakob Schleiden
(1804–1881) stated the theory that all living things consist of
cells. German pathologist Rudolf Virchow (1821–1902), investigator of circulatory diseases such as leukemia and phlebitis, declared that new cells are continually being generated in the human body to replace preexisting cells. In 1861 Max Johann
Sigismund Schultze (1825–1874) promulgated his classic doctrine that the body consists of protoplasm, the living substance in
plants and animals, a concept also suggested by the noted Czech
physiologist Johannes Evangelista Purkinje (1787–1869). (In
1851 Schultze had discovered the presence of chlorophyll in animal tissues.) Many biologists contributed to the ever-expanding
storehouse of knowledge about body cells in relation to the
mechanisms of heredity. (The contributions of Darwin, De
Vries, Mendel, and other pioneers are discussed in chapter 3,
pages 57–60.)

Investigations of physical structures in relation to the nervous
system progressed rapidly in the nineteenth and twentieth centuries. Although Erasistratus had differentiated sensory from motor nerves, it was not until about two thousand years later that
the Scottish anatomist and surgeon Sir Charles Bell (1774–
1842) in 1811 and the French experimental physiologist François Magendie (1783–1855) in 1822 proved that the common
belief in the combined sensory and motor functions of each nerve
was wrong and that Erasistratus was right. Another famous
nineteenth-century French physiologist, Pierre Jean Marie
Flourens, experimenting on pigeons, discovered that the cerebrum of the brain controls reflex actions as well as voluntary
movements. During the nineteenth and twentieth centuries, a
great number of scientists accumulated significant information
concerning the nerves, nervous systems, brain, and sense organs.

Among the most productive early studies were those by the
Italian physicists Luigi Galvani (ca. 1737–1798) and Count
Alessandro Volta (1745–1827), both of whom in the 1790s applied electrical currents to nerves in order to stimulate muscle
movements; and those by the British physician Marshall Hall

(1790–1857), who discovered reflexes (unlearned, involuntary reactions to stimuli) in 1832.

MÜLLER

The most influential of the nineteenth-century scientists who contributed basic information about physical structure and human behavior was the German physiologist Johannes Peter Müller, justly honored as the father of modern physiology.

Müller was born in Coblenz in 1801. During his teens, he studied at Bonn University, displaying such excellence in the biological sciences that he was eventually employed as a lecturer in physiology, earning a salary from tuition fees paid by his students. Within a few years, he became a professor of physiology, experimenting and teaching in the university until he accepted an appointment as professor of anatomy at the University of Berlin, where he continued his experiments (especially in comparative anatomy) and teaching until his death in 1858.

The most important of Müller's numerous publications was his *Handbook of Human Physiology* (1833–1840), consisting of reports and discussions of every major aspect of physical structure. In 1841, with his famous associate Henle, he issued a treatise summarizing the relationships between anatomical structures and the major diseases of mankind, a subject he had also emphasized in his own handbook. Henle, who assisted Müller's experiments by preparing the dissections for him, contributed substantially to knowledge about the nervous system, blood circulation, and other phases of physical structure and human behavior.

According to Müller's classic doctrine of specific nerve energies, each sense organ (for vision, hearing, touch, taste, and smell) provides the individual with only one specific kind of sensation even if it is excited by different stimuli. Thus the eye can be stimulated by light, a blow, electricity, chemicals, or blood congestion, but it will always react with the visual sensation of light. Moreover, if one kind of stimulus excites several sense organs, each sense organ will still always react in its own specific way. Electricity, for example, can stimulate the eye to see light and also can stimulate the ear to hear sound. The quality of sensation depends on the sense organ affected by the stimulus. From the sensations initiated by the sense organs and the nerve impulses they transmit to the brain, the individual obtains his ideas about the external and internal environment, though the ideas are shaped by his past experience.

In addition to his researches on perception, Müller's contributions included experimental investigations of blood circulation, embryonic kidney organs and ducts (Müllerian ducts), and other physical structures and functions. The methods and ideas he advocated were emulated by the physiologists Henle and Helmholtz and the biologists Mendel, Darwin, and Thomas Huxley, building solid foundations and speeding the progress of modern biology, physiology, and psychology. Biology and physiology became a principal basis for the rapid development of psychology. Müller traced the roots of these sciences to ancient philosophers, especially Aristotle, whose inductive methods he admired. He credited Aristotle with valid, consistent ideas about specific nerve structures and sense organs as the causes of perception, and he pointed out that Aristotle had even correctly attributed dreams to the activity and specific energy of the visual sense organs.

The noted German physiologist at the University of Leipzig, Ewald Hering (1834–1918), and other scientists demonstrated experimentally that Müller's doctrine of specific nerve energies is applicable to glands and muscles, as well as to sense organs. Salivary glands, for example, react by secreting saliva if they are stimulated by any of various chemical, mechanical, or electrical forces, while muscles always contract in response to these diverse stimuli. Certain stimuli can be used for inhibiting or depressing instead of stimulating the customary specific reactions of sense organs, nerves, glands, and muscles. But in all cases, Müller's doctrine that each sense organ maintains its own specific mode of action remains valid.

Müller himself could not explain definitely why each sense organ produces its specific type of sensation and perception, but he suggested two possible explanations: (1) that the nerve fibers extending from the sense organs differ in their structure and energy; and (2) that the nerve fibers transmit impulses to certain terminal areas of the brain and spinal cord, and that because those areas differ in makeup and activity, they produce their own characteristic types of sense experience. He thus raised a basic question about the mechanisms of perception, which became a challenge to later biologists and psychologists.

CAJAL AND VON WALDEYER

The two most successful investigators of the problem of specific sensation and numerous functions of the nervous system were Ramón y Cajal, professor of histology at the universities of Barcelona and Madrid, who in 1889 analyzed the connections among nerve cells of the brain cortex and spinal cord and in 1890 described the neuron as the main unit of the nervous system; and Wilhelm von Waldeyer (Wilhelm von Waldeyer-Hartz), a German anatomist who performed experiments verifying the findings of Ramón y Cajal and in 1891 formulated the theory of neurons as cellular units of the nervous system that transport nerve impulses to all parts of the body. Nerve impulses reach the cell body of one neuron through its bushy end (or dendrites); and then, through a long, fibrous extension (the axon), proceed toward a point of contact with the dendrites of another neuron. The nerve impulses travel only forward from one neuron to the next. The impulses thus establish pathways along which new impulses more easily travel to centers of perception in the brain.

SHERRINGTON

Sir Charles Sherrington (1861–1952) was a leading English physiologist, educated at Cambridge University, whose experiments contributed enormously to the progress of physiology and psychology. In 1895 he was appointed professor of physiology at the University of Liverpool, and he remained there until 1913, when he joined the staff of the Royal Institution of Great Britain. In 1917 he accepted an appointment as professor of physiology at Oxford University and taught there for the next twenty years.

Sherrington verified and supplemented the discoveries of Ramón y Cajal and Wilhelm von Waldeyer about the neuron. In 1932, jointly with another eminent English physiologist, Edgar Douglas Adrian, he received the Nobel Prize for pioneering researches on the structures and functions of the nervous system. (It was Adrian who, with his associate Keith Lucas, formulated in 1917 the *all-or-none law* stating that any adequate stimulus applied to a single, isolated nerve fiber elicits a maximum response. In other words, an unnecessary increase in the stimulus does not augment the action of the nerve fiber, although a sensation and reaction may intensify if multiple sensory fibers are stimulated together, or if the frequency of stimulation increases.) Sherrington formulated the theory of the synapse as the place of connection between the end brush (the terminations of axons) and the dendrites of two neurons.

Sherrington's principal ideas and discoveries were derived from his studies of animals. His surgical experiments on the brains of animals led him to conclude that there are three levels of neural reactions. (1) On the first level, or spinal level, neural impulses and pathways extending from the sense organs through the neurons of the spinal cord to muscles and glands result in automatic reaction (spinal reflexes), as in the withdrawal of one's finger from contact with a flame. (2) On the second level of neural pathways, impulses are conducted from sense organs and muscles through the medulla and brainstem so as to produce other automatic reactions, such as blinking, sneezing, or heart action. (3) On the third level, impulses along neural pathways from sense organs to specialized areas of the brain cortex and thence to the muscles and other organs produce voluntary movements, learning, remembering, and similar complex activities.

Sherrington's experiments disclosed significant facts about neural action, especially the role of cerebral areas. Since body organs, he said, are connected directly or indirectly to the central nervous system, the stimulation of one organ can affect many others. Furthermore, impulses generated in several organs may converge or reinforce one another, eliciting, facilitating, or intensifying responses. Contractions of one group of muscles may cause relaxation of other, antagonistic or opposing muscles, or may inhibit them. According to Sherrington, the different parts of the nervous system work together as a coordinated unit, adjusting sensory and motor organs to one another and integrating behavior.

Sherrington's researches, however, failed to explain adequately the phenomena of cerebral localization. The theory of cerebral localization states that sensory experiences and behavior depend on specific areas in the brain, which collect, organize, and modify or interpret neural impulses on their way to or from receptor organs and motor effectors. For over two centuries, psychologists investigated and debated this theory. Even in the seventeenth century, Thomas Willis and other anatomists had speculated that a vital spirit is localized in the gray areas of the brain cortex, rejecting the ancient idea that the soul resides in the pineal gland.

THE PHRENOLOGISTS

In the eighteenth and early nineteenth centuries, a group led by Franz Joseph Gall (1758–1828) and Johann Kaspar Spurzheim (1776–1832), the German physicians who founded phrenology, claimed that mental powers and even personality traits are localized in the brain and that they can be measured by examining the protuberances of the skull. Phrenology became a popular pseudoscience defending unsupported claims of this kind, which, however, impelled many scientists to seek better explanations of cerebral phenomena and localization.

BAIN AND FLOURENS

The Scottish philosopher Alexander Bain (1818–1903) at first adhered to associationist doctrines that attributed behavior patterns and reactions to relationships among specific physical mechanisms, but he later concluded that the body reacts as a single unit in controlling sensations, responses, emotions, and purposes. His view was shared by the French physiologist Flourens (1794–1867), who studied definite brain areas on which various perceptions seem to depend but then decided that the stimulation of one point in the nervous system has effects that spread to other points so that the nervous system acts as an integrated whole.

BROCA

The French surgeon Paul Broca (1824–1880), investigating the disease of motor aphasia, assigned motor speech to an association area in the left frontal lobe (Broca's area) of the brain. (He found that a patient with an injury in that area loses the ability to express ideas in spoken words even though he may retain normal functioning of speech muscles and memory.) His theory was not correct, however, for later investigators reported that several patients surgically deprived of Broca's area showed no symptoms of motor aphasia. Although some psychologists have associated motor aphasia with personality changes resulting from localized cerebral lesions in a wide speech area, others have attributed it to changes in the individual's entire mechanism of perception and reaction. Recent studies have indicated that severe injury to the left hemisphere of the brain frequently causes aphasic disorders.

FRITSCH, HITZIG, AND FERRIER

In 1870 the German surgeons G. Fritsch and E. Hitzig, applying electricity to the brain, traced connections between specific cerebral areas and numerous sensory and motor reactions. Similar researches were carried out more thoroughly by the Scottish neurologist Sir David Ferrier (1843–1928), locating many cortical centers of sensation. But the later discovery of "vicarious functioning," whereby one part of the brain cortex takes over customary functions of other parts previously injured, aroused skepticism about strict adherence to the theory of localization. (The problem has been further complicated by recent experiments and careful examination of brain waves, indicating that damage to a small area of the brain can profoundly affect other areas and the entire brain. The cerebrum as a whole seems to be involved in some neural reactions.)

JAMES AND McDOUGALL

At Harvard University from 1872 to 1910, the great philosopher and psychologist William James consistently portrayed the
nervous system as the chief instrument of habit formation and
trial-and-error learning from past experience. James held that
physical structures and neural processes cooperate so that some
neural and motor reactions are unified while others remain specific, multiple, and localized. At the same time, psychologists of
the functionalist school, such as John Dewey, in general accord
with the pragmatic views of William James, developed theories
that integrated and unified all neural and motor aspects of human behavior, including both subjective mental experiences and
objective overt reactions, as purposive series of psychophysical
activities.

As James had done, William McDougall, at Oxford, Harvard, and Duke universities, attributed behavior patterns directly or indirectly to inherited innate, unlearned drives or instincts,
a view accepted by some but modified or opposed by various
later investigators.

In his *Introduction to Social Psychology* (1908), *Body and Mind*
(1911), and later writings, McDougall held steadfastly to his view
that the human organism is a purposive, striving, unitary whole
served by or making use of localized physical mechanisms. Man
inhibits his instincts more readily than other animals do, and he is
born in possession of attributes, neural structures, and mental
gifts that make a higher plane of life possible. Only a foundation
of inherited instincts, said McDougall, enables higher organisms
to develop superior levels of thought, emotion, and behavior. It is
in this sense that all reactions are directly or indirectly derived
from instincts. (In 1930 at Duke University, McDougall established a parapsychology laboratory that conducted experiments in
extrasensory perception, researches based on the theory that living
organisms can become aware of, and also exert influence on,
environmental forces and the contents of the mind through psychic
mechanisms not always subject to laws of physics or to limitations
of the sense organs—a concept still being debated.)

FREUD

Inspired by the ideas of Jean Martin Charcot (the famous French neurologist who was investigating hysteria and hypnosis), Sigmund Freud formulated his psychoanalytic postulate of psychosexual energy as the dominant force operating on three levels or depths (conscious, preconscious, and unconscious) of human experience. His work with psychologically disturbed patients enabled Freud to cite considerable evidence to support his view. Several psychoanalysts eventually broke away from Freud's system, however, and postulated other dynamic life forces, which they regarded as less dependent upon genital structures and sexual experiences. Some critics among contemporary philosophers preferred the mystical *élan vital* (vital spirit) of the French metaphysician Henri Bergson (1859–1941) to Freud's *libido* as the basic force directing human behavior. It may be recalled that love and hate were the universal forces postulated in ancient times by Empedocles of Agrigentum (ca. 495–435 B.C.), that prophetic Greek thinker who speculated about such modern ideas as biological evolution and the survival of the fittest.

CANNON

During the 1920s, in analyses emulating theories promulgated seventy-five years earlier by the great French physiologist Claude Bernard (who discovered the vasodilator and vasoconstrictor nerves and many facts about digestion and the sympathetic nervous system), the American physiologist Walter Bradford Cannon of the Harvard University Medical School concluded that neural structures stabilize and regulate the entire internal environment, including chemical balance, emotions, and cerebral and motor mechanisms. Cannon termed homeostasis this process of physiological adjustment in which, although the higher centers of the brain play an important part, structures throughout the body participate in a coordinated manner, many of them with involuntary, automatic reactions.

WOODWORTH, THORNDIKE

One of Sherrington's students, Robert Sessions Woodworth (1869–1962), a noted American psychologist at Columbia University, asserted that mental activity is initiated and sustained by dynamic drives, streams of energy that impel the individual to satisfy his desires and felt needs. Conscious goals and drives invest or affect centers in the brain and spinal cord, causing some neural mechanisms to reinforce and unify while others modify or inhibit one another. All kinds of mental acts (including perceptions, emotions, and thoughts) and overt responses constitute fundamentally similar reactions to internal and external stimuli.

Woodworth joined his famous colleague, the leading educational psychologist Edward Lee Thorndike, in developing and popularizing the stimulus-response or S-R bond theory of neural connections and reflex reactions to explain much of human and animal behavior. Both Woodworth and Thorndike agreed with McDougall that potent instinctive drives exist, but disagreed with McDougall's claim that all drives are based on instincts. In his experiments, Woodworth produced evidence that the individual's mental attitude affects his perceptions and reactions. He asserted that two major types of reactions are set in motion by internal or external stimuli: *preparatory* reactions by the individual prepare him for *consummatory* reactions. Thorndike similarly noted that readiness to act and mental set facilitate reactions toward a satisfying goal.

Numerous experiments have disclosed relationships among physical structures, neural impulses, stimuli, perception, and human behavior. Investigators such as Ellis Freeman, Ragnar Granit, Selig Hecht, David H. Hubel, and Torsten N. Wiesel have traced connections among neural impulses, retinal images, and specific areas of the brain cortex. (For their researches, Hubel and Wiesel received the Nobel Prize in 1981, shared with Roger Sperry, who demonstrated that the left hemisphere largely regulates speech and certain motor functions in the right side of the body while the right hemisphere regulates certain spatial perceptions and various motor functions in the left side of the body.) Such experiments have contributed useful suggestions but do not explain the basic nature of cerebral and neural functions. Divergent views about cerebral localization still divide leading psychologists, as, for example, the disciples of Ivan Petrovich Pavlov and Karl Spencer Lashley.

PAVLOV

The Russian physiologist Pavlov (1849–1936), who served forty-six years as director of experimental researches, moving from one to another of several laboratories in Russia during both the czarist and the communist regimes, is best known for his contributions to the psychology of learning. He was the first investigator to conduct systematic experiments in the production of neuroses in animals.

Pavlov's discovery and applications of the conditioned reflex had broad implications for all aspects of physical and mental experience. In a classical experiment, he presented a dog with meat shortly after or during the ringing of a bell, and repeated this procedure a number of times. Each time the dog salivated on seeing the meat and hearing the bell. Then, when Pavlov rang the bell without presenting the meat, the sound of the bell caused the dog to salivate. The dog had been conditioned; his natural reaction to the meat had been transferred to an artificial stimulus, the sound of the bell. It was obvious that the dog had learned to associate the sound of the bell with the meat.

The classical philosophers in ancient and modern times (Plato, Aristotle, Locke, and James Mill, among others) had recognized the association of ideas as an aid to memory and learning. Applying conditioned reflexes experimentally, Pavlov discovered how association of ideas as well as other types of association function in connection with sensory experience and motor reactions. He concluded that even the highest forms of mental activity can be fully explained as the operations of conditioned reflex mechanisms. Reflexes operate in two ways, he asserted: (1) by means of conduction of impulses along neural paths to effector muscles and organs; and (2) by means of connecting impulses, a process learned from life experience of the individual. The nervous system analyzes and interprets stimuli and the external environment, a function performed in a simpler form by lower parts of the central nervous system and in a more complex form by higher centers in the cerebral hemispheres of the central nervous system.

For his physiological investigations, Pavlov received the Nobel Prize in 1904. The Soviet regime that had been inaugurated in 1918 welcomed his experiments and ideas, which they considered to be consistent with communist principles of materialism. Some Western critics thereafter accused him of allowing himself to be used as a tool of the government—an accusation inconsistent with Pavlov's long record of carefully objective scientific work accomplished during both the capitalistic and the communist regimes.

Pavlov discovered that conditioned reflexes can inhibit as well as stimulate reactions. In the experiments with dogs, he repeatedly used the conditioning technique to induce frustration and neuroses. He attributed the phenomena of sleep, dreams, and hypnosis to the spreading of intensified inhibiting reflexes from zones in cortical centers to other areas of the brain. Also, if stimuli repeatedly affect only one zone or brain center, Pavlov said, they may become monotonous and induce sleep, but if the impulses spread to other zones, new neural connections are formed and new reflexes created, not through psychic memory but only through new physical pathways of conduction. (Recently physiologists have learned that impulses reaching the reticular formation of the brainstem cause wakefulness by affecting the thalamus, which then activates neurons in cortical areas of the brain. Inhibition or a monotonous flow of the sensory impulses generally initiates sleep.)

Pavlov and the Behaviorists. Pavlov himself and many other investigators modified and supplemented the conditioning methods and findings utilized in his early experiments. John B. Watson of the University of Chicago and B. F. Skinner of Harvard University joined other prominent theorists adhering to the behaviorist school of psychology in accepting and applying Pavlov's view of conditioning as a primary mechanism of human behavior. According to the early behaviorists, the human organism can be analyzed objectively in all its aspects and can then be reconditioned through the reinforcement of desirable activity and the inhibition of undesirable activity. They emphasized therefore the objective aspects of behavior, developing hypotheses based on observable reactions; whereas adherents to the functionalist school of psychology, such as James Rowland Angell (1869–1949) and John Dewey, attempted to investigate and integrate subjective as well as objective operations of the organism in order to describe and explain human nature and conduct. (More recently, some behaviorists have regained interest in imagery and inner integrated thought processes not always observable or only partly analyzable as motor phenomena.)

Meanwhile, Pavlov's original claim that all important behavior changes depend upon the cerebral cortex seemed to have been considerably weakened by the discovery that some animals possessing no cerebral cortex learn through association and experience. Behaviorists maintained, however, that such animals have their own neural and other physical structures that reinforce successful reactions and condition them to meet their felt needs.

Pavlov and the Gestalt Psychologists. George Ellett Coghill (1872–1941), noted American anatomist, was among those who rejected Pavlov's assumption of a direct or indirect connection and causal relationship between specific neural areas or structures and reactions to stimuli. Coghill stressed the fact that, in many animals, mass movements or integrated actions often occur prior to specific reflexes; the latter then serve merely as aids to or subordinate adjuncts of mass action—a process he termed *individuation*. In his own criticism of the writings of Wolfgang Köhler of the Berlin Institute of Psychology, who was a founder of Gestalt psychology, which interprets behavior as a unified organic reaction to a total life situation, Pavlov insisted that the mass action cited by Gestaltists as proof of purposive integrated behavior is an illusion, that an animal usually seems to be reacting as a unit in a single purposeful way only because conditioned reflexes have inhibited all parts of the cerebral hemispheres except one dominant area.

Pavlov vs. Lashley and Other Critics. Among psychologists who analyzed and criticized Pavlov's theories were the American experimenters Shepherd Irving Franz (1874–1933), who observed the remarkable recovery of their normal functions by animals after severe brain injuries; Edwin Ray Guthrie (1886–1959), who referred to purposive motor reactions and cited the role of ideas and imitation and the limited effectiveness of conditioned reflexes in animal learning; and Karl Spencer Lashley (1890–1958), who continued the kinds of studies done by Franz and traced other organic activity besides conditioned reflexes as decisive factors in habit formation and learning.*

Pavlov rejected Lashley's conclusion, from experiments on rats, that reactions often depend on a total mass of organic tissue and the total activity of the central nervous system, not upon specific cortical areas or neural tracts and reflexes. The only way to prove such a contention, he said, would be to destroy all specific receptors and cortical areas and still find the animals to be responding in an integrated manner—an inconceivable procedure. He predicted that even the purposes and goals of animals and human beings, their anticipations or expectations and desires, which initiate and sustain reactions during a conditioned reflex, would ultimately be explained in physiological terms.

In 1929, in his influential volume *Brain Mechanisms and Intelligence,* Lashley reported his own experiments on monkeys in whom the motor cortex in one hemisphere and then in another hemisphere of the brain had been removed. The animals, previously trained to open boxes with one hand, transferred this skill to the other hand upon recovery from paralysis. Lashley also cited experiments in which animals substituted head or leg movements for arm movements prevented by surgical procedures. He asserted that interest, effort, and attitudes of an animal as a unitary organism control the initiation, rate, and results of neural impulses and reactions.

During the 1960s and 1970s, numerous American psychologists adopted Lashley's point of view, devoting less attention to

---

* Pavlov also defended his views vigorously against critics who favored the theory of the British psychologist Charles Edward Spearman (1863–1945) that intelligent action is basically a function of some kind of undifferentiated nervous energy.

the stimulus-response and conditioning aspects of behavior and more attention to integrated cognitive, conative (purposive) reactions involved in information processing, insight, and voluntary activities. They also accepted and elaborated on Freud's approach to the analytical investigation of consciousness and his subdivision of emotional, cognitive, and other psychical experiences into several levels of conscious, partially conscious, potentially conscious, and totally unconscious reactions.

The Swiss psychologist Édouard Claparède (1873–1940), joining other critics of behaviorism, asserted that the conditioned reflex works not merely because of neural connections and conduction of impulses but also because the individual understands the relationships among, and the implications of, multiple or successive stimuli, his own needs and desires, and the goals or satisfactions yet to be fulfilled.

Whether or not they agree with Pavlov's mechanistic interpretations, contemporary psychologists respect his advocacy of objective piecemeal research, careful observation, controlled experimentation, and free, disinterested investigation.

SCHOOLS OF PSYCHOLOGY

Six approaches to the modern science of human behavior evolved out of the observations, experiments, and theories of the preceding great philosophers and psychologists. (1) The introspectionist, *structural* school, perfecting and applying Saint Augustine's method of introspection, regarded behavior as consisting of states of consciousness discoverable and analyzable through experiments and self-observation. (2) This approach was counterbalanced by the conditioned-reflex theses of *behaviorists*, who described behavior as a series of machinelike observable responses to stimuli. (3) The *functionalists* emphasized purposive mental processes and overt reactions, useful activity, as the core of human behavior. (4) The *Gestaltists* ascribed action, motivation, and adjustment to the unified reactions of the organism as a whole to a composite configuration or total life situation, a view directly contrary to behavioristic atomistic interpretations. (5) The *hormic* school, as represented by William

McDougall, likewise condemning the behaviorists' view of organic responses as being too mechanistic and automatic, agreed with the gestaltist emphasis upon man as a unitary whole, also emphasized cognition, but attributed purposive reaction chiefly to innate tendencies or instincts. Cognitive psychologists such as Benjamin L. Whorf and psycholinguists such as Noam Chomsky shared McDougall's opposition to extreme behaviorism. (6) Freud and his early associates (including Alfred Adler and Carl Gustav Jung) in the *psychoanalytic* school regarded the unconscious as the central force in motivation and adjustment of behavior, but differed with one another about the nature of the unconscious drives, which were attributed by Freud to the id or psychosexual energy, by Adler to the will-to-power, and by Jung to physical and social compensatory mechanisms. It became apparent that each of the six schools of psychology contributed useful concepts and findings to the scientific study of behavior.

2 SENSATION, ATTENTION, PERCEPTION

In ancient times, great philosophers developed theories concerning the importance of the brain for neural responses and cognition, the role of the association of ideas and of memory in perception and thought, and the causal relationship between environmental objects and visual perception. However, despite fruitful experiments and observations by Aristotle (who regarded the perception of specific objects as the foundation of valid thought and scientific knowledge), most of the prevalent ideas about sensation and perception consisted of speculative, often erroneous, conclusions. Even Plato, who in the *Timaeus* described vision and audition as among the highest senses activated by the brain, condemned attempts to experiment with mixed colors, attributing color perception to divine intervention.

In medieval times, anatomists and other scientists, such as Berenger, Vesalius, Varoli, Harvey, and Willis, made significant physiological discoveries that paved the way for modern investigations of perception. But the dominant views were still mystical. Saint Augustine, who attributed knowing, willing, and feeling to God's power, declared that man would never be able to understand them.

Psychologists have discovered useful facts, however, about sensation, attention, and perception, the three primary psychological processes of the human organism. Among the earliest and most influential investigators of these processes were Müller's contemporaries Ernst Heinrich Weber (1795–1878) and Gustav Theodor Fechner (1801–1887).

WEBER AND FECHNER

At about the time in the 1830s when Müller was formulating his doctrine of specific nerve energies, Weber, professor of anatomy at Leipzig University, was experimenting with stimuli affecting the senses of touch and hearing. He discovered that when a stimulus increases in strength so that the increase becomes just noticeable, any larger stimulus must be increased proportionately in order to become noticeable. Thus if one holds a weight of forty grams in the hand and can just feel the difference when the weight is increased to forty-one grams, then a weight of eighty grams will have to be increased to eight-two grams before one can feel the difference in weight. In 1834 Weber reported this discovery, which became a fundamental law of experimental psychology. In his research reports, Müller cited the experiments by Weber concerning the sense of touch, noting Weber's discovery of wide variations in the perception of spatial magnitudes when different body surfaces are stimulated. Two objects may seem to be only one inch apart when touched by the fingertips, but as much as five inches apart when touched by the wrist. Skin surfaces have numerous sense organs or receptors for sensations of pain, heat, cold, pressure, and touch, and areas with the most numerous receptors exhibit the greatest sensitivity. The tip of the tongue is most sensitive, followed by the finger, nose, head, and neck. The abdomen, chest, and underarm are more sensitive than the face or limbs to heat and cold.

The researches of Weber became the basis for the pioneering work of Fechner, the German physicist who formulated Weber's law in mathematical terms. Fechner was educated in a small town in southeastern Germany, where his father was a Lutheran pastor. At the University of Leipzig, Fechner was a brilliant student and, beginning in 1834, served on the faculty for several years as professor of physics. While doing research on visual perception, he contracted a painful eye infection that forced him to give up teaching. Subsequently he recovered and devoted himself to the study of the relationship between physical stimuli and mental reactions.

It seemed to him that psychological and physical phenomena were two aspects of the same spiritual universe consisting of living substances, ranging from lower stages of life to higher stages of plant and animal existence, all being parts of a divine consciousness. This concept resembled the theory of the famous "God-intoxicated" philosopher Baruch Spinoza (1632–1677), whose works Fechner admired, that God is the cause and essence of all things.

Fechner formulated a law of perception (which he called the Weber-Fechner law in recognition of Weber's basic contribution to it) stating that stimuli increase in an arithmetical progression, whereas corresponding sensations that follow increase in a logarithmic progression. This law holds good only approximately and only for moderate intensities of the sensations of hearing, vision, and pressure. If a stimulus is either very slight or extremely large, the difference from another stimulus has to be proportionately much larger than the law requires in order for the difference to be appreciated. Moreover, for each sense organ, there is a lower limit or limen of intensity below which no sensation is mediated by that sense organ.

Fechner declared that it should be possible to measure sensations as well as stimuli. But James and other leading psychologists objected that while a stimulus can be measured because it consists of an aggregate of quantities or units that accounts for its total force or strength, a sensation is a single, indivisible experience the magnitude of which is not measurable in units of any kind. When one feels the pressure of a heavy object in the hand, for example, that feeling is not a composite or total of less intense feelings but rather a single, immediate experience.

Despite its apparent imperfection, Fechner's theory that the magnitude of sense experiences is measurable seemed logical to contemporary scientists. At about the same time, Helmholtz (Müller's most famous student) succeeded in measuring the speed of motor-nerve impulses in frogs and sensory-nerve impulses in human beings. The researches of Fechner and Helmholtz encouraged Wilhelm Wundt and other pioneering psychologists to establish experimental laboratories in order systematically to measure and analyze sensations, perceptions, and related psychological reactions.

HELMHOLTZ

Herman Ludwig Ferdinand Helmholtz earned an unrivaled reputation for versatility as a pioneer in physics, acoustics, optics, mathematics, chemistry, anatomy, physiology, medicine, and psychology. He was born in Potsdam, Prussia, in 1821 to parents in humble circumstances who nevertheless provided him with a well-rounded education. One ancestor on his mother's side was the renowned Quaker William Penn (1644–1718), founder of the colony of Pennsylvania in America. Helmholtz's father, a teacher in the local Gymnasium, encouraged the boy, who was rather frail, to study several branches of mathematics and science, subjects in which he displayed unusual competence and creativity. At the University of Berlin, he studied physiology under Müller, and at twenty-one completed and reported on his own fruitful researches concerning nerves and neural ganglia. Shortly thereafter, however, a lack of funds compelled him to accept a position as a physician in the Prussian Army, a post he filled creditably until in 1849 he was appointed as a professor of physiology at the University of Königsberg. Later he taught the same subject for several years at the University of Bonn, and thereafter for twelve years (1858–1870) at Heidelberg University. Beginning in 1871, he served as a professor of physics at the University of Berlin, and he remained there until his death in 1894.

Helmholtz made his most significant contribution to modern science in 1847 by presenting a theory (in a paper entitled "Concerning the Conservation of Force") to the Berlin Physical Society, closely reasoned and supported by evidence, about the conservation and indestructibility of energy. Although this principle (the first law of thermodynamics) had been suggested or implied by other scientists, namely, Julius Robert von Mayer, James Prescott Joule, and Baron Kelvin (Sir William Thomson who formulated the second law of thermodynamics in 1852), it was developed independently and elaborated most convincingly by Helmholtz in an epochal achievement comparable to Max Planck's quantum theory and Albert Einstein's special theory of relativity. The ideas of Helmholtz paved the way for revolutionary progress in physics, just as the law of the conservation of matter propounded by Antoine Laurent Lavoisier (1743–1794) had done in chemistry.

Contributions to Physics. The law of the conservation of energy developed logically from Helmholtz's researches into the metabolism of food. He measured the amount of heat generated by metabolic processes and showed it to be equal to the total energy received from the food ingested. In 1851 he invented the ophthalmoscope, containing a perforated mirror that enabled physicians to view clearly for the first time the retina and other structures deep within the eyes. He invented the opthalmometer in 1850 to measure astigmatism, built a binocular telescope, and contributed greatly to hydrodynamics and to knowledge about the characteristics and measurement of electricity, light, and heat. He also wrote profound works on epistemology and aesthetics. His treatise *Sensations of Tone* (1863) was universally acclaimed as a major contribution to the science of acoustics. He encouraged and guided his famous student of electricity Heinrich Rudolph Hertz to carry out investigations that made wireless telegraphy possible. In 1883, during the administration of Bismarck, who encouraged scientific studies in the universities, the German emperor William I honored Helmholtz with the title of nobility.

Researches on Vision and Hearing. Helmholtz approached the problems of psychology from the point of view of a physicist. His researches into the mechanics of vision and hearing resulted in monumental achievements, including especially his theories of color perception and audition.

In his comprehensive treatise on physiological optics (1856–1866), he described the chief mechanisms of vision, including the results of his own experiments, inventions, and observations. His book discussed the geometry of eye structures, eye movements and the factors involved in monocular and binocular vision, the three-color theories of Thomas Young, and his own conclusions about color perception, which are accepted, with various modifications, by most psychologists today.

Helmholtz elaborated on Young's theory that the retina of the eye has three kinds of microscopic elements particularly sensitive to the three primary colors of red, green, and blue, respectively. According to the Young-Helmholtz theory, light waves for two primary colors, by stimulating the millions of cones contained in the retina, produce intermediate color sensations (for example, yellow from red and green, purple from red and blue, and green-blue from green and blue). Stimulation of retinal cones by light waves for the three primary colors produces white or near-white hues as a composite of the entire spectrum of light waves: violet, indigo, blue, green, yellow, orange, and red. (The Swedish physiologist R. Granit in 1945 and other later investigators measured the electrical currents generated along sensory nerves by light waves and verified the main thrust of the Young-Helmholtz theory.)

Helmholtz concluded that light waves divide into three groups generating corresponding impulses in three independent neural processes along the optic nerve, and that these impulses are interpreted when they arrive at the sensory area of the brain to be fused and sensed as particular colors. He declared that cooperative and coordinated actions of light waves, of eye structures and nerves, and of the brain cortex all contribute to color perception, but that the blending and recognition of colors occur in the brain, not within the eye. (In 1895, G. E. Müller, of the University of Göttingen, discovered corroborating evidence that the sensation of gray originates in the brain cortex.)

Helmholtz and Hering. The views of Young and Helmholtz became most influential despite a rival theory in 1874 by Ewald Hering that attributed color perception to four primary colors combined in pairs and to chemical changes (catabolism and anabolism) in retinal cells or end-organs sensitive to specific light waves.

Hering's views were accepted by prominent psychologists, who noted that a great variety of physical and chemical factors affect some aspects of color perception. As early as 1825, Purkinje at Breslau University had conducted experiments which indicated that color sensations change with shifts in the energy of light waves. In his treatise on optics, Helmholtz himself cited other factors affecting color perception, such as fatigue of the visual organs, past experiences of the individual, and illusions of

judgment. In 1838 the English physicist Sir Charles Wheatstone, inventor of the stereoscope, had reported the results of his
investigations concerning binocular vision and binocular rivalry
(inspired by Leonardo Da Vinci's observations of differences in
the dimensions of an object when viewed with each eye separately and then with both eyes together). Wheatstone explained how
binocular vision results in perception of three-dimensional figures. He described binocular rivalry that causes the eyes to shift
rapidly back and forth from one color to the other when each eye
looks at a different color. Thus if one eye looks at blue while the
other eye looks at yellow, the brain will not see green (the usual
result of mixing blue and yellow) but will alternate between
blue and yellow. Helmholtz concluded that binocular rivalry depends mainly upon the mental set or deliberate purpose of the
individual as he divides his attention between the two colors.
Hering attributed binocular rivalry to chemical changes, a view
elaborated by Selig Hecht and other subsequent investigators.

   Helmholtz and Hering differed about the phenomena of complementary colors, afterimages, contrast colors, and color blindness. A primary color and its complementary color (for example,
red and green) are sensed as white when both are combined in
equal strengths. After the original stimulus for a particular color
disappears, the *same* color may persist or reappear as a *positive*
afterimage, but an *opposite* color may appear instead as a *negative* afterimage. Thus blue is seen as a negative afterimage of
yellow. Helmholtz attributed afterimages to fatigue in the sensory receptors of the retina, explaining that looking at green, for
example, may cause so much fatigue in green-sensitive receptors
that the red-sensitive or blue-sensitive receptors, which continue
to react vigorously, produce red and blue negative afterimages.
Complementary colors often seem to appear along the edges of a
principal color as contrasting hues, a phenomenon attributed by
Helmholtz to illusions of judgment. Hering claimed that all such
phenomena are caused by chemical changes. He also asserted
that, owing to chemical factors, partially color-blind persons are
blind to both red and green, whereas Helmholtz believed that
some are blind to red colors only, others to green colors.

   Christine Ladd-Franklin (1847–1930) of Columbia Universi-

ty attributed the perception of color to evolutionary changes in
the physical structure of receptor cells of the visual apparatus.
Her views supplemented the ideas of Helmholtz and Hering.
The evolutionary theory supported Helmholtz's emphasis on
structural factors in color perception as well as Hering's emphasis on chemical changes. Some of Hering's conclusions concerning chemical factors have been verified by recent investigators.
During the 1970s, Barry Honig, biophysicist at the University of
Illinois, suggested that the chemical retinal, contained in vitamin
A, when affected by light of different wavelengths binds itself to
proteins in the various light-receiving cells of the eye so as to
alter the electrical charges in the cells and thus changes the stimulus arousing color perception in the brain. Koji Nakanishi and
collaborators at Columbia University verified this theory experimentally and concluded that genetic defects may damage the
functions of proteins in the green, red, or blue cones of the eye,
resulting in color blindness.

In 1899 the American psychologist Burtis Burr Breese concluded from his experiments that overt movements of the eyes,
coordinated with the individual's mental set and purposive attention, control binocular rivalry, a view comparable to the theory of John Dewey that sensation, attention, and perception as
conscious reactions depend upon physical functions of the living
organism in its efforts to adapt itself to the internal and external
environment.

The Resonance Theory. Helmholtz's resonance theory states
that the basilar membrane of the inner ear (a membrane consisting of 24,000 fibers) reacts like a resonator to vibrations of
sound waves; that the membrane has three parts made up of
short, medium, and long fibers; and that each part vibrates in
response to corresponding low, middle, and high tones. Groups
of hair cells in the organ of Corti (identified by the nineteenth-
century Italian anatomist Alfonso Corti as the key organ of
hearing) vibrate within the inner ear in sympathy with the vibrations of the basilar membrane and transmit impulses along
the fibers of the auditory nerve to the brain for interpretation.

Loudness, said Helmholtz, depends upon the amplitude of vibrations affecting a particular section of the basilar membrane,

and timbre depends upon overtones (partial vibrations that accompany the fundamental tones, or complete vibrations) of musical instruments. Helmholtz analyzed the mathematics of vibrations and the order, intensity, and number of overtones as major factors that make musical sounds pleasing and harmonious. His theory of audition is still widely accepted.

Critics objected that the fibers of the basilar membrane were too small to function well as resonators, but Helmholtz replied that other structures reinforced the action of the membrane. (It should be noted that fishes have no basilar membrane but use a different structure of the inner ear, the sacculus, as the main organ of hearing.) Recently, Reissner's membrane of the inner ear has been identified as an important instrument for generating sound waves which concentrate in those specific parts of the basilar membrane attuned to the vibrations. Research findings concerning electric currents in neural structures have been consistent with the resonance theory. Helmholtz's friend Du Bois-Reymond became famous for his pioneering measurements of electric currents in auditory organs and animal tissues. Recent investigators, including E. G. Wever and C. W. Bray, have shown that electric waves transmitted along the auditory nerves oscillate at the same rate as the vibrations of the sounds being heard, a fact that seems to corroborate the Helmholtz point of view.

Factors in Perception. Helmholtz attempted to explain the paradox that every perception occurs as a single, immediate action that nevertheless contains, and depends upon, elements of past experience. He agreed with Aristotle that all organic behavior arises from interactions between body and mind, and that the association of ideas is a key factor in perception and reasoning. (Aristotle stated that ideas become associated by means of contiguity, similarity, and contrast.) The Aristotelian doctrine of the conscious association of ideas was accepted with various modifications by modern British philosophers, such as Thomas Hobbes (1588–1679), John Locke (1632–1704), George Berkeley (1685–1753), David Hartley (1705–1757), David Hume (1711–1776), and James Mill (1773–1836). Helmholtz noted the association of ideas as a factor in perception, but also pointed out that some associated ideas are conscious, others unconscious, and that the unconscious ideas play a part in the initiation of new perceptions. (James Mill had suggested a similar concept in 1829, citing forgotten reactions as stimulants of new ideas, perception, and feelings. In 1865 his famous son, John Stuart Mill, published a treatise reiterating this idea, which he called a law of oblivescence. In Paris during the 1890s, the first French experimental psychologist Alfred Binet attributed many psychological problems of mental patients to subconscious sensations, perceptions, and reactions.)

According to Helmholtz, perception depends not only upon immediate sensations but also upon past sensory and motor experiences, the association of ideas, and the influence of habits and training. All these factors, he said, make possible and modify the perception and interpretation of new experiences, and they account for the phenomena of common illusions and erroneous judgments—for example, those of a patient who continues to feel sensations in the absent toes of an amputated foot.

WUNDT

The German physiologist Wilhelm Wundt (1832–1920) has been widely regarded as the father of experimental psychology. The Wundtian structural point of view emphasized laboratory experiments, observations, measurements, and introspection as the chief methods of analyzing consciousness into simple elements. Although other investigators, including William James, had conducted laboratory experiments in psychology, Wundt's laboratory (established in 1879 at Leipzig University) became a widely emulated model.

Born and raised in Baden, southwestern Germany, Wundt received comprehensive medical training at the universities of Tübingen, Heidelberg, and Berlin, and specialized in physiological research. At the age of twenty-five, he lectured at Heidelberg University, where he was appointed assistant professor in 1864. After a decade of teaching and research, he accepted the position of professor of philosophy at the University of Zürich, taught there one year, then joined the faculty of the University of Leipzig in the same capacity and remained there forty-two years (1875–1917), directing the work of his laboratory and counseling psychologists from many lands who founded scores of similar laboratories. Although psychology was still widely regarded as a branch of philosophy, these centers of experimentation speeded its development into an independent discipline, the modern science of human behavior.

Wundt's Point of View. In formulating his basic approach to problems of psychology, Wundt was influenced by the work of Fechner, Helmholtz, and John Stuart Mill. He agreed with them that consciousness consists of simple elements that, like chemical compounds, can be analyzed and described by means of careful observation, measurements, and experiments. Wundt also agreed with Fechner that human ideas, purposes, and actions are not experiences separated from the rest of nature but inseparable aspects of a universal drive or will. Wundt held that oral communication is the decisive force that makes possible the acquisition and sharing of ideas among human beings, and that mental operations are not individual but social activities. In the 1920s, the pioneering social psychologist William McDougall asserted a comparable hypothesis. The pragmatic, instrumentalist philosophers George Herbert Mead and John Dewey also accepted Wundt's theory about the social character of mind and the nature of reality as an active, inseparable process, even though they did not adhere to Wundt's conclusion that all mental experience can be explained through introspection and the analysis of structural elements.

Experiments and Theories of Perception. Wundt's laboratory procedures and comprehensive, systematic investigations resulted in a well-rounded organization and integration of the subject matter of psychology and served as a guide for his students and disciples in their experimentation and teaching.

In Germany the laboratory experiments and techniques of psychological measurement used by Wundt inspired the same approach by Hermann Ebbinghaus in studying memory and developing the first sentence-completion test, and by Ernst Meumann (1862–1915) and his assistant Paul Rankov Radosavljevich in studying recall, learning, and methods of teaching. James

McKeen Cattell, Granville Stanley Hall, Charles Hubbard Judd, and Edward Bradford Titchener were prominent followers of Wundt's approach in America. Cattell, who worked as Wundt's assistant and also studied with Sir Francis Galton, analyzed reaction times and individual differences. He constructed various intelligence and performance tests, correcting some of Wundt's conclusions based upon similar tests. Hall, who carried on researches under Wundt in 1883, became famous for his investigations of religious belief, children's behavior, and adolescence. Judd, a noted specialist in learning processes, transfer, and the psychology of reading, translated Wundt's *Outlines of Psychology* in Leipzig in 1897. Titchener, inspired by the great physiologist Sir John Scott Burdon-Sanderson at Oxford University and by Wundt at Leipzig University, contributed to all fields of psychology, often disagreeing with Wundt but almost matching the versatility of Wundt himself. Among Wundt's world-famous German students were Emil Kraepelin, specializing in research concerning mental illness, fatigue, and the effects of drugs; Oswald Kuelpe, prominent in philosophy and experimental psychology, as well as in the study of cognition and feeling; and Hugo Münsterberg, a leader in experimental psychology and applied psychology.

To measure the reaction times required for mental operations such as purposes and ideas, Wundt made the mistake of merely subtracting the time needed for single sensory and muscular responses from the total time consumed by complex tasks. His error was corrected by Titchener, Cattell, and others, who pointed out that purposes and ideas cannot be added to or subtracted from other reactions entirely different in character. From his own observations and experiments, Wundt himself eventually concluded that sensation and perception cannot be explained by analyzing individual characteristics and adding them to arrive at a sum total or composite result. He developed the theory of structural psychology: that an inner psychic force integrates and synthesizes simple mental elements, restructuring them and thus creating new psychological experiences, which can be analyzed by subjective observation, the method of introspection. These conclusions failed to satisfy the Gestalt psychologists Max

Wertheimer, Kurt Koffka, and Wolfgang Köhler, who emphasized the whole pattern and unitary character of every mental
experience. The functionalist psychologists John Dewey and
James Rowland Angell, also criticizing Wundt's structuralist
view, described mental experience as an active process in which
all elements work together as inseparable sensorimotor responses
to fulfill a practical need or purpose.

Wundt postulated the existence of a specialized brain center
in the frontal lobes that directs the individual's attention to specific stimuli responsible for his sensations, perceptions, and reactions. This cortical center restricts attention to one stimulus at a
time merely by inhibiting possible reactions to other stimuli. According to Wundt, the stimuli vary in quality and for this reason
differ in their effects upon the individual. Stimuli of moderate
intensity are pleasant, whereas either inadequate or very intense
stimuli are unpleasant. Some stimuli are exciting, others depressive. In laboratory experiments, Wundt found high correlations
among the following multiple factors: intensities of stimuli,
pleasant and unpleasant feelings, muscular tension and relaxation, and pulse and respiration rates. Nevertheless, other experimenters concluded from their own similar experiments that
these factors vary widely with the particular sense organs being
stimulated and with different individuals.

Wundt's theory of space perception aroused further controversy. He believed that each point on the skin gives sensations of
pressure a special quality, or local sign, and that the local signs
combined with sensations of movements to produce spatial perceptions. The perception of space, he said, tended to assume a
rectilinear form only because the organism had become accustomed to sensations of movement toward environmental objects.
Neither Wundt's theory nor the variant but comparable theories
of Hering and other psychologists, however, explained how combinations of local pressure and sensations of movement could result in bidimensional or tridimensional space perception.

Wundt offered the same kind of explanation for time perception as for space perception. Sensations, he held, possessed no
quality of time. The perception of time depended upon a sequence of sensations that varied in intensity and were accompa-

nied by successive feelings of tension and relaxation. The individual interpreted the succession of sensations combined with his own alternating feelings of tension and relaxation as the flow or passage of time. Wundt's theory was rejected by other experimental psychologists, including Ebbinghaus, who attributed the perception of space and time not only to the individual's sensations but also to his general ideas of duration, extension, change, unity, and similarity. Recent studies, however, have verified the role of tension (in the form of muscular strain) postulated by Wundt as a primary element in the perception of time, citing, for example, the fact that time passes slowly for people subjected to pain or stress.

Each of several theories of space perception seems to possess a measure of validity. Wundt attributed common illusions in spatial perception to eye movements and a tendency to misinterpret external stimuli in conformity with previous experience. Thus a person looking at two equal lines with their slanted ends turned in opposite directions at top and bottom tends to keep his eyes moving in one direction so that he judges the line with the ends turned up and outward to be longer than the other line with its ends turned down and inward. But Ebbinghaus pointed out that an individual's past experience with such illusions will not make them disappear even when he does his utmost to visualize the lines correctly as equal in length.

Later investigators claimed that by constant practice and control of attention one could reduce or in some cases even eliminate an illusion. The observer's attitude or expectation could often modify or correct his interpretation of an object. The psychologist E. J. Rubin showed pictorially that a white figure on a black background (the Rubin figure) could be seen either as a vase or as two faces, depending upon one's deliberate choice between the white figure and the black background as the center of attention. The Austrian physicist Ernst Mach noted illusions of reversible perspective in which, for example, the movement of the eyes outward makes a line diagram of an open book represent the back of the book, whereas the movement of the eyes inward makes the same diagram represent the front of the book. In his discussion of mistaken or ambiguous perceptions, Titchener disagreed with Hering's explanation that different points on the retina have corresponding sensations of height, depth, and breadth. He held that there are no specific sense organs for these qualities, and he attributed the result in consciousness to the individual's concentration on specific features of the objects or figures being observed. Thus if an individual focuses his attention upon minor features of an object instead of its main feature, he often misjudges the object's dimensions.

To explain the perception of movement, Wundt postulated that when the individual becomes aware of a succession or stream of stimuli, each stimulus arouses a sensation that tends to persist as an afterimage. The sensations become less and less intense; the observer, noting the differences in their intensity, interprets the succession of these sensations as indicating the movement of the object. Other investigators disagreed with this theory. The German psychologist Korte measured the time between successive exposures of lines to an observer and the distances between the lines. He stated the mathematical relationship that governs the recognition of movement as follows: The time intervals must be decreased when the distances between the lines are increased before the observer can perceive the best movement of the lines. From another point of view, Gestalt psychologist Max Wertheimer declared that the perception of movement was simply an immediate unitary experience that required no further explanation or analysis.

Wundt's Analysis of Temperament. In his study of temperament (defined as a more or less permanent, dominant mood), Wundt accepted the four Hippocratic types, adding the comment that anyone can learn to control these dispositions. Ideally, said Wundt, one should adopt a sanguine temperament concerning minor life experiences, reserving choleric and melancholic moods for important events and interest, and a phlegmatic mood for long-term, well-defined plans and actions. Wundt agreed with Meumann in defining character as a disposition of the individual's will, a view shared by McDougall, who defined it as a complex of purposive tendencies. Meumann, however, analyzed temperaments on the basis, not of their importance, but of their degree of pleasantness or unpleasantness, ease of arousal, and persistence, describing the sanguine temperament as pleasing, difficult to excite, and less intense than the others; the choleric as unpleasant, easy to excite, and persistent; the melancholic as difficult to excite but persistent; and the phlegmatic as pleasing, easy to excite, and persistent. Wundt postulated three kinds of feeling: pleasantness and unpleasantness, dependent upon intensity of the stimulus; excitement and depression, also dependent upon intensity of the stimulus; and tension and relaxation, dependent upon duration of the stimulus.

TITCHENER

Wundt's eminent British student Edward Bradford Titchener was the leading representative in America of the Wundtian emphasis on introspection and analysis of consciousness into simple, structural elements—the two basic aspects of the structural school of psychology.

Titchener was born in 1867 in Chichester, England. He attended Malvern College, and at eighteen enrolled at Oxford University, where he studied philosophy, classical literature, biology, and physiology. At Oxford the eminent Regius Professor of Medicine Sir John Scott Burdon-Sanderson encouraged him to write an outline of psychology, which became a popular textbook for students in British and American universities. Having earned his Oxford degree in 1890, Titchener studied for two years under the direction of Wundt at the University of Leipzig, and in 1892 received the doctorate degree.

In 1892, after teaching biology at Oxford for a brief period, he accepted a position as assistant professor of psychology at Cornell University in Ithaca, New York. He attained the rank of full professor in 1895 and remained active on the faculty for thirty-two years thereafter until his death in 1927. He was a brilliant lecturer, drawing upon a remarkably rich life experience and a wide range of interests in psychology, philosophy, science, literature, numismatics, and music, all of which subjects he could have taught with distinction, and, in fact, he did teach music for two years at the university. For several years (1921–1925) he served as editor of the *American Journal of Psychology.*

Titchener promulgated and implemented Wundt's analytical methods of psychological research through his teaching, laboratory experiments, and writings. Although he frequently disagreed with Wundt, both in point of view and in specific conclusions, he became the acknowledged founder and leader of the American structural school of psychology.

His analysis of sensation, attention, and perception emphasized the factor of clearness. An increase in intensity of a sensation, he said, increases the degree of clearness even though a weak sensation can often be quite clear. The degree of clearness also depends upon the concentration of attention on external and internal stimuli. Directly or indirectly, attention dominates both conscious and unconscious experience. Titchener classified attention into three stages: (1) primary attention, dependent mainly upon the nature and force of the stimulus, especially its intensity, suddenness, repetition, movement, novelty, and familiarity; (2) secondary attention, dependent mainly upon the individual's own ideas and effort; and (3) derived primary attention, dependent mainly upon his purpose and interest. Learning involves a combination of alternating secondary and derived primary attention. Attention occurs on two broad levels, marginal and concentrated. Distraction makes a sound less intense and harder to hear, more likely to fade away and disappear. Sensations become clearer and stronger as the individual raises his attention to a high level of concentration. Since every conscious person is always attending to something, inattention to any specific matter means only that he is busy attending to other things. The brain can work unconsciously to organize past experience during sleep; consequently, a period of sleep, or a period of rest and inattention to all specific matters, can shut out distractions and thereby facilitate subsequent associations, recollections, and learning.

Titchener noted that even though a person might seem to have forgotten many experiences, such as learned information and skills, the subconscious or unconscious organization of those experiences could make relearning them more efficient and time-saving. For this reason, a public speaker should prepare his speech and set it aside a few days before delivery, for he will then discover that his brain has unconsciously done most of the work of integrating or organizing the material. Similarly, William James pointed out that every new sensation or impression becomes integrated into past associations, the ready-made stock of the mind, and is never completely forgotten.

Titchener and his colleagues and students at Cornell University applied the Wundtian structuralist and experimental approach to major fields and problems of psychology, including processes of thinking and reasoning. But William James, as the eminent apostle of an opposing functionalist point of view, asserted in 1890 that verbal symbols such as the words *if* and *but* reflected elementary imageless thoughts (feelings about relations) not amenable to structural analysis into simpler elements like sensations, stimuli, and reactions. The functionalist psychologist Robert S. Woodworth asserted that imageless thoughts were, in the same way as motor responses, simply the reactions of the individual to external or internal stimuli.

In Titchener's laboratory, however, E. H. Rowland, Margaret F. Washburn, and other experimenters repeated and supplemented the experiments of James and Woodworth. They insisted that the "imageless thoughts of relations" were not simple but complex processes involving kinesthetic images, unconscious forces, internal speech, organic sensations, and similar definite psychological and physical experiences subject to analysis by experimentation and introspection. They argued that the word *but* did not indicate any fundamental imageless feeling, that it merely stimulated or reflected an unsettled, suspended attitude caused by alternating attention to contradictory or incompatible ideas. Thought, feeling, purpose, and reasoning, said Titchener, involved changes in neural structures and were therefore subject to analysis as composites containing both physical and mental elements. Neural processes did not cause mental processes, he declared, but they were necessary links that played a part in and helped to explain the individual's ongoing mental experiences and actions. The mental processes, which preceded, accompanied, and followed one another in a stream of consciousness, were discovered and analyzed by introspection. (It may be recalled that the physiologist Pavlov arrived at the contrary conclusion that all mental phenomena consist of changes in physical structures. For Pavlov's behaviorist disciples, psychology should be the science, not of inner experience revealed by Wundtian introspection, but only of observable behavior.)

Titchener disagreed with Wundt's contention that tension is a simple feeling, asserting instead that tension involves a combination of feeling and sensations. As previously noted, Wundt had attributed to a specific cortical center the functions of inhibiting attention to distractions and concentrating attention upon a single object of perception. But Titchener declared that Wundt had been unable to prove the existence of that cortical center. He also joined other experimental psychologists in rejecting Wundt's tridimensional classification of feeling into pleasantness and unpleasantness, excitement and depression, and tension and relaxation. In Titchener's opinion, all sensations are subject to variation in space as well as in time, excitement is often followed, not by depression, but by calmness and cessation of feeling, and tension and relaxation are complex organic processes dependent upon kinesthetic and muscular reactions. Some complex feelings, he said, may be regarded as emerging sensations, while others may involve a great variety of nerve endings. He proposed a broad, two-dimensional classification of feeling into pleasure and pain.

PILLSBURY

Walter Bowers Pillsbury (1872–1960) won recognition as an authority on the relationships among sensation, attention, and perception. In his laboratory experiments and writings, he refined and supplemented many of the findings reported by Wundt and Titchener.

Pillsbury was born in Burlington, Iowa and attended public schools in Iowa and Nebraska, followed by two years (1889–1890) of education at Penn College in Iowa and enrollment in 1891 at the University of Nebraska. At the university, he studied psychology in the classes of Professor Wolfe, who had received his doctorate under Wundt at the University of Leipzig. After graduation, Pillsbury taught mathematics and English for one year at the newly organized Grand Island College of Nebraska, and then received a scholarship for graduate study at Cornell University. He studied at Cornell under the direction of Titchener and received the doctorate in 1896. The following year, he joined the faculty of the University of Michigan as an instructor in psychology, soon was appointed a full professor, and remained active on the faculty continuously until retiring as emeritus professor in 1942. Forty-five years of experimentation, writing, and teaching at the university won him an international reputation as an exponent of an eclectic point of view in expounding and evaluating the ideas of structuralist, functionalist, behaviorist, purposivist (hormic), Gestaltist, and psychoanalytic schools of psychology.

In his earliest laboratory experiments at Cornell University, Pillsbury traced the effects of visual attention on the individual's ability to localize tactile sensations. He demonstrated that attention to tiny internal parts as well as to the overall shapes of words is involved in meaningful reading. The reader's attitude, environmental setting, and deliberate acceptance of specific meanings and reactions among many other possible meanings and reactions control his reading and thinking processes. Learning from experience, said Pillsbury, is to some extent a matter of chance since it depends upon whatever stimuli the individual happens to choose for attention. Thus when one examines a drawing one's interpretation of its meaning will change if one concentrates one's attention on a main feature instead of a minor one; selective attention modifies the apparent design and identity of the objects portrayed. According to Pillsbury, other factors affecting perception include physical fatigue, especially fatigue of the cortical neurons; body movements of the observer requiring the adaptation of the sense organs to stimuli, a factor previously suggested by the French psychologist Théodule Armand Ribot (1839–1916); changes in respiration and circulation; mental anticipation, purpose, and organic needs; environmental and social conditions or distractions; and recalled events in the earlier education and experience of the individual.

The effects of previous experience as well as the resulting mental set of the observer upon his perception of objects were

explored experimentally by Adelbert Ames, Jr. (at the Dartmouth College Eye Institute in New Hampshire), and by other
research psychologists whose studies reinforced Pillsbury's
views. Ames demonstrated that when objects identical in size are
seen in distorted rooms with slanted floors, the observer judges
the objects to vary widely in size, an error explained by the fact
that he had become accustomed to seeing such objects in rectan-
gular rooms. Ames performed many experiments that proved
that the apperceptive background of the individual determines
major aspects of his perception. Similarly, numerous investigators during the 1950s and 1960s provided evidence supporting
Pillsbury's conclusions about the effects of fatigue, body movements, and drugs upon sensory reactions, attention, and perception.

Pillsbury performed some of the earliest experiments to determine the effects of concentrated attention by a learner attempting to master intricate motor skills. He suggested similar experiments to J. H. Bair, who in 1901 reported the same findings as
Pillsbury's: for example, the fact that motor learning improves if
the learner can forget or ignore incorrect or unnecessary movements and distractions while directing all his attention to correct
movements. On the other hand, Pillsbury himself later reported
the surprising fact that distractions can often increase learning
efficiency if the learner decisively rejects errors and intensifies
his efforts to master correct movements. According to Pillsbury,
there are three types of attention: (1) involuntary or spontaneous
attention as a reaction to a powerful sudden stimulus, often accompanied by a feeling of surprise; (2) nonvoluntary attention, a
response directed toward immediate purposes arising usually
from inherited or acquired needs or traits and accompanied by a
pleasant feeling of interest; and (3) voluntary attention, motivated by long-term aims and followed by sustained efforts to overcome obstacles, such as conflict with nonvoluntary attention
based on immediate impulses and needs. Pillsbury agreed with
Ribot that motor processes of the body and its sense organs influence or reinforce attention and perception—as, for example,
when the ciliary muscles of the eye contract to change the shape
of the lens for the sake of a clearer image of an object. The

individual's mental set, interest, and attention seem to accompany overt actions but usually precede and sustain them. The task or purpose in mind, resulting from organic, environmental, or social influences, modifies and controls attention and perception.

The same kind of mental set, the idea in mind, said Pillsbury, initiates or at least antecedes motor activities. Overt behavior also involves stimuli that affect a sense organ, prepare the individual for action, and adjust his reactions to the complexity and requirements of the situation. Reaction times vary with the particular sense organs affected by a specific stimulus. Individuals differ widely in reaction times. On the average, touch and hearing are the quickest senses to elicit reactions, faster than sight, smell, warmth, and pain. Reaction times slow down under the following conditions: when the individual has to discriminate among several stimuli before reacting; when he needs to consider more relationships and associations among stimuli and situations; and when he is not adequately prepared for a reaction. In judgments of duration, short periods under three-fourths of a second are usually overestimated while longer periods tend to be underestimated. Muscular contractions, especially during periods of anxious waiting and inactivity, create a feeling of strain that affects one's estimates of time intervals.

DEWEY, KOFFKA, WATSON

Oswald Kuelpe's statement in 1893 that many different kinds of conscious and partly unconscious ideas can motivate or initiate voluntary action reflected the growing interest of psychologists concerning relationships among ideas, sensations, attention, and perceptions. Thorndike wrote in 1909 that any mental state whatever may be followed by intentional, purposive action. Titchener considered Thorndike's view extreme, yet superior to the traditional theory that the individual's motive to obtain pleasure or avoid pain is the immediate, direct cause of his overt behavior. Functionalist psychologists, including Harvey A. Carr and John Dewey, rejected the structuralist view of sensations, feelings, and perceptions as subjective, interconnected units of consciousness. For them, psychological experiences depend upon utility, the attempts of every living organism to perform useful functions. Experiments by Carr at the University of Chicago explored the way in which individuals control and redirect their sensory responses and perceptions, selecting useful and eliminating useless reactions in order to accomplish motor tasks successfully—the principle of adaptation for the sake of utility or functionalism. John Dewey expounded this basic idea and also delineated certain principles acceptable to Gestaltist psychologists, such as Kurt Koffka, as well as concepts adopted by exponents of behaviorism, including its founder John B. Watson.

John Dewey. According to John Dewey, an objective stimulus, such as light waves or sound waves, plays an effective role in the individual's psychological experience only if he acts by sensing, organizing, and interpreting it and using it to make his next reaction possible. *Thus if a child sees fire as part of a dangerous situation, he may quickly move away from it.* The work of his nervous system and visual apparatus enables him to sense the fire in its entire surroundings so that it becomes a conscious subjective stimulus functioning usefully as part of a sensorimotor circuit or reflex arc connecting the stimulus with cognition (understanding), and the reaction to it, all constituting a unified stream of responses directed toward a purpose or goal, the avoidance of injury. The circuit is unbroken, a unity in experience, inseparable from the whole situation; the subjective stimulus is itself a motor activity, and sensation is united with action. All these factors are responsible for the composite mental experience, and all perform a useful function. Dewey's position was therefore quite different from that of the structuralists. For structural psychologists, neural processes are involved in sensations, feelings, and other subjective units of consciousness but do not cause them.

Koffka. Kurt Koffka (1886–1941) expounded the Gestaltist principle of insight (by the organism as a whole) into a whole situation, a principle similar to Dewey's concept of the inseparable stimulus-response circuit consisting of reactions organized and used for a purpose. For Koffka, not only are objective and subjective stimuli and responses inseparable parts of a unitary circuit, but even physical and unconscious as well as conscious mental reactions belong together as parts of an all-embracing psychophysical process. These reactions cannot be explained adequately, said Koffka, by those psychologists, such as the behaviorists, who try to analyze them as if they were separate bits of activity, nor can they be explained satisfactorily by structuralist psychologists who regard every sensation and perception as a separate mental element revealed by introspection. In fact, introspection is a unique additional activity quite different from the original sensation and perception; it provides insight into the whole psychophysical process and situation of the organism. Koffka cited an experiment of his colleague Wolfgang Köhler (1887–1967) in which a chimpanzee was taught to react positively to a dark shade of color but to ignore a lighter shade. When a still darker shade was substituted for the lighter shade, the animal transferred its positive reaction to the darkest color, proving that it had insight into the whole situation, the entire range of color shading. Such facts of psychology, said Koffka, are revealed only by observation of the individual's entire pattern of behavior, during which he reorganizes his perceptions of, and insight into, the life situation in all its relationships.

A percipient perceives not only a whole object or situation but also parts or features. Max Wertheimer (1880–1943, cofounder of Gestalt psychology with Koffka and Köhler) attempted in 1912 to explain, on the basis of his previous experiments, why stationary lights, each displayed separately at a high rate of speed, were perceived as a set, configuration, or stream of moving lights. The same problem of interpretation is involved in the fact that a triangle consisting of three individual lines is seen bound together into a single design or object. Gestalt psychology, applying careful observations and experiment, formulated general principles of perception to account for such relationships among whole objects or situations and their parts. Its principles were consistent with Dewey's emphasis on the unity of sensorimotor reactions to a complex situation. The Gestaltists rejected the traditional view that stimuli cause immediate sensations, memories, and associations that impel the individual to connect separate impressions with one another so as to create new perceptions of objects and situations.

The following were important principles set forth by Gestalt psychologists to account for the unified patterns and configurations of perception. (1) Figures close together tend to be seen as a unit—the principle of proximity. (2) Things that resemble one another closely tend to merge into a single configuration—the principle of similarity. (3) Objects combined so that they become continuous are perceived as a configuration—the principle of continuity. (4) Objects and figures containing tiny gaps will seem to be perfectly continuous if each is exposed to the observer for only an instant—the principle of closure. (5) Small details in a complex figure or object are interpreted by the observer, not as separate entities, but only as organic elements contributing to and subordinate to the entire figure or object—the principle that the whole controls the perception and interpretation of its parts.

In 1924 Koffka published a report classifying whole objects and situations into two types: (1) stable objects and situations, those not readily changed by the observer when he perceives them; and (2) less stable objects and situations, those that the observer tends to change by making them simpler or more complex, by unifying or disuniting them, or by amplifying or reducing them in scope.

Watson. Dewey's hypothesis that each mental experience is a unit in which sensory stimuli, interpretations, and motor responses are inseparably bound together as coordinated behavior to achieve a purpose was applied (beginning in 1913) by John B. Watson (1878–1958) and his behaviorist colleagues. Why, they asked, should psychologists even attempt to investigate subjective mental experiences, which are supposed to include (in Dewey's theory) coordinated stimuli, ideas, and reactions, if all mental experiences are fundamentally motor activities? Psychology, said Watson, should adopt the method of the physical sciences, investigating behavior only by means of objective observation and laboratory experiments. He declared that (in scientific analyses) introspections, subjective ideas and impressions, and inner experiences should be excluded from consideration because, even though they may actually be implicit motor responses, they cannot be observed objectively in controlled experiments. What indeed, he asked, could be learned from the introspections of infants or animals unable to communicate subjective feelings or images?

In his objective observations and experimental investigations of animal and human behavior, Watson applied the conditioning techniques devised by Pavlov. Watson's contemporary critic, William McDougall, insisted that the individual's purpose and motive affected profoundly what he saw and how he interpreted it. Count Alfred Habdank Skarbek Korzybsky (1879–1950) founder of the semantics movement in the 1930s, accorded to language experience a decisive role in all aspects of human nature and conduct. Cognitive psychologists, such as George A. Miller and Jerome S. Bruner, founders of the Harvard University Center for Cognitive Studies, Edward Sapir, and Benjamin L. Whorf pointed out that, besides sensations and diverse stimuli affecting perception, new elements of thought and communication are introduced, based upon the individual's previous experience, whenever he perceives, interprets, and reacts to each situation. Language and other meaningful symbols, said Whorf, determine our ideas and our perceptions of the environment.

In the judgment of many present-day psychologists, verbal and physiological responses often depend upon attitudes, ideas, goals, and expectations of the percipient. Watson's behaviorist doctrine has been accepted, therefore, only within narrow limits, as a partial explanation of some aspects of perception and behavior. In the broader view, language, experience and thinking processes of the individual reflect and alter the way in which he senses, perceives, interprets, and reacts. Contemporary psychologists place more emphasis than Watson did on the organism's purposive striving and on cognitive integrated actions of the individual as he attempts to cope with his internal and external environment—a point of view that considers not only behaviorist but also functionalist, Gestaltist, structuralist, psychoanalytic, and cognitive schools of psychology.

3 HEREDITY AND ENVIRONMENT

The great philosophers of the ancient world speculated about the inheritance of physical characteristics and attempted to account for resemblances between children and their parents.

Some attributed heredity to the production of minute particles that circulate in the body and replicate the characteristics of individual body parts.

EMPEDOCLES AND ARISTOTLE

Empedocles of Agrigentum (ca. 495–435 B.C.), who formulated a theory of biological evolution stating that man evolved through random, uncontrolled admixtures of body organs and the survival of the fittest (with physicians and prophets as the highest beings), asserted that seminal fluids from both parents flow throughout their bodies and thus reproduce similar organic structures and characteristics in the embryo. The driving forces in this process, he said, are love and hate, which unite, separate, and change the proportions of all substances in the universe. Physical structures inherited in this manner control sensation and other mental functions. The body receives particles from external objects as the basis for visual perception.

Aristotle adopted a somewhat different view of heredity. He compared the popular biogenetic theory to the notion that walls are built by materials, tools, and energy without the purpose, design, and work contributed by the builder. God (as pure contemplation) and nature, he declared, create nothing at random but everything for a purpose. All substances consist of both form and matter in reciprocal action for a definite end—that is, to

54

perform a function. The function of reproductive substances flowing from a specific type of parents is to produce the same type of offspring. Since the substances on the earth are never pure entities but only manifold combinations, the fruits of reproduction must usually be imperfect specimens. Moreover, said Aristotle, nature stops short of completing its work and achieving its goal, thereby producing weak or useless organs. Most parts of animals, however, are reproduced correctly so that they will be able to adapt to the environment and their life situation and needs. Aristotle explained in this way the phenomena of legs, wings, fins, and unique defensive organs of various animals. He noted that in the process of reproduction, the eye is so formed as to make it sensitive to a certain range of stimuli, including colors. But there are structural limitations; thus if the object seen is extremely small, its color is no longer visible. An object is felt through contact with the hand, but cannot be seen unless light separates it from direct contact with the eye.

Aristotle's ingenious speculations about heredity contained numerous errors. He asserted that semen was produced by the father's blood and impelled the female to create embryonic parts out of her menstrual fluids, a theory widely accepted during medieval times. He knew nothing about the role of the ovum in reproduction. He believed in spontaneous generation of plants and certain animals. Nevertheless, he pioneered in raising many perplexing problems of heredity, and his classification of animals was not excelled until the epochal work of Linnaeus in the eighteenth century.

THEOPHRASTUS AND LUCRETIUS

Theophrastus and Lucretius, Roman intellectual leaders, proposed noteworthy theories about heredity. Theophrastus (372–287 B.C.), who succeeded Aristotle as head of the Lyceum in Athens, achieved merited fame as the founder of botany as a systematic body of knowledge. He agreed with Aristotle's general thesis that all things in nature, including the inherited characteristics of animals, are designed to fulfill a purpose and to perform a definite function. Theophrastus, however, corrected

Aristotle's assumption that plants reproduce by means of spontaneous generation. He discovered plant sexuality and described
the process of pollination. The poet Lucretius (96–55 B.C.), the
famous Epicurean philosopher whose atomic doctrine (similar to
that of the Thracian philosophers Leucippus and Democritus in
the fifth century B.C.) foreshadowed modern physics, postulated
the transmission of individual physical traits through the passage
of germinating seeds from parents to their descendants. He defended the Empedoclean view that organisms must evolve and
adapt themselves to the environment in order to survive.

EARLY MODERN SCIENTISTS

Throughout the Middle Ages, biological sciences made virtually no progress. The thirteenth-century theologians Albertus
Magnus and Saint Thomas Aquinas, who regarded Aristotle as
their authority on biology and pyschology, accepted his theory
that species reproduce without basic changes in structures or
functions, a theory consistent with biblical references to divine
creation and the begetting of animals after their own kind.

In the seventeenth century, the Italian naturalist Francesco
Refi (1626–1697) proved experimentally that Aristotle's hypothesis of spontaneous generation was incorrect, and the English
naturalist John Ray (1627–1705) constructed a system of classification for many thousands of plants and animals, paving the
way for the more elaborate work of the great Swedish botanist
Carolus Linnaeus (1707–1778) whose method of binomial no-
menclature was to be modified but never superseded. Linnaeus
listed six classes of animals (insects, worms, fish, reptiles, birds,
and mammals). He accepted the biblical view that each species
had been created by God in an immutable form.

In the seventeenth and eighteenth centuries, advances in the
study of heredity were made as a result of experiments by William Harvey (1578–1657) in England, Anton van Leeuwenhoek
(1632–1723) in Holland, Regnier de Graaf (1641–1673) in
Holland, and Kaspar Friedrich Wolff (1733–1794) in Germany.
Harvey reported gradual changes in the form of the embryo during its development. Van Leeuwenhoek observed animal sperms

in his microscope and attributed the embryo to the union of sperms with eggs. De Graaf noted eggs in the human ovary and suggested the process of fertilization through the union of eggs and spermatozoa. In 1759 Wolff, the founder of modern embryology, proposed his epigenetic theory that the embryo is not preformed but develops in an orderly manner as a result of spontaneous interaction between internal energy and internal environmental conditions, a correct but incomplete concept inasmuch as he failed to postulate or identify the organizing, causative factors operating within the germ cells.

NINETEENTH-CENTURY BIOLOGISTS

The nineteenth century witnessed significant investigations into heredity by Lyell, Lamarck, Darwin, Weismann, De Vries, and Mendel.

In 1830 the British geologist Charles Lyell, father of modern geology, began to publish geological evidence, including descriptions of fossil remains, indicating the great age of the earth and supporting the conclusion that natural processes have gradually produced continuous changes in its structures and life forms, a principle that had been suggested by the French naturalist Georges Leclerc Buffon in 1779 and by the Scottish naturalist James Hutton in 1785.

In 1809 and 1815, the French naturalist Jean Baptiste Pierre Antoine de Monet Lamarck (1744–1829) had published his influential theory that the inheritance of acquired characteristics produces evolutionary modifications in organisms. According to Lamarck, environmental conditions compel animals to make extensive use of some parts of their bodies in order to meet life needs, eventually those parts develop more fully in this way, and the modified parts transmit their new characteristics to descendants who continue to make further adaptations so that more and more complex forms emerge.

Charles Robert Darwin (1809–1882) gave up preparation at Edinburgh University for a medical career and enrolled at Cambridge University where he studied geology and other sciences. Shortly after graduation in 1831, he joined a five-year geographical expedition to South America and oceanic islands as a naturalist on H.M.S. *Beagle*. During this voyage he made a large collection of plants, fossils, and animals, and noted the structural modifications, the excessive multiplication, the changing food habits, and even the disappearance of species inhabiting coastal areas. The probable causes of these changes occurred to him in 1838, when he read the newly published volume *Essay on Population*, by the English economist Thomas Robert Malthus, which stated that increases in human population were held in check by wars, famine, accidents, and disease. Darwin concluded that the struggle for existence and the survival of the fittest individuals in that struggle account for the variations and evolution of species. He announced this revolutionary theory in 1858 jointly with the surveyor, architect, and naturalist Alfred Russel Wallace, who had also read Malthus's book and had arrived independently at the same conclusion.

In 1859 Darwin published his classic *The Origin of Species*, presenting detailed corroborating evidence that he had accumulated and organized over a period of twenty years. He did not correct Lamarck's theory of the inheritance of acquired characteristics, but elaborated on his own mistaken theory of pangenesis (that small particles from all parts of the body pass into reproductive cells and thus reproduce the same kinds of body parts as those of the parents). In fact, in or about 1827 the great Estonian embryologist Karl Ernst von Baer had announced his discovery of the mammalian and human ovum, proving by observation that the origins of lower animals and man are quite similar, and he also had described the embryonic layers out of which the various body organs, structures, and systems are derived. The basic ideas of Buffon, Hutton, Lamarck, and Darwin were ably defended and popularized by the renowned British philosopher Herbert Spencer (1820–1903), a friend of Darwin's who applied a comparable theory of evolution to the entire universe.

The German scientist August Weismann (1834–1914), after serving as physician to the royal Austrian family, turned to biological studies. He taught for many years as professor of zoology at Freiburg University. His numerous reports on heredity were published in 1882 as a composite volume with a preface by Darwin. Weismann formulated the germ-plasm theory according to which stable germ cells combine with other unchanging germ cells to form body structures and transmit characteristics to succeeding generations. In 1888 Wilhelm von Waldeyer identified the chromosomes as the colored materials in germ cells, and Weismann concluded that the chromosomes contain hereditary materials that transmit characteristics from parents to offspring. (The unchanging hereditary units were subsequently named *genes* by the Danish scientist Wilhelm Johannsen.)

Hugo De Vries, the Dutch botanist trained in Germany, published in 1900 his discovery of sudden changes, or mutations, in the mechanism of heredity which were responsible for "sports," or new types of organisms. His experiments in crossing unusual forms of evening primroses proved that new forms can reproduce themselves systematically, a result now attributed to modifications in their chromosomes.

The Austrian monk Father Gregor Johann Mendel (1822–1884), devoting spare time to experiments with pure-breeding peas in a garden of his Augustinian monastery in Brünn (Brno in modern Czechoslovakia), discovered the precise quantitative relationships, mechanisms, and laws of heredity that became the foundations of the science of genetics. During a period of eight years he observed and carefully recorded the inheritance by the peas of each of seven pairs of characters, such as forms and colors of seeds and pods, lengths of stems, and flower distribution. He demonstrated that each pair of "factors," or genes (units of heredity) separates during the cell division that produces the germ cells, each member of a pair going to a separate germ cell, and later reuniting in random fashion—under the *law of segregation*; that two or more pairs of "factors" determining inheritance of traits segregate independently of each other, thus transmitting those traits independently of all other units and traits—under the *law of independent assortment*; and that one member of a pair of factors may be dominant over the other and thus be expressed when the two come together.

Mendel's reports and conclusions, originally published in 1866, attracted little attention until 1900, when Hugo De Vries, Erich Tschermak, and Karl Erich Correns, attempting to ac-

count for the occurrence of mutations, rediscovered and publicized Mendel's work. The science of genetics developed rapidly
upon the foundations built mainly by Lamarck, Weismann, De
Vries, Darwin, and Mendel.

GALTON, PEARSON, DUGDALE, GODDARD

Sir Francis Galton (1822–1911) was a pioneer in the genea-
logical study of heredity, the founder of the science of eugenics, a
famous explorer, a noted meteorologist and inventor of weather
charts that became models for modern weather maps, the inventor of a system of fingerprinting for identification, and a contributor to the art of portraiture.

Galton was born into a distinguished family in the vicinity of
Birmingham, England. He pursued scientific and medical studies at Birmingham Hospital, then at King's College in London,
and finally at Cambridge University from which he graduated in
1843. However, he gave up his plans for a medical career in
order to pursue the scientific researches through which he
achieved international fame, fellowship in the Royal Society,
honorary degrees from Oxford and Cambridge universities, the
Darwin Medal, and knighthood.

Galton concluded from his unprecedented studies of family
histories of famous men that heredity was responsible for many
physical and mental traits of individuals. Using questionnaires
returned by large numbers of people and a method of statistical
correlation, he discovered that close family relationships, compared with distant or negative relationships, were accompanied
by much greater similarity in the ability and character of individuals. He completed pioneering studies of twins, demonstrating great similarity in their physical and personality traits. He
analyzed the records of his own family antecedents (including
the Wedgwoods of pottery fame; his grandfather Erasmus Darwin, the noted poet and naturalist; and his renowned cousin
Charles Robert Darwin), and found an abundance of scientists
in his family history.

The English mathematician Karl Pearson (1857–1936), applying and refining Galton's statistical method, traced the

Wedgwood-Darwin-Galton family back hundreds of years and arrived at the same conclusion as Galton concerning the potent influence of heredity. Pearson, who devised the statistical technique that used correlation coefficients to indicate relationships among sets of data, such as test scores, found the same degree of correlation (.5) among siblings in their personality traits as in their physical traits, such as eye color. Since such physical traits as eye color are inherited, it seemed evident to him that personality traits are also inherited.

In 1875 and 1877, the American sociologist Richard Louis Dugdale (1841–1883) reported the family history of the Juke family, which seemed to show an unusually high incidence of crime, poverty, and prostitution among numerous members throughout seven generations, a result he attributed to heredity. It has been pointed out that he failed to consider adequately the possible effects on their behavior of their poor social environment. On the other hand, since the same adverse social environment afflicted other families exhibiting a much lower incidence of antisocial behavior, many psychologists concluded that hereditary as well as environmental factors had contributed to the Jukes' bad family history.

In 1912 the psychologist Henry Herbert Goddard (1866–1957) of the Vineland, New Jersey, Training School for feebleminded children traced the genealogy of two collateral branches of the "Kallikak" family (a fictitious name), the first stemming from the mating of one man apparently of normal intelligence with a mentally retarded woman, the second from lawful marriage of the same man with a woman regarded as mentally normal. He found a stream of hundreds of mentally retarded descendants from the first union contrasted with a long line of hundreds of superior descendants from the second union. Goddard also analyzed the family backgrounds of 327 retarded persons and stated that about half these cases were attributable to heredity. He concluded that heredity was more potent than environment in the determination of physical and mental traits, and that a general mental ability, or intelligence, contrasted with knowledge, was entirely inherited. But geneticists opposed to Goddard's views pointed out that the father of the Kallikaks must have transmitted similar recessive genes both to the first, mentally retarded, mother and to the mentally normal mother. Consequently, if inheritance had been the basic influence, many descendants of the second, normal mother would also have been mentally retarded due to the inheritance of defective genes from the father.

The conclusions of Galton, Pearson, Dugdale, and Goddard have been criticized for their failure to take environmental influences sufficiently into consideration. Moreover, their data were suspect inasmuch as public reputation, secondhand reports, biographies, and court records do not provide adequate scientifically valid evidence of any person's intelligence, character, merit, or personality traits.

It should be noted that Galton meant by *heredity* all the factors affecting the infant before birth, and by *environment* all the postnatal influences that strengthen, thwart, or supplement native equipment and natural tendencies.

The relative importance of heredity and environment for most aspects of human behavior remained scientifically undetermined. Nevertheless, the views of these early investigators had a profound influence on the psychology of heredity, especially stimulating the analysis of apparently inherited mental deficiencies and pathological defects.

Galton and his associate Pearson claimed that sufficient knowledge about heredity would enable human beings to improve inherited equipment by means of selective breeding, just as breeders of animals have done. Critics pointed out that the breeding of an animal species to develop a superior single trait is relatively simple but frequently results in the inheritance of undesirable traits as well. Knowledge about human heredity, they said, is far too limited to justify extensive restrictions upon individual choice of mates. Furthermore, increases in relevant knowledge may make it possible to counteract inherited deficiencies or even to directly repair abnormal genes.

TWENTIETH-CENTURY SCIENTISTS

Twentieth-century biologists investigated intensively the prenatal structures, internal environments, and genetic mechanisms involved in reproduction and heredity. Sociologists studied environmental factors affecting inherited "original nature." Psychologists observed and correlated behavior patterns, using biological discoveries to explore the hereditary and environmental roots of human nature and conduct. From their respective points of view, biologists, sociologists, and psychologists developed mutually helpful data. In some cases, as in the studies of twins, color blindness, crime, and various mental disorders, the methods of investigation of these disciplines were almost identical despite differences in emphasis.

Among outstanding accomplishments in biology during the early decades of the twentieth century were the findings of Thomas Hunt Morgan and Hermann Joseph Muller concerning gene structure. Morgan demonstrated an exchange of materials among genes. Muller, who had studied with Morgan at Columbia University, utilized X rays to modify gene structure in such a way as to produce inheritable mutations.

In the 1940s, the American microbiologist O. T. Avery and his colleagues at the Rockefeller Institute, experimenting with pneumococci, identified and isolated in genes DNA material (consisting of pure nucleic acid) that transmits hereditary changes to such bacterial cells. The American chemist Linus Pauling delineated the way in which abnormal chemical and electrical forces modify the capacity of protein to bind substances in blood cells and thus cause the inherited disease of sickle-cell anemia. Subsequent researchers at Cambridge University traced the disease to abnormal changes in the shapes of red blood cells owing to a lack of glutamic acid.

In 1951 the biochemists Francis C. H. Crick, and James D. Watson constructed a widely accepted theory postulating the double-strand structure of the DNA (deoxyribonucleic acid) molecule and its functions in controlling the transmission of inherited characteristics. In 1955 Heinz Fraenkel-Conrat, an American biochemist working at the University of California with tobacco-mosaic viruses, broke them into nucleic acids and protein material, destroying their ability to infect cells, then reassembled and reconstituted them to restore a degree of infectivity. He induced mutations in cells by chemical means so that they reproduced in the new form. In 1956 the American biochemist Arthur Kornberg of Stanford University separated enzymes active in DNA cell division to synthesize DNA, the molecules that work together with RNA (ribonucleic acid) molecules to transmit inherited traits. In 1958 the American geneticist Joshua Lederberg proved that bacteria combine sexually and thereby exchange genetic substances. In 1959 the zoologist R. A. Brink of the University of Wisconsin demonstrated that genes, though unalterable by the external environment, can sometimes be altered by the action of other genes.

In 1968 the American scientists H. Gobind Khorana of the University of Wisconsin and Marshall W. Nirenberg of the National Heart Institute showed how enzymes, chains of amino acids, control various genetic functions of cells. In 1969 the American biologist Solomon Spiegelman of the University of Illinois synthesized RNA in a test tube; and in 1969 David Kohne at the Carnegie Institute isolated and purified selected genes, forecasting the possibility of replacing defective genes in order to modify inherited traits.

American biologists at Rockefeller University and at the National Institutes of Health in the 1970s restored the impaired ability of living cells to produce useful enzymes, by injecting genes into the cells. In 1978 the Nobel Prize in physiology was awarded to Werner Arber of the University of Basel and Daniel Nathans and Hamilton O. Smith of the Johns Hopkins University for their discovery that enzymes as biological catalysts cut parts of the chemical strands of genetic material (DNA or deoxyribonucleic acid). Genes within cells can be cut, spliced, and reorganized for the study of chemical factors determining hereditary characteristics. (A typical cell contains twenty-three pairs of chromosomes carrying a total of perhaps forty thousand genes, the basic units of heredity.) Researchers working with Swiss biologist Charles Weissman of the University of Zürich and with the American biologist Walter Gilbert of Harvard University used gene-splitting techniques for the artificial production of interferon, a complex family of protein molecules normally produced by the body as a defensive substance, especially against viruses. This discovery raised the possibility of large-scale laboratory production of various biological materials useful for combating certain inherited defects as well as acquired diseases. In 1980 differences in the chemical structure of bacterial and animal genes were discovered. At Yale University, Francis Ruddle and his associates transplanted genes successfully into mouse embryos.

STUDIES OF TWINS

Titchener at Cornell University, who accepted Darwin's theory of human evolution through natural selection, asked how it had been possible for the first living organisms to evolve out of nonliving substances. He concluded that there were intermediate stages of partly living organisms that from time to time developed roots, rudimentary bits and pieces eventually working together to create purposive reactions and mechanisms for advanced species, and that only introspection could reveal clearly and fully the end result—conscious behavior. Nevertheless, as a disciple of Wundt, Titchener admired the laboratory experiments of his contemporary, the Columbia University psychologist Edward Lee Thorndike, who advocated analysis of the observed reactions of individuals under controlled conditions in preference to introspection.

Thorndike. Thorndike implemented his own point of view by completing many significant experimental studies of animal intelligence and learning. In 1904 he wrote the first textbook on the subject of mental tests. In 1905 he began a notable study of twins, using his own mental tests instead of depending on records, reports, and statistical data as Galton and Pearson had done. He tested pairs of twins and pairs of other siblings. Each pair of twins had similar high, average, or low scores, whereas the pairs of siblings had much more divergent scores. Environmental backgrounds seemed to be rather similar for twins and siblings. Consequently, Thorndike concluded that only their similar inherited mental traits or inherited intelligence could account for the greater similarity of test scores among the pairs of twins, and that only their differing inherited traits could account for the greater differences in the test scores among pairs of siblings. The environment, he asserted, provides stimuli that may either develop or to some extent modify and redirect the individual's inherited equipment (neural mechanisms and inborn reactions), but it does not eliminate certain basic, unlearned drives and characteristics passed on from parents to offspring. He listed more than forty unlearned reactions as instincts, a view of heredity disputed by most later psychologists. (Thorndike discounted the factor that the home environments of twins are generally more alike than the home environments of pairs of siblings.)

Many psychologists, however, interpreted Thorndike's data as indicating that both heredity and environment contribute substantially to superior or inferior mental abilities. (In 1929, using the method of co-twin control, L. C. Strayer and Arnold L. Gesell completed an experiment in which a pair of mentally subnormal twins remained remarkably alike in their motor skills and educational achievements even though they had been given very different amounts of training. The twin given only two weeks of delayed training equaled the twin given six weeks of training, indicating that the native equipment and stage of maturation were responsible for the end results. Furthermore, despite a great deal of extra training, both twins continued to be greatly inferior in achievement to younger children of normal intelligence who received much less training.)

Newman et al. During the 1920s and 1930s, the American zoologist Horatio Hackett Newman (1875–1957) of the University of Chicago, who wrote *The Biology of Twins* in 1917, pioneered in the experimental study of twins. He repeatedly administered intelligence tests to pairs of identical twins reared apart, and pairs of fraternal twins reared together. The test scores of the pairs of identical twins reared apart in different environments differed only slightly more than the test scores of identical twins reared together. It seemed to Newman that the variations in the environments of the identical twins reared apart had therefore only slightly modified their inherited mental abilities and that heredity was the most important factor. The test scores of ten pairs of fraternal twins reared together differed markedly from one another, apparently reflecting wider differences in their heredity.

In 1937 Newman and his colleagues Frank N. Freeman and

Karl J. Holzinger published the results of a significant study dealing with nineteen pairs of identical adult twins, some of whom had lived apart in different environments from early childhood while others had lived together in the same environment. Once again the data, including physical measurements and mental test scores, indicated the potent influence of heredity. But some new facts emerged from his study. Pairs of identical twins reared either together or in very similar environments were found to be amazingly alike in body build, appearance, personality, interests, behavior patterns, and family histories. However, some identical twins brought up in similar environments who had experienced substantial differences in health and education developed similar physical characteristics but quite different personality traits and mental abilities.

In 1962 James Shields of the London Institute of Psychiatry reported the results of a similar study of forty-four identical twins reared apart, and arrived at the same conclusion as previous investigators: that multiple hereditary and environmental factors contribute to the development of adult personality traits and that inherited genes should be regarded as possibly decisive influences.

Wingfield. These conclusions were consistent with the correlations among eight classes of persons studied by A. H. Wingfield and his colleagues in numerous studies of subjects ranging from identical and fraternal twins to cousins and entirely unrelated individuals. Similarities in personality and mental ability appeared to increase steadily with the increase in the closeness of family relationships. The concordance (similarity) on the average among twins of different sexes, for example, was found to be about double that among cousins, while the concordance among identical twins appeared to be on the average nearly double that among siblings. In 1976, a summary report by J. C. Loehlin and R. C. Nichols stated that in nearly all aspects of personality and skill, similarity among identical twins was found by all researchers to be greater than similarity among fraternal twins. However, in the early 1960s the American psychologists P. H. Mussen, J. J. Conger, and J. Kagan had reviewed numerous studies of personality development and mental ability and had concluded that close family relationships often were accompanied by similar environmental influences as well as similar heredity, and that either heredity or environment or both might be decisive causes of various adult abilities, interests, and traits.

Kraepelin and Kallmann. Studies of mental disorders such as schizophrenia have shed light upon genetic factors as well as biochemical, physical, psychological, and various environmental influences affecting the development of abnormal personality traits, neurotic symptoms, and related behavior. The Swiss psychiatrist Eugen Bleuler (1857–1939), who in 1911 used the term *schizophrenia* (instead of the old term *dementia praecox*) to denote "split personality," attributed that disorder mainly to inner emotional conflicts (ambivalence) initiated most probably by toxic or pathological conditions. Emil Kraepelin, on the other hand, who studied schizophrenic patients during several decades, concluded that such illnesses were caused mainly by hereditary structures or predispositions intensified by endocrine, metabolic, and other biological abnormalities. Kraepelin's view of hereditary factors was reinforced by the American psychiatrist Franz J. Kallmann and his colleagues at the New York Psychiatric Institute, who studied hundreds of twins and other relatives of schizophrenic patients. In one study of nearly seven hundred pairs of twins, Kallmann reported that about one-third of fraternal twins were alike in their resistance or lack of resistance to schizophrenia, whereas about 95 percent of the identical twins were alike in this respect.

Scientific studies of adopted children of schizophrenic parents by the British psychiatrist L. L. Heston in the 1960s and by the Danish psychiatrists D. Rosenthal, P. H. Wender, S. S. Kety, B. Jacobsen, and H. Schulzinger in the 1960s and 1970s indicated that schizophrenic diseases, as well as paranoid and schizoid disorders, are at least in part caused by or rooted in hereditary factors. The studies showed that a large proportion of children born to schizophrenic parents but reared by normal adoptive parents developed similar psychoses, whereas children whose natural parents were normal but who were reared by schizophrenic adoptive parents did not become psychotic. (These investigators found inherited genetic forces as well as the environment of adopting homes to be important influences on criminal behavior of adopted individuals, also that inherited biological factors are more potent than environmental conditions as causes of extreme alcohol addiction.)

Bouchard. In Rome, Italy, in 1974, an International Society of Twins Study held its first meeting to discuss research problems and findings concerning the estimated world population of 100 million twins. For many years, the famous Gregor Mendel Institute for Medical Genetics and Twin Studies, with its headquarters in Rome, has collected information about thousands of pairs of twins. In the United States, the National Research Council has maintained records for twins who have served in the armed forces. In recent years, the University of Minnesota has conducted research programs under the direction of the psychologist Thomas J. Bouchard, Jr., to investigate the heredity of identical and fraternal twins. Repeated intelligence tests, periodic health examinations, and analyses of observed habits and reactions revealed, as had previous investigations, that identical twins remained very much alike permanently in physical and mental abilities, interests, and personality even if they had been separated from each other in infancy and had been reared in quite different homes and communities. Bouchard emphasized the need for further long-term investigation of the future descendants of identical twins reared apart. Like Newman's data, Bouchard's information included coincidences such as reports that pairs of identical twins, though long separated, used the same names for pet dogs.

ENVIRONMENTAL STUDIES

During the first half of the twentieth century, a new emphasis became apparent in the views of social scientists concerning heredity and environment. Surveys of urban and rural communities and institutions, such as the family and the school, and scientific analyses of education and health, crime and poverty, ethnic conflicts, and human relationships provided rich information about the potent influence of the environment. It became increasingly clear that intelligence could not be attributed exclusively to heredity, nor could maladjustments such as delinquency and crime be attributed mainly to innate biological defects. The majority of social scientists did not accept the hereditarian conclusions of anthropologist Earnest Albert Hooton (1887–1954) of Harvard University, who simply studied the physical and genetic characteristics of antisocial individuals and then assumed that inherited inferiority was mainly responsible for criminal behavior. Many psychologists joined the behaviorist school, which rejected the instinct theory and asserted that the environment was responsible for all aspects of human nature and conduct.

Leading American psychologists accepted this emphasis on the environment in developing comparatively new fields of psychological study, such as educational psychology, child psychology, industrial psychology, business psychology, mental hygiene, and social psychology. Despite wide differences in the degree of importance they attached to heredity and to other biological factors, they all recognized the profound effects of drastic changes in the physical and social environment of individuals. Thus McDougall, a firm exponent of the instinct theory and the role of biological motivation, rejected behaviorism but stressed the modifiability of innate tendencies and instinctive behavior patterns through education, the physical environment, and social institutions. Among the most widely disseminated early environmental researches were those of Jean Itard, Kingsley Davis, Lewis Madison Terman, the Gluecks, and Jean Piaget.

Itard. Philippe Pinel (1745–1826), advocated and practiced humane treatment of the insane. In 1799 a twelve-year-old boy, entirely uneducated, who had been running wild and almost naked in the woods, was brought to Pinel for examination. (The boy's earlier background and previous human contacts were largely unknown.) Pinel pronounced him an incurable idiot. The boy had been living like an animal in the fields, capable of bare survival but apparently unable to speak, to feel intense heat or cold, to react normally to loud noises, or to distinguish and identify common objects by means of sight, taste, and touch. His filthy habits and crude, impulsive movements earned him the appellation "The Wild Boy of Aveyron."

Jean Marc Gaspard Itard (1775–1838), a young colleague of

Pinel's, inspired by John Locke's theory that only life experience develops mental ability, attempted patiently over a period of more than five years to teach the boy, whom he named Victor, the rudiments of speech and to improve his sensory perceptions, intellectual functions, and relationships to people. Although the results of Itard's kindness and training were limited by Victor's mental deficiency—which according to Itard was an inherited handicap so severe as to make normal progress impossible—the boy showed considerable improvement until he could understand spoken words and written instructions, identify and remember the uses of familiar objects, spell a few words by rearranging cutout letters, and solve very simple problems requiring judgments about similarities in the colors and designs of objects. Despite episodic temper tantrums and destructive, at times epileptic, seizures, he developed a sense of cleanliness and order and affectionate disposition. Itard's crude, unscientific, but useful experiment proved that greatly improved environment—especially humane social communication and cooperative human relationships—can influence for the better the physical, constitutional, psychological, and social makeup of even severely retarded individuals.

Davis. During the 1940s, sociologist Kingsley Davis of Columbia University reported his extensive observations of two girls who had been kept in isolation, almost totally deprived of human communication from birth to the age of six years, at which time they began to receive normal care and training.

The first girl, Anna, had been confined in a secluded room by her indifferent mother, who fed her just enough to keep her alive but never spoke or showed affection to her. The child stayed in bed, unable to feed herself or speak, malnourished and unhealthy, incapable of normal perceptions or mental reactions. Nevertheless, when she was removed to a decent environment and provided with good though not expert care and instruction, Anna improved rapidly, began to speak and walk, and cooperated with other children in everyday activities. Prior to her death at about eleven years of age, she had attained mental and social development comparable to that of a normal two- or three-year-old child.

The second girl, Isabelle, had been isolated in a dark room

with her mother, a deaf-mute, for the same reason as Anna, namely, to avoid the disgrace of illegitimate birth. Isabelle, however, existed in a somewhat better environment despite malnutrition and lack of oral communication, for her mother showed her some affection or at least friendly attention. After being removed from the isolated environment, Isabelle benefited from skillful care and training provided by psychologists and teachers. She progressed more rapidly than Anna had done, so that within two or three years she reached the same level as normal children of her age in mental ability, education, and personality.

These two cases of retarded isolated children were regarded by many psychologists as evidence that the social environment is a major determinant of human nature and conduct. Both girls began their new experiences at a very low mental level, reflecting extreme inherited and environmental handicaps. For one girl, a fairly good new environment brought moderate improvement. For the other much more favorable new environment and careful training produced remarkably rapid and extensive progress.

Terman et al. Lewis Madison Terman (1877–1956) began to study gifted children in 1911 at Stanford University. In 1913 he reported unexpected results of his investigations, emphasizing the gifted child's superiority in health, physical and mental capability, and personality adjustment. In 1922 Terman was appointed head of the psychology department at Stanford University. During the 1920s, he and his colleagues selected 1,000 gifted children for intensive study out of 250,000 children who had been rated by their teachers and had also been tested by two standardized intelligence tests. Terman considered heredity a significant factor among these gifted children, citing high correlations between their intelligence scores and the accomplishments of their parents in education and the professions. He noted that a large proportion had parents who had emigrated from northern and western European countries and also that a large proportion were Jewish children, while a much smaller proportion were blacks and children in various other minority groups.

Terman's conclusion that intellectually gifted children are often better adjusted, superior in character, physically healthier and stronger, and educationally more advanced than average children of normal intelligence appeared justified by his data, which included anthropometric, medical, and educational information as well as psychological test scores. But his assumption that racial and geographical origins correspond to specific levels of inherited intelligence was rejected by critics who maintained that high scores of gifted children probably reflect favorable cultural and environmental backgrounds, for example traditions and customs of Jewish families.

Terman could provide no evidence that hereditary deficiencies, rather than educational and social disadvantages, were responsible for the small proportion of gifted children in families of the laboring class. In 1959 he and his associate M. H. Oden agreed that the successes of gifted children, at least in later years of development, depended more upon family associations, intense interest in vocational and economic leadership, and character traits such as persistence than it depended upon inherited mental ability. In 1960 Terman and Maude A. Merrill reported that intelligence tests administered at an early age did not provide a good basis for predicting the future intellectual achievements of individuals. (Studies by Nancy Bayley in 1949 and 1960 arrived at a similar conclusion even though she also noted that the intelligence quotient of many individuals tended to remain about the same during the period of eleven to seventeen years of age.)

Terman's earlier contention that the child's basic mental capacity is inherited and remains relatively constant was rejected by investigators at the University of Iowa, including Beth L. Wellman and George D. Stoddard, who held that mental ability changed substantially with large shifts from poor to excellent environments. It seemed probable that children taking intelligence tests are penalized if their previous social environment, urban or rural, has made them unfamiliar with specific words, logical manipulations, and other factors involved in test questions. Furthermore, many aspects of mental ability are difficult to measure by verbal or nonverbal intelligence tests. Children with broader and richer life experience have an advantage over other children in taking tests or in otherwise demonstrating intellectual capacity.

Barbara S. Burks, one of Terman's co-workers, compared the mental ability of foster children with the educational and occupational backgrounds of their biological parents and also of their foster parents. The results, published in 1928, showed much greater similarity between parents and their biological children than between parents and their foster children. In the same year, however, Frank N. Freeman and his colleagues stated that in their studies of foster children, the test scores ranked them about midway in intelligence when compared with their natural parents and their foster parents. Sigmund Freud and other psychiatrists emphasized the fact that internal and external environmental conditions and related experiences during the first year after conception have profound and lasting influence on the mental and emotional makeup of the person. Leading anthropologists pointed out that genetic differences among national, regional, or racial groups are slight, relatively unimportant compared to the effects of diverse environments, very early biological factors, nutrition and health, and familial, economic, cultural, and social conditions.

During the 1940s, J. H. Rohrer reported that when Osage Indian children were removed from poverty-stricken families to more prosperous foster homes, their intelligence test scores rose from considerably below normal until they equaled or exceeded the scores of average white children. Various studies indicated, too, that in poor environments the older children tend to earn the lowest intelligence-test scores compared with the IQs of younger children in those environments, apparently reflecting the longer period of exposure to adverse environmental conditions.

According to the psychologist Carl Ransom Rogers of the University of Chicago, a good new environment in foster homes can help many children with emotional and behavior disturbances to gain self-understanding, self-confidence, and better social adjustment. Inner conflicts, fears, suspicions, and resentment directed against parents or others can often be remedied as the child begins to express his feelings freely and then sees himself in a more favorable light. In the 1940s and 1950s, Rogers applied his technique of client-centered counseling as therapy for

adults who similarly needed self-expression to gain self-understanding and self-confidence.

Eleanor and Sheldon Glueck. In the area of delinquency
and crime, the emphasis in research also shifted from hereditary
to environmental causes. Cesare Lombroso (1836–1909), an
Italian physician and criminologist, was a foremost exponent of
the view that antisocial behavior can be predicted from the presence of inherited physical traits, such as high cheekbones; reced-
ing chins; small, lobeless, or malformed ears; low foreheads; and
crooked noses—a view Karl Pearson easily disproved through
careful examination of criminals and comparisons with others.

Significant researches into causes of delinquency and crime
were carried on during four decades beginning in the early
1930s by the American criminologists Sheldon Glueck (1896–
1980) and Eleanor Touroff Glueck (1898–1972) under the auspices of Harvard University. The Gluecks concluded that most
people who live in adverse environments ignore or reject opportunities for delinquency and crime. Most of those who persist in
antisocial behavior do so primarily because of psychological and
social factors, cultural conflicts and difficulties of adjustment,
strains of present-day society, and their own developed habits
and temperaments. In 1968 the Gluecks, reporting on a fifteen-
year follow-up study (a sequel to a ten-year study in 1950) of
one thousand delinquent and nondelinquent boys in slum areas
listed forty influences in the development of delinquency, including family background, social conditions, discipline, permissive-
ness, and affection on the part of parents, as well as personal
health problems and body types and defects. Delinquents, they
said, are more aggressive, stubborn, energetic, impulsive, and
emotionally less stable than other children. Although boldness
and bodily strength may become ingredients of complex situations leading to antisocial attitudes and aggressive behavior, the
main causes are personality disturbances and environmental
conditions rather than retarded or inherited mentality. In fact,
many known criminals are ingenious and clever, and doubtless
many are so superior in mental capacity as to escape detection.

Many contemporary psychologists endorsed the emphasis
placed by the Gluecks on environmental influences, especially

rejection of children by the family, overindulgence by parents, and other deficiencies in their human relationships. They concluded that personality disturbances and antisocial reactions were frequently attributable to physical, biological, and social environments interacting with the inherited genetic equipment of individuals.

Jean Piaget. The relative importance of heredity and the environment for the individual's level of mental ability cannot be properly evaluated without considering the basic nature and development of intelligence. The renowned Swiss child psychologist Jean Piaget (1896–1980) of the University of Geneva investigated the growth of intelligence in children over several decades and made significant contributions to the study of mental processes. His *Psychology of Intelligence,* published in France in 1947, reviewed critically the ideas of leading thinkers concerning the nature, genesis, and development of intelligence, especially the concept of Lamarck and Darwin that human equipment and abilities have evolved from lower forms of life.*

Piaget asserted that perceptions and motor reactions are learned through the application of intelligence to experience, and that thoughts are products created by the individual as he organizes and separates or reorganizes elements of language, symbols, meanings, actions, events, values, and objects into classes and groupings. The scope, efficiency, and applications of mental operations change with age and with each stage of development. Some persons perform the classifying and grouping functions more effectively more often than others do and therefore, as Charles Spearman contended, possess relatively superior general intelligence. But human relationships, communication, and the social environment are central factors in the operations of the mind and the development of mental abilities. Piaget observed that an infant may at first be only intuitively, vaguely aware of external stimuli and be unable to discriminate among words, physical objects, pictures, and people. Eventually he mas-

---

* During the 1920s, William McDougall at Harvard University, experimenting with white mice, investigated again the old Lamarckian theory that animals sometimes transmit acquired modifications and behavior patterns to successive generations, but the results of his experiments were uniformly negative.

ters language, space and time relationships, and other aspects of experience that help him to make complex distinctions and to assimilate and utilize new concepts, meanings, and patterns of thought. The social environment, especially close human relationship and communication, interacting with basically identical inherited equipment, is mainly responsible for the way the child thinks and learns to think, acts, and grows in mental powers during each period of his life-span.

Thus Piaget's cognitive views reinforced the conclusions of Itard, Davis, Freeman, Rohrer, and the Gluecks concerning the potent influence of the external social environment, particularly language and communication, upon the level and growth of intelligence. The cognitive psychologists Edward Sapir, Benjamin L. Whorf, George A. Miller, and Jerome S. Bruner, and students of semantics, including Count Alfred H. S. Korzybski, Wendell Johnson, and S. I. Hayakawa, contended that reasoning, emotional adjustments, and many aspects of behavior depend upon language experiences of the individual.

Other Recent Investigators. The infinite number and variety of interactions between hereditary and environmental forces vastly complicate attempts to identify and explain the sequential results upon the individual's mind and personality at different stages of his life. During the 1930s, the Gestalt psychologist Kurt Lewin, analyzing key factors in the development of human motives and personality, formulated a theory of tensions and a topological or quantitative method of measuring stresses and drives as responses to a total environment or life space. Similar analyses were developed by the Gestalt psychologist Koffka. During the 1920s and 1930s, the leading American sociologist Robert E. Park and his associates at the University of Chicago investigated the relationships between human behavior and geographical, industrial, ecological, urban, economic, and social environments. In the 1930s and 1940s, Henry Alexander Murray of Harvard University and Eugene Chace Tolman of the University of California analyzed effects of geographical and ecological environments upon personality development and cognition.

Contemporary psychologists have undertaken many researches

into the influence of environmental forces upon behavior, and into the perceptions and interpretations of individuals regarding various types of environmental factors. These studies have been much more diversified than the older laboratory experiments by Watson and other behaviorists exploring the effects of specific external stimuli on organic reactions. Recent investigators have dealt with the psychological effects of crowding, air pollution, noise, space and privacy, landscapes and architectural characteristics, natural resources, and the like, as well as the psychological motives, reactions, and behavior of individuals and groups in relation to their whole environment. Typical reports and theories, to mention a few, were published during the 1970s by D. Stokols, E. Sundstrom, J. Schopler, and others on the physical, social, and other effects of crowding; by R. H. Moos on community settings and social ecology; by W. H. Ittelson, H. M. Proshansky, and R. M. Downs on the individual's perception and interpretations of the environment; and by N. D. Weinstein and others on the effects of noise on individuals.

It seems safe to conclude from the bulk of numerous recent research studies that inherited genetic structures cannot be expected to develop properly or even to function in a completely hostile environment. Even an infant perfectly endowed genetically must depend upon a wholesome initial environment, the mother's warm affection and nutrients provided in the womb as well   challenging stimulants of experience. But psychologists have scarcely begun to unravel the intricate interrelationships between the hereditary and environmental factors responsible for any aspect of normal or abnormal human development and behavior. Research and experimentation in the field of heredity and environment are i a primitive stage in which the basic unsolved problems far outweigh the problems already solved.

4   GROWTH AND DEVELOPMENT

The development in plants and animals of parts or organs and the processes of growing, maturing, and aging have absorbed the attention of leading thinkers throughout history. The Greek philosopher Democritus declared that all things, living or nonliving, consist of indestructible atoms that move continually and change their structures in accordance with eternal natural laws. Aristotle held that animals grow differently than plants because nature gives animals organs that enable them to move about and perform numerous functions, whereas plants are restricted in the spread of their roots and the scope of their activities, which consist mainly of growth and spontaneous generation (an error corrected by Theophrastus). According to Aristotle, the earliest stage of human growth depends upon nutrition provided by surplus blood of parents; the embryo grows because its inner energy and the father's semen have stirred up movement in the mother's reproductive system. Attempting to explain memory and the development of intelligence, he declared that universal truths constantly enter into and control every person's mind until his thinking powers weaken in old age and disappear. In Aristotle's view, the basic elements responsible for human growth are nutrition supplied by the blood and heart; the functions of sense organs; and the work of the soul or reason. Medieval and early modern thought associated growth and aging with the four temperaments or humors described by Hippocrates. Vigorous blood circulation and an enthusiastic temperament were supposed to dominate in childhood and youth, a mixture of choleric and melancholy dispositions in later years, and retarded, phlegmatic reactions in old age.

FROEBEL, PREYER, COOLEY, AND BÜHLER

The great German educator Friedrich Froebel (1782–1852) described growth as a natural process whereby the inner powers of the child unfold, just as plants grow from within. His doctrine had a profound influence on psychology and education, changing ideas about the nature and needs of children emphasizing their inner drives and self-expression, a point of view generally accepted by modern psychologists.

The German Darwinian physiologist and psychologist Wilhelm Thierry Preyer (1841–1897) carefully and systematically observed his own child's daily growth in physical powers and mental ability, progress described in his classic volume *The Mind of the Child* (1890). He reported, for example, that at eighteen months the child still tended to confuse parts of his own body with external things; thus he attempted to give away his foot as if it were a toy. Preyer's observations set a precedent for subsequent researches. A more subjective but popular anecdotal book, *The Biography of a Baby*, by Millicent W. Shinn published in 1900, described a child's first year of growth and stimulated wide interest among parents and teachers in the facts of human development.

In 1902 the American sociologist Charles H. Cooley analyzed infant communication and agreed with Preyer that it takes many months for neonates to become aware of various differences between the self and external objects. The infant learns such distinctions, said Cooley, from the speech and behavior of his parents. He imitates parental language and actions, broadening the scope of his attention to objects around him, thus growing intellectually through communication and other face-to-face contacts in the family. Cooley declared that, to live and grow successfully in any society, a person must develop sympathy for other people and understand what is in their minds. From their reactions to him, the individual constructs a conception of the way he looks to others, a self-image (or looking-glass self) seen just as if he were looking at himself in a mirror. According to Cooley, growth is thus mainly a social phenomenon.

On the other hand, in 1933 Karl Ludwig Bühler (1879–1963) a leading psychologist of the German Würzburg school of psychology, classified mental activity into instinctive, learned, and intellectual types, and pointed out that during the first weeks of life the infant often reacts to objects in the same way as to people, that he senses and thinks without being aware of many environmental and social influences, and, moreover, that his thoughts often seem to consist of sudden, independent insights instead of depending upon communication or instruction.

COMENIUS, ROUSSEAU, AND PIAGET

Among the earliest investigators to delineate stages of physical and intellectual growth was the seventeenth-century Moravian bishop John Amos Comenius (1592–1670), who divided the period of growth into four stages and recommended appropriate education for each stage: (1) infancy to six years; (2) six to twelve years; (3) twelve to eighteen years; and (4) eighteen to twenty-four years.

The revolutionary French educator Jean Jacques Rousseau (1712–1788) contended that there were five natural stages of growth: (1) birth to five years of age; (2) five to twelve years; (3) twelve to fifteen years; (4) fifteen to twenty years; and (5) twenty years and older. Physical and mental powers grew, said Rousseau, through self-expression, learning from experience and nature, and freedom of the individual to obey his natural impulses.

In the 1920s and for five decades thereafter, Jean Piaget, who respected the views of Comenius and Rousseau, investigated three stages of intellectual development: (1) birth to one and one-half or two years of age, marked by increasing perceptual awareness and improving sensorimotor reactions to objects in the environment; (2) early and middle childhood, from one and one-half or two to eleven or twelve years, featuring symbolic and preconceptual thoughts, simple concepts based on experience, some ability to organize ideas and anticipate results, and concrete thinking (especially from seven to eleven years) about immediate situations and problems; and (3) late childhood, eleven or twelve years and older, emphasizing abstract thinking, comparisons, deductions extending beyond experience into imagination, and formal operations of logical thought perfected during adolescence.

Piaget discussed the important role of the social environment in the growth of intelligence. The six-year-old, for example, tends to regard rules of conduct as mere expedients, while eight-year-olds accept them completely, and older children consider them to be somewhat flexible. Piaget rejected the view of the British philosopher Bertrand Russell (1872–1970) that the mind is a set of mathematical and logical relationships constituting the realities of the universe. He also disagreed with the concept of Alfred Binet that mental experience arises from internal unconscious activity. He discounted the importance of Aristotle's doctrine of the association of ideas to explain intelligence. The child, said Piaget, does not merely recognize associations and relationships among things but also learns to anticipate what may happen; tries to explain why; constructs his own ideas about objects, events, and experiences; and improves, broadens, and refines his mental operations during infancy, childhood, and adolescence.

GRANVILLE STANLEY HALL

The period of adolescence became the subject of intensive investigations by the eminent American psychologist Granville Stanley Hall (1846–1924), who wrote his classic two volumes, *Adolescence,* in 1904. As early as 1891, in a significant article ("The Contents of Children's Minds"), Hall had introduced his unprecedented questionnaire method of investigating the growth of infants and young children. His numerous publications gave impetus to the child-study movement in the United States.

The doctrine of mental faculties had been espoused by the German rationalist philosopher Christian von Wolff (1679–1754) and the idealist philosopher Immanuel Kant (1724–1804), but had later been rejected by the noted German educator Johann Friedrich Herbart (1776–1841) and his disciples. This doctrine assumed that children at birth possessed compartmentalized powers, or faculties, such as memory, will, judgment, and perception, which could be developed by drill and exercise. Inspired to adopt a new approach by Darwinian methods of scientific observation and analysis of facts, and the unique discoveries of the Freudians about the roots of personality in the unconscious, Hall and his colleagues turned to the investigative techniques of Weber, Fechner, Helmholtz, Hering, and Wundt, and the statistical methods of Galton and Pearson, to pursue the scientific study of growth and development.

Hall studied under Wundt at the University of Leipzig in 1882, and in 1883 joined the faculty of The Johns Hopkins University in Baltimore, Maryland (formally opened in 1876), where he immediately organized along Wundtian lines the first psychological laboratory in the nation. He taught at the university as professor of psychology and pedagogy from 1883 to 1888, then accepted the position as president of the newly formed Clark University of Worcester, Massachusetts. During Hall's presidency from 1889 to 1919, the work of his faculty in the field of child psychology received worldwide recognition. (In 1887 he founded and edited the *American Journal of Psychology,* the first American journal dealing with research studies in psychology, and in 1891 the *Pedagogical Seminary,* a journal emphasizing related problems of education. Also in 1891 he became the first president of the American Psychological Association.)

Among the theories advocated by Hall was that of recapitulation. The nineteenth-century biologists Karl Ernst von Baer and Jean Louis Rodolphe Agassiz analyzed the physical features of vertebrate embryos and noted remarkable resemblances between those features and the characteristics of fossil remains. In 1864 the German zoologist Fritz Müller, attempting to account for the resemblances, suggested that the growing embryo passes through a shortcut series of changes duplicating features developed by the species over long periods of its evolution. Shortly thereafter, German biologist Ernst Heinrich Haeckel, an ardent defender and popularizer of Darwin's ideas, set forth his famous principle that ontogeny recapitulates phylogeny—that is, the life history of each human being corresponds to the history of successive ancestors during the long course of evolution. The statements of Müller and Haeckel became widely known as the recapitulation theory.

A related concept expounded by von Baer and Haeckel, that

evolution proceeds from simple to more complex forms, was publicized by Herbert Spencer, who applied it to human physical, mental, institutional, and cultural development. Spencer asserted that natural selection and competition have developed superior mental powers and higher forms of existence and that the teaching of such scientific facts should be accorded priority. Followers of Herbart, especially Tuiskon Ziller (1817–1883) and Wilhelm Rein (1847–1929), attempted to apply their interpretations of the recapitulation theory to education. They advocated the teaching of legends, myths, fairy tales, and history, subjects that would reproduce or reflect "culture epochs," the past stages of human nature and civilization.

Hall, who became a most enthusiastic exponent of the recapitulation theory, repeatedly pointed out that the earliest movements of the infant, as in biting the nails, pulling and twisting, and hanging down and balancing, are simply echoes of the behavior of primitive ancestors who had to depend on such actions in their struggle for survival. Ancestral voices can still be detected in the utterances of the child, and even children's play and games mirror the hard labor of primitive mankind.

Another of Hall's influential doctrines was his theory of saltatory development, or sudden spurts in the growth process. Some aspects of this theory, particularly in its applications to mental traits, still receive serious consideration by psychologists despite its rejection by many investigators, including Edward L. Thorndike and Louis A. Pechstein. Hall cited as evidence for this hypothesis the drastic changes apparent during adolescence when the sex organs and reproductive functions rapidly mature. He pointed out that, although adolescents display extreme individual differences in rates of growth, the typical adolescent becomes rapidly subject to intense sentimental and religious feelings, confusing spiritual and emotional experiences, and fluctuating interests as he approaches adulthood and serious responsibilities of self-direction. In the 1920s and 1930s, the psychologist Harry Levi Hollingworth (1880–1956) of Columbia University, elaborating on Hall's views, classified the basic needs of the adolescent into (1) the need for independence or self-direction; (2) the need for communication and association with the opposite sex;

(3) the need for serious vocational interests pointing toward self-support and successful living; and (4) the need for ethical ideals, models to emulate, and religious convictions.

On theoretical grounds, supplemented by casual observations, Hall spread the notion that large families provide a wholesome social environment for the character development of children, that an only child in a family becomes selfish, domineering, jealous, aggressive, and egotistical. This widely accepted assumption was eventually disproved by John C. Claudy and other psychologists in their studies of 400,000 adolescents during the years 1960 to 1980 in California. Their periodic evaluations of only children showed them to be relatively more intelligent, more ambitious, and better adjusted than children in large families.

Still another of Hall's theories stated that each of an individual's mental powers, such as memory and reasoning, had its own best stage for development; that some powers developed rapidly in early years whereas others developed best in later years. This theory was disputed by leading psychologists, including Thorndike, Dewey, and Judd, who adhered to the view that mental powers grow concomitantly, constantly and in unison, from one period of childhood to the next.

Hall was immensely impressed by Sigmund Freud's method of psychoanalysis and, as Freud had done, attributed the genesis of certain mental disturbances to repressed impulses in the unconscious mind. He agreed with the Freudians about the value of sublimation as a defense mechanism for the transformation of unacceptable into acceptable forms of behavior. He also agreed with Freud's early associate Carl Jung that the primary life energy or *libido* of primitive man, which expressed itself in reactions of anger and aggression, was inherited and used by all future generations in order to survive and to fulfill drives for mastery and success.

THORNDIKE, DEWEY, WATSON, AND JUDD

Edward L. Thorndike (1874–1949), John Dewey (1859–1952), and Charles Hubbard Judd (1873–1946) contributed important research findings and theories to the study of growth and development. Thorndike and Dewey achieved worldwide fame during their careers at Columbia University, where they served for forty-five and forty-eight years, respectively, as professors of psychology, beginning in the same year of 1904. Judd taught at New York University for several years and later at the University of Chicago from 1909 to 1938.

Thorndike's adherence to the instinct hypothesis had an impact on the views of psychologists regarding growth and development. Growth begins, he said, on the foundations of innate, unlearned, instinctive tendencies, and continues during reactions and experiences that perpetuate, modify, or redirect those tendencies. By changing his responses to stimuli and applying them repeatedly, the individual substitutes new, more positive intellectual and attitudinal traits for less desirable or less satisfying ones. Thus he develops gradually from one stage of growth to the next. According to Thorndike, some innate tendencies are simple reflex actions, difficult to modify as the individual matures; others are less rigid, somewhat more modifiable basic instincts; and still others are extremely flexible, indefinite, and complex, highly modifiable through natural processes of experience and growth.

For Hall's recapitulation theory, Thorndike substituted a utility theory, which states that the behavior tendencies appearing very late in human evolution (because they were then most useful for survival) appear very early in the life of the child today. Innate tendencies vary considerably in regard to when they first appear and when they best develop. Growth is a gradual process wherein the child changes his behavior patterns steadily and enlarges his powers and intellectual horizons. As he grows, he builds upon and modifies his inner tendencies in order to satisfy personal needs and cope with life situations.

In Thorndike's view, there are no specific stages during which some instincts lie dormant or suddenly become potent: For example, the sex instinct and the ability to reason do not mature abruptly but over long periods and at varying rates among individual children. Thorndike pointed out that some children display greater mental capacity for solving intellectual problems than average children twice their age. From his studies of adult learners between the ages of twenty and seventy years (reported in his *Adult Learning* in 1928), he concluded that a peak in mental and motor learning ability is reached during the early twenties, followed by a slight decline until the fifties and a greater rate of decline during the fifties and sixties. (In the 1960s, studies by the National Institute of Mental Health in Maryland, however, found that men sixty-five to ninety-two years of age in good health were superior in verbal intelligence and equal in alertness, vigor, and verbal ability as compared to young men about twenty-one years old.)

Dewey agreed with Thorndike that growth is a gradual process, but rejected Thorndike's concept of numerous separate instincts. In Dewey's opinion, the whole person, interacting with an ever-changing physical and social environment, participates in every human reaction. This is true, said Dewey, of all activities, including those apparently blind and impulsive and those seemingly repressed, modified, or sublimated. The child grows by reorganizing his own habits, conduct, and thinking in the light of his past experience so as to cope with new situations or problems. He develops powers and attitudes by attempting to accomplish definite purposes and by implementing his ever-changing ideas, sometimes emulating models or accepting suggestions, but always making decisions and learning from the consequences. In this way he progresses from one stage of life to the next, as, for example, from childhood to adolescence when he broadens his personal interests, social relationships, and intellectual concerns but still applies the same kinds of reasoning and testing of ideas that he used in childhood years. Growth, said Dewey, depends upon successful purposive functioning to fulfill immediate needs and to deal with present life situations; consequently, if an individual grows well psychologically at any age of childhood or youth, he is likely to grow well at any age of adulthood. This view concerning exploration, discovery, and self-direction as the best means of growth and development was shared by Jean Piaget and many other contemporary child psychologists and educators.

Dewey's statement that sensory, motor, and emotional reactions are inseparable, integrated functions of the whole organism in responding to a total life situation reinforced the views of the Gestalt psychologists Kurt Koffka, Max Wertheimer, Kurt Lewin, and Wolfgang Köhler. In asserting the important role of structural relationships between the whole person and the total situation or configuration of things to which he reacts, Koffka and Köhler cited their research findings on patterns of visual perception and reasoning among animals. Wertheimer emphasized the integrated perception of movement. Lewin analyzed personality as a unified composite and the genesis of inner conflicts of the individual. For Gestaltists, the child's intellectual growth involves both sudden insights and gradual understandings as he interprets and reacts to patterns in his environmental situation and life experiences.

John B. Watson reiterated Dewey's conclusions that sensation is a motor as well as a sensory activity and that all reactions are produced by the organism as a whole, not by isolated or separate, cumulative parts. Watson insisted that behavior patterns and growth depend entirely upon training that improves motor reactions. In his view, all physical and mental abilities, habits, emotions, ideas, temperaments, and personality traits originate and develop through the uses the individual makes of innate equipment beginning in embryonic and fetal periods of life. Growth and development result from the person's activity as he responds to changing internal and external environmental forces. The newborn, for instance, smiles as he responds at first to the mother's caresses, then later to the mere sight of her in the distance, and still later to recollections of their relationship. For Watson, growth is a product of condition; social conditioning develops personality.

Elaborating on Watson's conclusions, leading advocates of behaviorism, such as Walter Samuel Hunter, E. R. Guthrie, and B. F. Skinner, investigated various types of conditioning as instruments of growth. Hunter compared the conditioning of emotions in human beings with similar conditioning in animals. He noted, for example, that man introduces complex acquired reactions, such as sublimation, to modify instinctive patterns, and also that the maturing person is seldom aware of the original instinctive impulses being modified to achieve ideals, skills, and social relationships. Guthrie highlighted the role of bodily structures and positive or negative adaptation of the nervous system to a stimulus as key factors in conditioning and growth. Skinner traced the mechanisms of conditioning somewhat differently than Pavlov had done, describing the variable rates and frequencies of responses to stimuli and discussing methods of strengthening, weakening or inhibiting reaction patterns (by means of operant conditioning through reinforcement of reactions irrespective of particular stimuli) involved in the growth of animals and human beings.

Judd, at the University of Chicago, emulated Wundt in the practice of laboratory experimentation, and Dewey in adherence to functional psychology and in emphasis on education as the means of growth and development. Judd asserted that human behavior patterns, though based on inherited instinctive tendencies, develop through purposive reactions directed at the achievement of self-sufficiency, self-direction, and self-control. These reactions, especially through the use of language and the arts, reach a much higher level than the simple behavior of animals can attain. He noted common features in the development of man and animals: For example, animals as well as children play, but the child steadily acquires superior skills and intellectual mastery. The infant at first merely moves his limbs rhythmically, later uses a rattle, still later imitates adult conduct during games, then participates in competitive and cooperative play—all parts of a gradual, natural, orderly progression. In adolescence some aspects of growth are intensified and accelerated, often resulting in awkwardness and even unsocial attitudes. These traits are eventually superseded by clearer self-understanding, increased self-assurance, and better adjustment to the social environment. With the exception of a few periods of sudden spurts, however, growth is gradual, coordinated, and cumulative. Growth in self-discipline and personality, necessary in order to meet the challenges of routine tasks and serious life responsibilities, proceeds in the same gradual manner and sequence of stages as play. All growth processes involve the individual as a whole during each period of development. According to Judd, every aspect of human growth and, in fact, every change in experience, whether initiated by an external sensory stimulus or by an inner feeling or idea, is accompanied by muscular tension and physical as well as mental and emotional reactions.

FREUD AND FROMM

Sigmund Freud (1856–1939) divided psychosexual personality development into three stages: (1) the infantile stage, from birth to six years of age, subdivided into the oral period of eighteen months (marked by swallowing, sucking, and biting reactions), then the anal period, to four years (marked by pleasure-seeking related to excretory activity and some awareness and testing of reality), and the phallic period, four to six years (with genital, sexual reactions dominant, accompanied by repressed sexual fantasies); (2) the latent stage, to twelve years, during which the individual grows in moral, intellectual, and social aspects of personality; and (3) the genital stage, the years of adolescence, beginning with change from self-love to either homosexual or heterosexual attraction to another person and soon thereafter usually progressing to heterosexual satisfactions (in accordance with the pleasure principle) so that the demands of the id, the unconscious inner psychic force, though modified by the reality principle reflecting the demands of society, are gratified.

The psychoanalyst Erich Fromm (1900–1980) rejected Freud's three stages of personality growth and cited a variety of basic forces molding personality, namely, organic instincts, desires for influence and prestige, and sentiments, ethical standards, and religious goals.

RANK, ALLPORT, AND ERIKSON

Among leading social psychologists and psychoanalysts whose views on the growth and development of personality have been widely disseminated were Otto Rank (1884–1939), Gordon Willard Allport (1897–1967), and Erik H. Erikson (1902–).

Rank, one of Freud's earliest disciples in Vienna, and well known for his concept of birth trauma as the root cause of emotional disturbances, asserted that the growth of personality depends upon inner adjustments of the individual, not upon merely external circumstances or conditions. The person matures as he corrects illusions he has formed about himself and faces reality, even though such illusions may sometimes be unavoidable and necessary. As he develops, the child learns to trust himself to make new decisions, reduces his dependence upon parents or others, and assumes increasing responsibility for his own choices and tasks.

Allport, a noted psychologist at Dartmouth College and later at Harvard University, held that the motive power energizing conscious behavior (the *libido* of the Freudian *ego*), though grounded in the native equipment of the individual, consists of the impulses, habits, values, and goals experienced or accumulated during his entire life-span. Not behavior patterns but inner drives rooted in past motives result in orderly growth of a unique personality that is integrated, always maturing and learning from experience. The child is forever becoming a different person as he repudiates past disappointments, illusions, and failures and improves his adjustments to people and life situations.

For the Freudian psychoanalyst Erikson of Harvard University, the superficial manifestations of growth must not be confused with the deeper forces, mainly psychosexual, operating in successive periods of the life-span. The child matures normally through psychological adjustments to his mother and others. Periods of growth correspond to stages of organic maturation of psychosexual zones from the time of birth onward. Thus the infant develops a sense either of trust or of mistrust during his relationship to his mother, while she may develop a sense of exclusion or excessive concentration on her own desires and interests. Erikson postulated six psychosexual stages of growth: (1) oral-respiratory-sensory-kinesthetic earliest mother-child contacts involving mainly trust and mistrust; (2) anal-urethral-muscular functions, involving mainly self-reliance, obedience, doubt, and shame; (3) infantile-genital-locomotor functions, as in play, involving mainly self-assertion and guilt; (4) latent persistent habits of confident performance and also feelings of inadequacy;

(5) puberty, involving mainly relations to peers and a leadership role in groups; and (6) genital maturity, involving mainly partnership relations to another person, accompanied or followed by periods of mutual care and shared experience of crises or adversity. Characteristics dominant in each stage are not exclusive but blend into the total personality of the growing individual.

The views of Rank, Allport, and Erikson were reflected in the writings of sociologists concerning human growth and development, but with more emphasis on the role of social environmental factors and social experience. Thus in the 1940s Kingsley Davis noted that growth requires integration of personality through the individual's changing self-images. These self-images depend chiefly upon social organization, social forces, and social interaction, from which personal ideas and aims are derived, as well as upon the individual's reactions to the physical environment, his recall of past experiences, and the continuous development of his organic systems. During the 1950s, 1960s, and 1970s, family studies, such as those by Philippe Aries, Michel Foucault, and Jacques Donzelot in France, indicated that historical changes culminating in the modern nuclear family lengthened the period of childhood, created many aspects of adolescence, and transformed human relationships.

ADLER, MOWRER, KLUCKHOHN, HORNEY, SULLIVAN

During the 1940s and 1950s, several leading psychiatrists, anthropologists, and educational psychologists proposed variant theories about personality development. Alfred Adler (1870–1937) pointed out the importance of all-round integrated reactions of the individual to biological and social influences affecting personality traits. Orval H. Mowrer (1907–) and Clyde K. M. Kluckhohn (1905–1960) attributed personality growth to continual, irregular adjustments and changing habits of the whole individual as he senses entire social situations, encounters conflicts, and tries to achieve health, satisfactory relationships, and feelings of consistency and success to abate or replace his fear, feelings of insecurity, and anxiety. At the same time, Karen Horney (1885–1952) emphasized the significant effects upon personality growth of the child's inner feelings and conflicts, especially his successful or unsuccessful attempts to adjust to a frequently hostile, contradictory, and unpredictable adult world. The psychiatrist Harry Stack Sullivan (1892–1949) attributed personality growth to the individual's entire history of relationships to others. He postulated six periods of development: (1) infancy, featuring the mother's love and care; (2) childhood, opening up social relations to other children; (3) juvenile years of adjustment to associates and peer groups; (4) preadolescence, years of initial interest in close relationships or to contacts with others; (5) adolescence, dominated by sexual interests; and (6) maturity in sexual and other human relationships.

GESELL AND OTHER CHILD PSYCHOLOGISTS

Many behaviorists, psychoanalysts, and social psychologists have disparaged the traditional view that character and personality develop from the pursuit of ethical values or rational appreciation of moral standards. Piaget and other cognitive psychologists, however, have noted the significance of the very young child's ability to distinguish right from wrong behavior and to sense the difference between constructive, or consistent, and destructive, or inconsistent, behavior patterns and human relationships. Gesell and other leading child psychologists used rating scales, questionnaires, personality inventories and tests, association tests, firsthand observations of behavior, interviews, and controlled experiments to obtain evidence about the physical, mental, emotional, and social development of children.

Arnold Lucius Gesell (1880–1961), a native of Alma, Wisconsin, earned his medical degree in 1915 at Yale University, where he had already served on the faculty beginning in 1911 and in the same year had founded the Yale Clinic of Child Development. During five decades, he reported his numerous studies of infancy and childhood in major works of which he was the author or coauthor, such as *Infancy and Human Growth*, 1928; *The First Five Years of Life*, 1940; *Infant and Child in the Culture of Today*, 1943; *The Child from Five to Ten*, 1946; and *The Years from Ten to Fifteen*, 1956.

Gesell and his associates delineated the patterns of behavior that develop during the life stages of infant and child. They defined growth as an ongoing functioning of the whole person that begins immediately upon conception and continues as a process of maturing through interaction between the individual and his internal and external environment. Each element and sequential period of growth results from hereditary and environmental influences that stimulate, support, and direct or redirect the person's functions so that he progresses toward and eventually reaches full maturity.

Gesell concluded that maturing occurs in four interrelated types of behavior: language, motor activity, adaptive adjustments, and personal-social reactions. Physical structures and behavior patterns develop in accordance with the following principles: (1) Physical parts grow at different rates but continuously (except for brief intervals of fluctuation and retrogression); (2) physical parts grow in harmony so that organs, limbs, and muscles, for example, parallel or oppose one another whenever necessary, thus achieving balance and coordination; (3) physical parts function together as they grow, thereby achieving efficient movements; (4) the various types of behavior progress and attain maturity at specific times of the life cycle in an orderly sequence; and (5) growth is continuous but sometimes irregular and often interrupted by setbacks before recovering and advancing again toward maturity.

Gesell reported numerous facts about the growth of children in each of the four types of behavior. The normal six-month-old child recognizes and reacts to familiar voices and repeats vocal sounds, while the year-old child uses one or two words. The two-year-old uses a few clauses or very short sentences. Motor development proceeds steadily so that the child holds his head up at two months, sits without help at eight months, walks with help at twelve months, climbs stairs at eighteen months, and runs at twenty-four months. During the first few months, the head region grows more rapidly than the limbs, and thereafter the lower limbs and body as a whole grow fast while the head region slows down to nearly a standstill reached within the next two years. (These are average measurements and are subject to wide variations among individuals, attributed in part to economic or other environmental influences.) Gesell's observations of children's behavior during the first five years of life revealed that certain personality traits—such as friendliness, pride in accomplishment, and application of energy—tended to persist from the beginning to the end of that period. A research study by Mary M. Shirley at the University of Minnesota disclosed similar persistence of personality traits such as aggressiveness among nineteen children during the first two years.

Gesell's careful methods of research, his measurements, observations, tests, and experiments, were typical of techniques utilized during the 1920s to 1970s by hundreds of investigators who verified or modified and supplemented many of his findings about growth and development. Among the best-known research studies were those by Smith, Osgood, Shirley, Jersild, Baldwin, McGraw, Thorndike, Miles and Miles, Jones and Conrad, Thurstone, Hartshorne and May, Bridges, Sallenberger, and Peck and Havighurst.

Madorah E. Smith, investigating the development of the sentence and the vocabulary of young children, reported in 1926 that, on the average, children at the age of one year know 3 words, at two years 272 words, at three years 896 words, at four years 1,540 words, at five years 2,072 words, and at six years 2,562 words. In 1953 Charles E. Osgood of the University of Illinois reported that the one-year-old child makes all possible sounds of ordinary English speech and that progress in oral language thereafter is the result of social learning; association of words with new objects, ideas, or situations; and imitation of adults.

Mary M. Shirley reported in 1931–1933 her observation of the motor development of twenty-five babies during their first two years of life. According to her findings, the average child is able to raise his chin in the first month while on his stomach, to sit with assistance in the fourth month, to creep and also to walk with assistance in the tenth month, to stand alone in the fourteenth month, and to walk by himself in the fifteenth month. Arthur T. Jersild at Columbia University studied the growth of equated groups of children two to eleven years of age in intellectual, motor, and musical performance, reporting during the 1930s that although specially trained children were superior in achievement during the training period, the untrained children soon thereafter equaled them in most respects, a result attributed to the natural maturing process of both groups. Jersild concluded that premature early training produces only temporary advantages.

Reports on the maturation of preschool and elementary-school children in the 1920s by psychologists Bird T. Baldwin, Lorle I. Stetcher, and others at the University of Iowa compared the growth of boys and girls. Boys were found to average about 20.5 inches in height at birth, 37.6 inches at two years, 42 inches at five years, 45.4 inches at six years, 51.5 inches at nine years, and 59.5 inches at thirteen years. Boys were taller than girls at all ages except eight to eleven years, the period when girls tend to spurt ahead. Growth in social attitudes and group cooperation was rapid during the period of two to four years of age. Ten-year-old girls were equal or superior to twelve-year-old boys in sexual maturity.

Myrtle B. McGraw conducted several experiments in a study of identical twins, the results of which (reported in 1940) appeared to justify Gesell's emphasis on natural maturation processes as the most significant factors in the development of behavior patterns. Thus a twin who received toilet training from birth to eighteen months achieved only the same performance as the twin who received no training. Neither the trained twin nor the untrained one learned this skill until they both reached a level of maturity at which the untrained twin mastered the necessary skill as rapidly as the trained one. McGraw reported similar results for training in the use of a tricycle.

At Cleveland, Ohio, in 1927 Thorndike reported, on the basis of his extensive experiments with persons thirty-five years old and over, that middle-aged adults possess on the average superior mental ability to study motor skills and languages as compared to children eight to twelve years old, and that normal adults of any age can learn a variety of skills and information related to their personal interests. Old people learned an artificial language about five-sixths as fast as young adults.

A study by C. C. Miles and W. R. Miles and another by
E. H. Jones and H. S. Conrad indicated rapid growth in intellectual performance during the years from early childhood to
adolescence, with mental ability at a peak level from approximately seventeen years through the twenties, followed by a small
gradual decline until the fifties and a somewhat greater decline
thereafter. Miles and Miles also noted that the average highly
intelligent adult retains a maximum of mental capacity even
during the seventies, a conclusion reinforced by the researches of
Louis Leon Thurstone in 1955 indicating that many aging
adults, despite slow progress in various other fields, continue
readily to improve their linguistic skills.

In their *Studies in Deceit* in 1928, Hugh Hartshorne and
Mark A. May at Columbia University, after testing eleven thousand children over a period of five years, concluded that the development of honesty as a trait dominant in school, home, and
playground activities is not attributable to preaching by adults.
Rather it develops mainly from personal relationships and social
situations that often make ethical instruction, behavior controls
or discipline (to inhibit impulses), and imitation of adult or peer
models highly effective. Lying, cheating, and stealing do not always go together. Individuals differ widely in all age groups,
and the influence of the family environment is usually decisive,
as shown, for example, by the fact that properly supervised children of well-to-do parents tend to cheat less than relatively neglected children in poverty-stricken homes.

In 1966 Gesell's associates Frances L. Ilg and Louise B.
Ames, analyzing children's behavior and personality growth,
concluded that individuals differ considerably in basic temperaments and general attitudes toward reality and people in their
environment; some young creative children find it difficult to differentiate between fact and fiction. Play activities and imaginary
situations are serious concerns of the growing child. Play patterns develop steadily from the stage of simple handling of toys
to group games, then to constructional and dramatized projects,
with all forms of play eliciting maximum attention and sustained interest during late childhood and with some types continuing into adolescence and beyond.

In the 1930s, Katherine M. B. Bridges of Montreal determined from her observations of infants that during the first
month their reactions and mass movements do not indicate basic
emotions of anger or fear, as Watson had assumed, but only a
diffuse state of restlessness and excitement; they develop numerous other, more familiar reaction patterns only as they mature
and have to cope with new stressful life situations. R. T. Sallenger reported in 1940 that hormones have a significant effect
on personality development during adolescence; thus adolescent
boys possessing more male hormones (measured in their urine)
were found to form and maintain more mature interests and
attitudes than boys with fewer hormones. In 1960 R. F. Peck
and R. J. Havighurst studied the personality development of
thirty-six children ten to seventeen years old and were impressed
with the fact that, despite normal changes in behavior practices
during maturation, the basic ethical standards and attitudes of
the children remained uniform throughout the years. A child
who displayed inconsistency and opportunism at ten proved to
be similarly inconsistent and opportunistic at seventeen, while
the most obedient, the reliable and conscientious, and the altruistic children likewise tended to retain their original character
traits from the beginning to the end of the period, most uniformly in the later years.

These research studies appeared to justify the claim that the
personality traits of young children are predictable through observation and analysis of their past characteristics. John Dewey
attributed this remarkable stability in the dispositions and moral
values of children, not to theoretical principles or adult instruction, but to repeated, purposive, meaningful experiences and behavior practices that make socially approved standards and attitudes habitual. In the late 1970s, P. B. Baltes and other
researchers formulated theories of life-span human development
through stages from birth to death, identifying multiple interacting forces of continuous growth, including biological influences
that affect large groups of people during specific historical periods, and significant drastic events or episodes impinging upon
the individual at critical times during his entire life career. The
relative potency of these influences changes considerably as the

individual progresses from infancy through childhood, adolescence, adulthood, and old age. At the University of Chicago, R. J. Havighurst and B. L. Neugarten were among the research gerontologists who devoted special attention to the cumulative factors operating from early childhood through later stages of the life-span to account for personality traits of individuals in advanced old age. Such insights are valuable contributions, but precise descriptions of the numerous factors affecting human life-span development and experience, factors determining changes in intelligence, short-term and long-term memory, and personality traits, remain largely unexplored, challenging areas of investigation confronting contemporary psychologists.

5 INDIVIDUAL DIFFERENCES, TESTS, AND MEASUREMENTS

Differences among individuals in character and behavior patterns have been discussed from very early times in the works of philosophers and educators. In the fourth century B.C., Plato proposed that citizens should be divided into three classes (craftsmen, warriors, and rulers) in accordance with their native, natural differences in ability. Aristotle declared that unborn natural differences fit some people to be free, others to be slaves. He stated further, however, that power does not prove merit; that a slave can be intelligent; that no highborn, superior person should be enslaved by conquest; and from a remarkably modern point of view, that all conclusions about human nature should be subject to modification on the basis of careful observations of facts.

In the first century B.C., the Roman philosopher Cicero commented on the wide differences among individuals in interests, beliefs, skill, knowledge, and character. He warned that a democracy would treat superior persons no better than those possessing inferior intelligence and ability. Quintilian (b. A.D. 35), the foremost educator of ancient Rome, devoted many years to observing carefully the attitudes, personalities, mental capacities, and behavior of boys, and recommended that teachers should always adapt instruction to individual differences among students.

The medieval Church hierarchy was usually not concerned about individual differences in attitude among Christians, except those differences that might induce heresy or disobedience to Church authority. However, Charlemagne's educational adviser, Alcuin (735–804), attempted to establish a merit system for the appointment of the best-qualified clergymen to high ecclesiastical posts. Later, Quintilian's ideas about individual differences inspired humanist educators, especially Erasmus (ca. 1466–1536) in Germany and the famed educators Guarino da Verona (1370–1460) and Vittorino da Feltre (1378–1446) in Italy, who insisted that pupils in every age group differed in interests and learning abilities and that the pace of instruction should be adjusted accordingly.

In early modern times, the great educators Mulcaster, Comenius, Locke, and Rousseau emphasized the need for adaptation of instruction to individual differences in the interests and capacities of learners. Their view stimulated the study of such differences during the nineteenth and twentieth centuries. The first scientific analyses of individual differences are credited to Sir Francis Galton, who described in quantitative terms the varying abilities of adults to remember shared experiences, a procedure that gave impetus to the development of statistical methods as an effective tool of psychological research. Karl Pearson and James McKeen Cattell (who had studied with Wundt and Galton) pioneered in the experimental and statistical study of individual differences.

GALTON, PEARSON, STERN, CATTELL, AND FARRAND

In the late eighteenth and early nineteenth centuries, the French astronomers and mathematicians Pierre Simon de Laplace (1749–1827) and Joseph Louis Lagrange (1736–1813) and the famous German astronomers Karl Friedrich Gauss (1777–1855) and Friedrich Wilhelm Bessel (1784–1846) built the mathematical foundations for statistical studies of individual differences by Galton and Pearson. Laplace, Lagrange, Gauss, and Bessel are credited with developing measures of variability (including the curve of normal distribution) that became useful tools of psychological research and experimentation. In 1869 Galton utilized statistical analyses in his genetic studies of individuals, correlating their mental characteristics with their family histories. In 1879 Wundt opened his unprecedented psychological laboratory. The following year, Galton began to experiment with word-association tests, tracing word associations statistically to past experiences of the individual. He also discovered variations in the number forms and calculating methods, such as shortcuts, used by individuals for solving mathematical problems. Galton's work was soon followed by similar experiments with word-association tests by Wundt, Kraepelin, and Jung to explore complex mental reactions. In 1910 the American psychiatrists G. H. Kent and A. J. Rosanoff reported on their use of word-association experiments to discriminate between normal persons and mentally disturbed patients.

New techniques enabled investigators to compare one individual with a large random group of individuals in regard to specific abilities and traits. Pearson developed formulas for estimating the probability that an individual or small group will earn scores above or below any given point on the base of a normal distribution curve. Thus if there is a high correlation (a high degree of relationship) between intelligence-test scores and reading-test scores, there will be a specific probability, ascertainable statistically, that a person with high verbal intelligence will also be a highly skilled reader. Using statistical calculations, psychologists can determine whether and to what extent a particular ability or trait has been found more often in some individuals or groups than would be expected to occur by mere chance.

In 1877 Galton suggested that all human characteristics should be analyzed by measurements of individuals and comparisons with relevant data about large numbers of other individuals. His suggestion failed to discriminate adequately among the various types of individual differences, lumping together intelligence, character, physical powers, and temperaments. Nevertheless, his views influenced other investigators and contributed to the development of differential psychology, a new discipline attributed mainly to the efforts of the noted German psychologist Louis William Stern (1871–1938) of Duke University, who, beginning in 1900, analyzed types of individual differences. Stern was the first to use the intelligence quotient, the familiar IQ, to designate the ratio between mental age and chronological age. He constructed a picture test to measure the immediate visual memory of individuals. (In 1938 Stern changed his emphasis from the analyses of separate traits of the individual to the study of the whole person acting as a unit, an approach reflecting the views of McDougall's hormic school of psychology.) Pearson, in his *Grammar of Science* (1890), explained the scientific basis for the new statistical methods, the principles and limitations involved in them, and their proper applications to biological and psychological research.

In 1891 James McKeen Cattell (1860–1944) and Livingston Farrand (1867–1939) began a program of testing their students at Columbia University. After completing graduate studies in 1883 at Lafayette College (where his father was president from 1863 to 1883), Cattell studied under Galton, subsequently under Wundt, receiving the doctorate degree in 1886 at the University of Leipzig. He taught psychology at the University of Pennsylvania from 1888 to 1891, constructing and administering tests to measure the sensory and motor reactions of students, then joined the faculty at Columbia University, where he remained until 1917. He became the editor and publisher of widely used reference works in psychology, education, and science, the editor of professional journals, and the president of a book-printing establishment. Farrand received a medical degree at Columbia University in 1891, taught psychology there from 1893 to 1903 and anthropology from 1903 to 1914, then served as president of the University of Colorado from 1914 to 1919 and as president of Cornell University from 1921 to 1937.

Cattell and Farrand pioneered in the construction and administration of objective tests to measure differences in mental abilities; speed of responses to stimuli such as light and sound; abilities to discriminate among and estimate relationships of space, time, and weight; visual and auditory acuity; sensitivity to pain; reaction times; attention span; memory; and physical strength. They verified and elaborated on the conclusion of Galton and Pearson that individuals differ considerably in all characteristics, possessing the same fundamental traits but in amounts that vary, depending upon the particular trait, for each person and among the members of any random group. They concluded that, in any characteristic, the majority in a large, unselected group will, if properly tested, earn scores that cluster around a central point on a scale and will be distributed in the middle range between two extremes, even in physical attributes such as height and weight as well as in skills, reaction times, and mental abilities.

The researches of Pearson, Cattell, and Farrand indicated that a person who excels in a particular type of ability or task is apt to excel also in closely related similar abilities or tasks. A skillful athlete may be a good or poor academic student, but he will tend to be superior in several forms of athletic activity. If pupils are grouped in homogeneous classes on the basis of verbal intelligence, they will usually still differ in physical, emotional, social, and other characteristics. Owing to individual differences of this kind, the standards of accomplishment by large groups may not be applicable to any one person, and consequently it is necessary to study the individual as a whole in the light of all his characteristics and needs.

EBBINGHAUS, BINET, AND TERMAN

Cattell and Farrand had assumed that intelligence consisted of a complex of separate mental abilities, each measurable by means of objective tests. Other eminent psychologists, including Hermann Ebbinghaus (1850–1909) and Alfred Binet (1857–1911), believed that an individual's behavior reflected a general power to think and reason correctly, an inseparable capacity applicable to a variety of tasks or situations.

Ebbinghaus, the German experimental psychologist best known for his pioneering studies of memory, attempted during the 1880s to construct tests to measure individual differences in native intelligence. For this purpose he devised short-answer, sentence-completion tests, a type of examination still in common use, consisting of sentences containing one or more blanks to be filled in by the examinee. These tests required an ability to reason correctly and discriminated well between superior and inferior students of academic subjects. However, they appeared more useful for measuring knowledge and recall of specific facts than for evaluating individual differences in mental power 'or intelligence.

Alfred Binet was the director of the physiological psychology laboratory at the University of the Sorbonne in Paris and also served as president of the Free Society for the Study of Children. He devoted many years to observation and experimentation on behalf of retarded children. In 1904, upon the invitation of the French minister of education, he organized a commission to investigate the mental abilities of all types of children in order to identify subnormal pupils and place them in special classes suited to their abilities.

Binet decided that a graded test of intelligence (requiring boys and girls of different ages to perform various tasks of the type they normally performed and to answer questions about information usually acquired at their respective ages), would disclose individual differences in mental ability. For Binet, *intelligence* meant the ability to make valid judgments, to comprehend life situations, and to reason correctly about everyday things. In the measurement of intelligence, he thought, a typical task for a five-year-old would require him to compare two weights; a typical question would require him to repeat a sentence of ten syllables. In Binet's view, the standard for judging overall intelligence should not be the individual's ability to perform any particular kinds of tasks, such as reciting from memory, but his ability to do many things that average children at his age are able to do. The average performance of individuals at each age should be the standard of measurement. Each person should be rated by comparison with the intelligence level of the entire population on his age level.

In 1905, assisted by the French physician and psychologist Théodore Simon (1873–1961), who was highly esteemed as an authority on child development, Binet constructed a set of thirty test questions (selected on the basis of firsthand observations as well as parental reports about their children's behavior). He administered the test to each of 203 Parisian children three to fourteen years old, divided into one group regarded by their teachers as mentally superior and another group considered mentally subnormal. He discovered that at every age the answers discriminated between the mentally superior and the mentally subnormal individuals, verifying the teachers' judgments. He then arranged the questions in order of their difficulty, as determined by the ages at which most pupils answered them correctly, thereby making it possible to assign a mental age to each child by comparing his accomplishment on the examination with the accomplishments of all other children. A child eight years and six months old, for example, who could correctly answer the questions that were usually answered by most children ten years old was given a mental age of ten years and considered to be eighteen months above normal (or above average) in intelligence.

In 1908 Binet and Simon constructed a revised test containing fifty-four questions and tasks, and in 1911 they again revised and republished the test. In both revisions, questions were arranged in separate groups for the various ages, beginning with three-year-olds up to and including adult years. The set of five questions, for example, given to ten-year-olds required them to (1) arrange five blocks in order of their weight, (2) copy drawings from memory, (3) identify illogical reasoning in sentences, (4) answer ordinary informational questions, and (5) use three given words in two sentences. Each child taking the test received credit in years and months according to the total number of questions he had answered correctly, a feature that made the examination the first age-scale intelligence test ever devised. Binet's method of grouping questions according to age, then using each group of questions as a standard of measurement, established a precedent followed by many later investigators.

The hereditarian psychologist H. H. Goddard revised the Binet-Simon test and administered it to diagnose the extent of mental retardation among children at the Vineland, New Jersey, Training School for the feebleminded. Goddard's revision (published in 1911) adjusted the questions and scoring system to obtain readily calculated mental ages, and thus assisted psychologists in many institutions to provide diagnosis and suitable training for mental defectives. For use with the general population of American children, the most important revisions of the Binet-Simon test were those made by Lewis Madison Terman, by Frederick Kuhlmann, and by Terman and Maude A. Merrill, his associate at Stanford University. Terman emphasized the ability to understand, think, and express abstract ideas as the core of mental powers.

Terman's revision in 1916 became the most widely used intelligence test in the United States and also the basis for numerous revised editions and translations in foreign countries. Owing to a high correlation between the test scores earned by pupils and their successes in academic studies, American school administrators developed great confidence in the first Terman revision as an aid in the evaluation of mental ability and the proper classification of pupils. (Terman had tried out the questions and determined the average scores by administration to nine hundred children, mainly in California cities.)

A 1937 Terman-Merrill revision, known as the Stanford-Binet Scale, with a total of 129 items, was based on the trial scores of three thousand children in eleven states; it included questions for children only eighteen months old, twelve subtests instead of six for each of the lower grades, ten additional subtests for ages eleven to fourteen years, and twenty-six instead of the previous twelve subtests for adults. In a 1960 revision, the test items, arranged in groups, were designed to measure mental ability from two years to the superior adult level.

The original Binet tests and the Terman revision were criticized because the questions in the subtests for each age were very brief and not well balanced between verbal and nonverbal tasks; the subtests were therefore not regarded as sufficiently comprehensive to be given separately. Many questions involved academic information and everyday experiences of children in particular environments, with little emphasis on abstract thinking and other forms of mental activity. To counteract this limitation, common to most of the mainly verbal tests of intelligence, Terman and Merrill introduced performance tasks in their 1937 and 1960 revisions. (New norms were developed in 1972.)

In 1920 Terman constructed a group test of mental ability; and in the 1930s, with Catharine Cox Miles, an attitude-interest personality test (developed during eleven years of research) for adolescents and adults, featuring word-association questions, to identify individual differences in so-called masculinity and femininity, also questions for men and women about their vocational and social interests.

KUHLMANN, PINTNER, ARTHUR, AND GOODENOUGH

Frederick Kuhlmann (1876–1941) in a 1922 revision of the Binet-Simon test featured new questions requiring the child to make comparative judgments, to arrive at inferences from data, and to define words to be used in reasoning by analogy. These aspects of mental ability had not, in his opinion, been sufficiently measured by the original examinations. In Kuhlmann's revision, the child was asked, for example, to compare pictures; to give reasons for, or causes of, events; to solve puzzles; and to explain what action might well be taken to cope with unexpected life situations. The Kuhlmann-Binet test was acclaimed by psychologists as a carefully prepared, useful examination. In 1916 Kuhlmann and R. G. Anderson had begun work upon new mental tests, and for about a decade thereafter had tried out test questions with about thirty thousand children. The resulting Kuhlmann-Anderson Intelligence Tests, containing ten tests and first published in 1927, could be used for testing either an individual or a group, with ages ranging from six years to maturity. Kuhlmann also constructed tests of general intelligence for use with infants, measuring the child's visual coordination and the ability to hold objects, to imitate movements, to identify objects shown in pictures, to obey simple instructions, to remove food wrappings, and to feed himself.

Rudolf Pintner (1884–1942), a native of Lancaster, England, was a pioneer in the field of intelligence testing. He came to the United States in 1912, taught at Ohio State University, and served for many years as professor of educational psychology at Teachers College of Columbia University. Among his numerous important works were the Pintner-Paterson Performance Tests (with Donald G. Paterson of the University of Minnesota, 1917); a drawing-completion test (with Herbert A. Toops at Ohio State University, 1918); *Intelligence Testing* (1923, 1931); *Educational Psychology* (1929); and *An Outline of Educational Psychology* (with others, 1934, sixth edition, 1970). Pintner was an authority on the education of handicapped children and author of the standard work *Psychology of the*

Physically Handicapped. His keen interest in the education of physically handicapped children impelled him to devise tests that would measure the mental abilities of deaf, illiterate, and mentally retarded individuals. These tests included a battery of form board tests patterned after the materials of instruction used in the late nineteenth century by Édouard Seguin in France; a manikin test; the Knox-Kempf feature-profile tests; a picture-completion test; and a cube test—items requiring the child to deal with a variety of standard, familiar, or well-established tasks. Pintner pointed out that nonverbal and nonlanguage tests reduce or often eliminate the influence of academic learning on the child's scores and therefore measure basic mental power, which he believed to be largely inherited. He asserted that only extreme changes in the environment could modify hereditary differences in intelligence, a general capacity not always well measured by verbal tests. On the other hand, he regarded individual differences in interests, attitudes, temperament, and personality as largely dependent upon instruction, emulation, and other environmental factors.

In 1931 Mary G. Arthur, psychologist at the University of Minnesota, constructed an abridged series of tests entitled the Point School of Performance Tests, which contained many of the Pintner-Paterson items and was used by psychologists for testing exceptional children five to fifteen years of age. In 1937 Pintner and his colleague Gertrude H. Hildreth at Columbia University also constructed a shortened scale of the same performance tests for administration to children four to fifteen years of age. (Form board tests used by Pintner, Hildreth, and Arthur were similar to those devised around 1800 by Itard for teaching the "Wild Boy of Aveyron.") Devices of this kind were utilized beginning in 1907 by the Italian educator Maria Montessori in Rome as part of her methods of sensory training of feebleminded children.

In Switzerland the psychologists E. Claparède (1907) and E. Ivanoff (1909) undertook programs of testing children to determine whether spontaneous drawings would reveal individual differences in intelligence, aptitude, and personality. They found significant correlations among drawing skills, academic accomplishments, and ethical standards. In Germany during the early

1900s, the educator G. D. Kerschensteiner analyzed nearly 100,000 drawings by children, identified three stages in the development of drawing skills, and noted that the artwork of boys was in many respects superior to that of girls. In 1908 the German educator C. Kik reported that the creative artists among children were much more successful than the mere copyists in their academic studies.

Scores of psychologists and educators began to analyze children's drawings for cues to individual differences in mental ability and personality development. In 1926 Florence L. Goodenough (1886–1959), of the University of Minnesota Institute of Child Welfare, constructed, with Terman's assistance, a test entitled the Measurement of Intelligence by Drawing, which came to be widely used and was considered more valid as a measure of intelligence among deaf children and the foreign-born than the Binet-Simon and other tests. The Goodenough test required the child to make a single drawing of a man on white letter-size paper, a task taking less than ten minutes on the average and designed for boys and girls two to fifteen years of age. In 1935 William E. Hinrichs of Columbia University reported positive relationships between scores on the test and individual differences of children in problem behavior and delinquency. Goodenough suggested that in some cases the drawing made by an individual during this test could be analyzed and scored in such a manner as to reveal the presence and degree of mental disturbances. Clinical psychologists have since often used the test as one of several criteria for tentative judgments about the individual's sensory and motor reactions and personality integration. Sensory or motor disturbances might, for example, be indicated by missing parts in the final drawing. (The popular projective Draw-a-Person Test devised by Karen Machover to evaluate personality traits is comparable in some respects to the Goodenough test.)

PORTEUS, MARIE, GRAHAM, AND KENDAL

The Porteus Maze Tests devised by Stanley D. Porteus at the University of Hawaii in the 1930s require the subject to trace a course on a printed maze to measure his visualization and spatial imagination. The subject must visualize what will happen if he chooses particular successive paths instead of following other paths in the maze. Porteus asserted that the results of tests administered to primitive peoples in Australia and South Africa proved that racial factors have an influence upon levels of intelligence. His maze tests, however, have been regarded as most suitable for use with deaf children and non-English-speaking children.

The Marie Three-Paper Test, devised by the French physician Pierre Marie (1853–1940), measures ability to retain and recall information. The subject receives three pieces of paper and is instructed to dispose of them in different ways. Failure to follow the instructions may indicate severely deficient retention.

The Memory-for-Designs Test constructed by the American psychologists F. K. Graham and Barbara S. Kendal measures the ability to coordinate perceptions with motor reactions. It is a short test requiring immediate recall of design features and is used as a cue to possible brain injuries causing mental disturbances.

WECHSLER

In 1939 David Wechsler (1896–1981), chief psychologist at the Bellevue Hospital of the New York University College of Medicine, constructed the Wechsler-Bellevue Intelligence Scale, which was revised in 1955 and then published under a new title, the Wechsler Adult Intelligence Scale. The Wechsler tests, quite similar in content to the Stanford-Binet scale and designed for use with individuals ten to sixty years of age, consists of eleven tests: six verbal tests on vocabulary, information, comprehension, digit span, mathematical calculations, and similarities; and five performance tests on picture completion, picture arrangement, object assembly, block design, and substitution of digit symbols.

Wechsler stated that the intelligence level of individuals appears to vary with chronological age up to the age of fifteen years, then remains about the same to the age of twenty-five years, and thereafter declines, at first slowly, later more rapidly.

For adolescents and adults, his tests have been regarded as valid measures of mental capacity and also as a partial clue in the diagnosis of mental disturbances. Only one of the subtests in the adult scale measures memory (and aspects of attention as well), but Wechsler also constructed and standardized a special memory test. In 1949 he devised a separate intelligence scale for children five through fifteen years of age, a scale revised in 1974 for ages six through sixteen years.

Wechsler classified the intelligence levels of individuals in terms of their IQs as follows: 128 IQ or over, very superior (scored by 2.2 percent of the general population); 120–127 IQ, superior (scored by 6.7 percent); 111–119 IQ, above normal (scored by 16.1 percent); 91–110 IQ, average (scored by 50 percent); 80–90 IQ, dull normal (scored by 16.1 percent); 66–79 IQ, borderline (scored by 6.7 percent); and 65 IQ or below, mental defectives (scored by 2.2 percent). (Terman used a genius classification for IQs above 140, and he subdivided mental defectives into morons, with 50–70 IQs, imbeciles, with 25–50 IQs, idiots, with IQs of 24 or below.)

GROUP TESTS BY YERKES, OTIS, TERMAN, PINTNER

The great expansion of psychological testing in the United States and Great Britain during recent decades could not have occurred without the development by pioneering psychologists of standardized group tests, which were timesaving and much less costly to administer than individual tests. Among the earliest group tests of intelligence used on a large scale were the verbal United States Army Alpha Group Examination and the nonverbal Army Beta Examination, both of which were point-score tests administered to recruits during the First World War.

The Army Alpha Examination, consisting of eight parts and a total of 212 questions, was a test of power and speed, measuring the ability to follow directions, reasoning, mastery of general everyday information, word relationships, and memory. About 1.5 million copies were administered to army recruits who could read on a sixth-grade level. The Army Beta Examination, in seven parts, was a performance test primarily for recruits with inferior reading ability, to whom instructions were given in pantomime by the examiner.

The biologist Robert M. Yerkes (1876–1956), professor of psychology at the University of Minnesota, served as head of the committee (whose members included Otis, Goddard, and Terman, among others) that constructed and directed the administration of the Army examinations. Yerkes had pioneered in the study of animal psychology, especially the mental ability and behavior of apes, as well as in intelligence testing of children. As early as 1915, he had developed a point-scale test of intelligence with James W. Bridges and had reported a significant statistical relationship between the IQs and the social conditions of children, particularly the occupations of their fathers. In 1924 he joined the faculty of Yale University and thereafter directed researches in comparative psychology at the Anthropoid Research Station of the university at Orange Park, Florida. In his experiments with apes and chimpanzees, he found that the imposition of tasks beyond the animals' mental ability to comprehend created in them frustration, intense anger, and neuroses. Critics of standardized tests and competitive examinations have pointed out that children often experience similar frustration and tension when they are compelled to cope with difficult questions, problems, or tasks.

In 1916, while Kuhlmann and Anderson were developing their well-known intelligence test, Arthur S. Otis was constructing his group mental tests (published in 1918), which paved the way for the Army examinations. Otis revised his tests and issued them as the Otis Self-Administering Primary, Intermediate, and Higher Examinations, and later as the Otis Quick-Scoring Mental Ability Tests. Otis's quick-scoring system, using a punched stencil, foreshadowed machine-scoring methods. Each verbal test contained eighty questions, all multiple-choice, including vocabulary, analogies, opposites, logical reasoning, and a few nonverbal problems. In contents they thus reflected Otis's recognition of the primary factors involved in verbal intelligence.

In 1920 Terman published his Group Test of Mental Ability for Grades 7 to 12, divided into ten subtests (information; best answer; word meaning; logical selection; arithmetic; sentence meaning; analogies; mixed sentences; classification; and number series). Later, with Quinn McNemar, a colleague at Stanford University, he developed a revised popular test entitled the Terman-McNemar Test of Mental Ability for high-school students and college freshmen.

Terman maintained that the scores earned on his intelligence tests were valid, useful aids in the classification and promotion of pupils and in educational and vocational guidance. He cautioned teachers, however, to supplement test results with information about the individual's health, interests, habits, and social status as the bases for the improvement of instruction. He noted that students enrolled in Latin or algebra classes tended to earn much higher scores than those studying shopwork or domestic science. He reported (just as Yerkes had done in 1915) that the children of fathers working in the learned professions generally earned higher scores than the children of unskilled laborers. (N. Stewart's analysis in 1947 of scores on the U.S. Army's General Classification Test during the Second World War—a test measuring arithmetic reasoning, word meaning, and judgments about spatial relationships—duplicated the previous findings of Yerkes and Terman that men with a professional family background displayed the highest verbal intelligence. According to Stewart, the general level of intelligence of recruits in that war was considerably higher than the comparable level in the First World War.)

Beginning in 1919, the Ohio State University Psychological Test by Herbert A. Toops set a pattern for many similar examinations administered by colleges to applicants for admission. His test was designed for grades 9–16 and for adults and consisted of three subtests: same and opposites; analogies and verbal or grammatical relations; and reading comprehension.

In the 1920s, Rudolf Pintner developed a verbal group intelligence test for kindergarten and the primary grades (the Pintner-Cunningham Test) and also a nonlanguage test for grades 4–8. During the 1930s, he constructed a series of verbal group intelligence tests for elementary grades entitled the Pintner General Ability Tests, Verbal Series, similar in many respects to Terman's Group Test of Mental Ability for Grades 7 to 12.

In the 1950s, there were numerous contributors to the development of group intelligence tests, among them E. T. Sullivan, W. W. Clark, and E. W. Tiegs, of the University of Southern California, who constructed the California Short-Form Tests of Mental Maturity, featuring subtests for spatial relationships, arithmetic reasoning, logical thinking, and verbal comprehension. A later extensive revision contained twelve subtests with eight final scores. The California tests and a comparable battery, the Academic Promise Tests published in 1961–1962, reflected significant researches in factor analysis completed in preceding years by Spearman, Thorndike, and Thurstone.

SPEARMAN, THORNDIKE, AND THURSTONE

In 1917 the Dutch neuroanatomist C. U. A. Kappers formulated a theory of neurobiotaxis that attributed the growth of neural structures to changing relationships between the axons and the dendrites of neurons. The American psychologist Edwin Bissell Holt (1873–1946) applied the theory to the analysis of intelligence and intelligent behavior. A vast number of changing neural connections in an electric field, said Holt, account for the existence of the specific mental capacities measured by subtests in standardized intelligence examinations. In *Brain Mechanisms and Intelligence* (1929), however, Karl S. Lashley, who had devoted many years to experimentation in this field, elaborated on his theory of equipotentiality, which attributed intelligent reactions mainly to the general, unitary organization of the brain and to synaptic resistance to neural stimuli.

From another point of view, the British psychologist Philip B. Ballard stated in *Mental Tests* (1920) that the majority of psychologists agreed upon the following characteristics of intelligence: (1) It is innate and operates in manifold ways; (2) it becomes most evident during higher mental processes; (3) it is most active in connection with novel situations; (4) it functions mainly when the individual analyzes or dissects information, and plans or modifies a series of activities; and (5) it reaches its maximum level at sixteen years or younger.

Charles E. Spearman, in *Abilities of Man* (1927), advocated a two-factor theory stating that intelligent behavior depends not only upon a *general* mental ability (G) but also upon *specific* mental abilities (s). Spearman's general factor seemed consistent with Lashley's integrated, unified brain-action concept. According to Spearman, individuals with high IQs, for example, tend to be superior both in general mental capacity and in a variety of specific mental abilities (as in solving mathematical problems, reasoning by analogy, and the like) measured by subtests. (Raymond B. Cattell, one of Spearman's disciples, and Truman L. Kelley applied factor analysis to statistical investigations of personality traits.)

In another development affecting intelligence testing, Thorndike formulated a multiple-factor theory in contrast to Spearman's hypothesis. Similar mental abilities, said Thorndike, may possess common elements or be closely associated and should therefore be grouped together as factors to be measured by subtests of intelligence examinations. Thorndike elaborated on this concept in his well-known work *The Measurement of Intelligence* (1927). In the 1935 *Harvard University Studies in Education*, Kelley asserted that the most important traits in mental life and personality growth were not Spearman's general factor (G) but vigorous health, abstract reasoning, motor coordination, and emotional stability.

In 1940, having devoted forty years to the study of mental abilities, Thorndike classified them into three broad or composite types: abstract or verbal intelligence, most evident in mathematics, language, and science; mechanical intelligence, required for, and most useful in, skilled vocations and practical, manipulative work; and social intelligence, needed for successful relationships to other people. Thorndike constructed verbal group intelligence tests called CAVD tests to measure abstract intelligence in its applications to sentence-completion questions (C), arithmetic reasoning (A), vocabulary (V), and following directions (D). During the 1950s, he and his colleague Irving Lorge at Columbia University constructed batteries of verbal and nonverbal intelligence tests for children. In subsequent researches during the 1960s, Joy O. Guilford and P. R. Merrifield of the University of Southern California, applying statistical methods, identified about 120 factors involved in the three broad types of mental reactions postulated by Thorndike.

Spearman and his disciples in the 1920s at the University of London had been prime movers in the development of factor analysis as an aid to research in the field of tests and measurements. In the United States, Louis Leon Thurstone at the University of Chicago delineated a seven-factor theory of intelligence in *Vectors of the Mind* (1935) and took the lead during the 1950s and thereafter.

In 1973 and 1978, R. B. Cattell and A. K. S. Cattell developed the Culture Fair Intelligence Test, designed to minimize the influence of specific cultural backgrounds of the individual on his responses and scores, including, for example, questions in the form of nonsense material. If a test contains much subject matter most familiar to rural people—such as references to cows and sheep farming—it should also include many items most familiar to urban people—such as references to subways and skyscrapers. Ideal test items should discriminate between greater and lesser mental capacity among all persons irrespective of cultural environment. In the absence of such an ideal test, testmakers appeared justified in attempts to achieve a fair balance of items so as to reflect the cultural backgrounds of all individuals in any mixed group.

During the 1970s, several psychologists, as, for example, K. G. Jöreskog, P. M. Bentler, and C. E. Werts, utilized sophisticated mathematical, probability, and statistical techniques (with computers in some cases) to supplement traditional applications of factor analysis to psychological testing. Investigators attempted to analyze mathematically numerous multiple and latent factors, both psychological and environmental causes, related to the construction of tests and the reliability of test results. They investigated the conditions of testing programs, the continually changing attitudes and moods of examinees, and the variations, strengths, and limitations of tests and test batteries (especially in regard to their up-to-dateness and the familiarity of the subject content), as well as diverse environmental influences on test procedures, scores, and interpretations and applications of results.

The American Council on Education began annual publication of a Psychological Examination for College Freshmen in 1924 and annual publication of a Psychological Examination for High School Students in 1933—two mainly verbal group examinations constructed by Louis Leon Thurstone and Thelma G. Thurstone. These scholastic aptitude tests, in annual revised editions, were used by hundreds of four-year liberal arts colleges, two-year colleges, teachers' colleges, some technical schools, and many high schools as aids in the selection of students, the prediction of scholastic success, and educational guidance. The Thurstones emphasized language elements as the most useful basis for predicting success among students in liberal arts colleges. Later, L. L. Thurstone developed the SRA (Science Research Associates) Test of Primary Mental Abilities for ages 5–7, 7–11, and 11–17, and the Chicago Nonverbal Examination for age seven to adulthood. In 1955 he reported test results indicating that, for the majority of people, the speed of perception reaches its peak level sooner than general verbal intelligence and spatial discrimination, which attain their highest level at fourteen years of age, and that adults continue to improve indefinitely in their language comprehension and expression. He noted that children grow most rapidly in general intelligence during their early years as they encounter an abundance of new experiences requiring adjustments and exercise of intellectual capacity.

Thurstone's SRA Test of Primary Mental Abilities featured six groups of factors: arithmetic; speed of spatial perception; rote memory; verbal comprehension; language fluency; and logical reasoning. He concluded that each group of factors has its central core or special primary element which spreads across and connects the six groups of factors—a conclusion similar to Spearman's theory of a general basic mental ability (G).

TESTS OF APTITUDES AND INTERESTS

In the 1920s and 1930s, standardized tests were developed to measure individual differences in aptitudes and in personal interests. These tests are still used to assist teachers and counselors in their predictions of academic and vocational success and in guidance programs. Pioneers in this development were E. K.

Strong, Jr. of Stanford University; G. F. Kuder of Duke University; G. K. Bennett of the Psychological Corporation; John L. Stenquist; T. W. MacQuarrie; H. H. Remmers of Purdue University; Lawrence J. O'Rourke of the United States Civil Service; and Carl E. Seashore and Norman C. Meier of the University of Iowa.

Strong's Vocational Interest Blank for high-school students and adults (revised in 1974 as a combined test entitled E. K. Strong–D. P. Campbell Test) consisted of two tests, one for men, the other for women, each with a total of four hundred questions. The individual indicated his preference, indifference, or distaste in regard to specified skilled occupations, school subjects, and leisure activities and also chose between pairs of given activities, occupations and abilities. Included were questions to evaluate masculinity and femininity. (A similar short test by Thurstone consisted of seventy-two questions about occupational interests.)

The Kuder Preference Record-Vocational, constructed in 1939, measured the individual's interest in ten kinds of occupations. A revised version published in 1964 as the Kuder Occupational Interest Survey was widely used for evaluating the interests of high-school and college students in outdoor (recreational), mechanical, computational, scientific, sales, artistic, literary, musical, social-service, and clerical activities. A set of comparable Differential Aptitudes Tests constructed by G. K. Bennett and his associates in the Psychological Corporation measures intelligence as well as basic aptitudes and skills regarded as important in various occupations.

The Stenquist examination to measure mechanical aptitudes was designed originally to test men drafted into the United States armed forces during the First World War. It requires the individual to reassemble parts of mechanical devices, such as pumps and locks, and to state how he would cope with certain mechanical tasks and mathematical problems. The MacQuarrie Test for Mechanical Ability and the SRA Mechanical Aptitude Tests are similar popular examinations testing perceptual speed, manual dexterity, spatial judgments, and the like. Holland's Vocational Preference Inventory of 1970 attempts to associate vocational interests with personality traits, including questions about occupational interests, educational subject preferences, and personal qualities. It is a self-administering test for persons fourteen years and older.

During the 1930s and 1940s, numerous tests measuring the aptitudes needed in commercial occupations of special interest to high-school boys and girls were constructed and standardized. H. H. Remmers at Purdue University directed programs of test construction in bookkeeping, shorthand, typewriting, chemistry, and other subjects. Municipal, state, and federal civil-service agencies developed their own examination in addition to using national standardized tests. The United States Employment Service administered a battery of General Aptitude Tests for high-school students and adults measuring verbal intelligence, spatial perception, motor coordination, and clerical aptitude. O'Rourke's popular Junior Clerical Test emphasized arithmetic, proofreading, alphabetization, and language usage. Other useful similar tests include SRA clerical aptitude tests, the Minnesota Clerical Tests, and the Beginner's Clerical Test.

The Seashore Measures of Musical Talent, constructed by Carl E. Seashore (1866–1949) at Iowa University in 1919 (later revised), was based upon its author's extensive researches and experiments to identify abilities in discrimination of pitch and loudness, judgments of time, timbre, rhythm, and tonal combinations, and musical memory. The subject listens to recordings and answers true-false questions. The tests have been found effective for identifying persons lacking in musical aptitude and also those with exceptional talent. A similar approach is utilized in the Musical Aptitude Profile and in the Wing Standardized Tests of Musical Intelligence.

The Meier-Seashore Art Judgment Tests constructed by Meier and Seashore in 1929 measure the individual's appreciation of works of art by requiring him to examine pairs of similar pictures and art objects and to choose which is the better production. The Graves Design Judgment Test utilizes the same approach. These tests were intended to measure appreciation of artistic creations without reference to skill in performance. In the early 1930s, L. W. Kline and G. L. Carey of The Johns Hopkins University devised the Measuring Scale for Freehand Drawing for elementary-school pupils and used a scoring system for comparing the individual's freehand drawing with specimen drawings for many types of themes, illustrations, posters, borders, and designs.

Many Middle State colleges used the Ohio State University Psychological Test as an admissions examination. Thousands of high schools and colleges in the United States and in other English-speaking countries utilized the College Entrance Examination Board Scholastic Aptitude Test (SAT) for this purpose. In every state, many colleges administered to applicants the American College Testing Examinations (ACT), first developed in 1959 as a battery of four forty-minute tests in English, social studies, mathematics, and science, combining aptitude- with achievement-test questions. These tests emphasized language-aptitude questions (antonyms, analogies, and sentence completions) and mathematics-aptitude questions (arithmetic principles and computation, algebra, and geometry).

Aptitude tests in physical education included the Brace Motor Ability Tests, the Rogers Physical Capacity Tests, the McCloy Tests for Appraising Physical Status, and the MacCurdy Test for Measuring the Physical Capacity of Secondary School Boys. Tests of this kind required the use of simple gymnasium equipment, as in measuring the strength of grip, "push" and "pull" strength, and the like, supplemented by records of athletic accomplishments.

Also noteworthy among hundreds of aptitude tests in print were the Jensen Educational Aptitude Test, the annual National Teacher Examinations of the Educational Testing Service, and the Coxe Orleans Test for Teachers, for administration to prospective teachers. These tests measured the ability to analyze professional materials and to solve problems in school situations. Useful aptitude tests were developed for other professions, such as the Medical Aptitude Examination, the Minnesota Medical Aptitude Test, and the Scientific Aptitude Test by Zyve at Stanford University. The George Washington University Test of So-

cial Intelligence by F. A. Moss, constructed in 1925, measured
the ability to cope with problems of human relationships and to
remember names and faces.

PERSONALITY TESTS

The word-association method of analyzing mental activity,
used by Galton about 1880, was soon thereafter applied by
Wundt and Kraepelin in Wundt's laboratory. Galton studied the
ideas that came into his mind when he thought about specific
words, and he recorded the ideas as well as the reaction times
between the words and the associated ideas. Many of the same
ideas occurred to him repeatedly in response to stimulus words.
Listing seventy-five words and the ideas associated with each of
them, he noted that the majority of ideas related to events of his
youth and early adulthood, very few to events of recent years.

In Munich, Kraepelin and his disciple J. Lange used the
same word-association technique to discover some of the recollections and associations disturbing mental patients. In 1910
Jung constructed another word-association test requiring the individual to respond to each of a series of stimulus words with the
first word that occurred to him, a procedure that eventually became a standard technique. If the individual requires an above-
average time to respond to a word, or responds too rapidly, the
cause may be an emotional or intellectual disturbance; similarly,
perseveration (continued repetition of the same responses) or an
idiosyncratic (bizarre) response may indicate abnormality; and
mental blockage during the test may indicate guilt feelings and
emotional difficulties. Jung assumed that word associations usually revealed the individual's thought patterns and many of his
prior unconscious mental experiences. Also in 1910, G. H. Kent
and A. J. Rosanoff used Jung's method to discriminate between
normal and abnormal individuals. They constructed a test consisting of 100 stimulus words commonly associated with emotions and administered it to 1,000 normal people and to 247
mentally ill patients. The responses of the latter group were frequently more uncertain, hesitant, repetitive, and variant than
those of the normal group. Word-association tests are projective

tests widely used by contemporary psychologists and psychiatrists to discover an individual's inner conflicts and bring his repressed experiences and emotions to the surface.

Questionnaires and personality inventories, often supplemented by behavior samplings, are popular tests of moods, attitudes, beliefs, preferences, temperaments, and character traits. In 1918 Robert S. Woodworth constructed a Psychoneurotic Inventory that was administered to army recruits during the First World War to identify men most likely to break down under the stress of combat. In the 1920s, character tests (accompanied by observed behavior samples) were devised by R. F. Voelker, V. M. Cady, June E. Downey, and Hugh Hartshorne and Mark A. May. The questions in the Downey Will-Temperament Tests were designed to measure the individual's firmness and speed of decision; persistence; motor coordination; carefulness; and attitudes toward contradictions, suggestions, and opposition. Other personality tests included test papers and procedures allowing individuals to cheat while enabling the examiner to detect them. In 1926, after administering seven of their tests of this kind to hundreds of children, Hartshorne and May reported that cheating, lying, and stealing do not tend to go together; also that what individuals do depends usually upon the entire situation facing them, including the importance of success, the difficulty of using dishonest tactics, and the children's previous training and home backgrounds. In 1928 Gordon W. Allport's Ascendance-Submission Test was published to measure the tendency toward dominance and submissiveness. The following year, Thurstone constructed a Personality Schedule designed to measure individual differences in emotional stability, attitudes, opinions, and sensitivity.

Many excellent tests in this field were developed during the 1930s. The Willoughby Emotional Maturity Scale provided evidence that self-control and social maturity increase with age throughout the period of general growth and development. The Allport-Vernon Study of Values to measure the individual's attitude toward the ethical standards in his society, published in 1931, was revised and reissued as the Allport-Vernon-Lindzey Study of Values in the 1950s. R. G. Bernreuter's Personality

Inventory, containing 125 questions to measure self-reliance, extroversion and introversion, dominance and submissiveness, and neurotic tendencies, could be used either with groups or with individuals. Results often agreed with individuals' psychiatric histories and provided cues to potential, incipient, or developing personality maladjustments. Allport constructed a psychographic chart of fourteen personality traits, each trait to be rated by observers on a scale of 1 to 100; a profile of the individual's total personality was shown graphically by a curve joining the scores for the fourteen traits. The Bell Adjustment Inventory was used extensively to evaluate the seriousness of emotional and social maladjustments among adolescents, teen-agers, and young adults. The Vineland (New Jersey) Social Maturity Scale by E. A. Doll consisted of 117 items measuring personality traits related to self-direction, self-help, communication, social mobility, and social relationships, traits revealed by the overt behavior of feebleminded and normal children as they reacted to life situations. Doll's test, revised in 1947, became a popular individual test as well as being used for special classes of handicapped children. (The information called for in this test could be obtained from parents or other observers instead of from answers supplied by the children.) An Attitude-Interest Analysis Test prepared by Terman and C. C. Miles in 1936 was actually a disguised test of tendencies toward masculinity and femininity.

Raymond B. Cattell at the University of Illinois devised a Self-Analysis Scale that questioned the individual's motives and goals, leaving him alone as he reflected upon and answered the questions. A similar approach was used in the Minnesota Multiphasic Personality Inventory constructed in 1943 by S. R. Hathaway and J. J. McKinley, which consists of 550 items obtained from the case histories of psychiatric patients and includes questions about intimate relationships and personal habits. Each true-false question is printed on a card, and the individual is instructed to put the cards in the correct "yes," "no," or "do not know" boxes. Scores may indicate tendencies toward depression, personality disorders, masculinity and femininity, and sociability.

In the 1960s, questionnaires to measure social maturity were prepared by A. Mehrabian and others. A scale developed in

Norway during the 1970s to measure drives to achieve success and drives to avert failure attracted favorable attention among contemporary psychologists and educators. During the 1970s, Douglas N. Jackson, of Ontario, Canada, constructed personality scales measuring self-esteem, anxiety, social participation, tolerance, and other traits. H. J. Eysenck published a personality inventory and a personality questionnaire, both including measures of introversion and extroversion. Scales of masculinity, femininity, and androgenic tendencies were developed by S. L. Bem, J. I. Berzins, A. B. Heilbrun, J. T. Spence, and others. Many recent scales, questionnaires, and inventories benefited from impressive statistics regarding their validity and reliability as well as ingenious experiments and observations of behavior attesting to their predictive values.

Nevertheless, critics of personality scales, questionnaires, and inventories assert that an individual's answers to questions, even when supplemented by necessarily limited observation, may not correspond to his customary behavior under stress, that he may not even fully understand the implications of questions being asked or know the answers. Moreover, some persons answering test questions possess and apply more imagination than others. Some may answer carelessly without adequate reflection. In 1980 the Canadian psychologists Douglas N. Jackson and Sampo V. Paunonen of the University of Western Ontario suggested that computers (to calculate intricate statistical correlations and other relationships of data in minutes instead of many years otherwise required) should be used to investigate complex aspects of personality. But conclusions regarding personality based upon elaborate statistical methods, with or without computers, are viewed with skepticism by conservative psychologists. They hold that the validity, utility, and predictive value of many questions in personality tests should be carefully evaluated in terms of the wording of questions, the social and cultural environment of individual examinees, periodic modifications in the testee's self-judgment and perceptions of other people, and actual long-term behavior patterns. The testmakers justify continued use of their examinations as valuable psychological instruments supplementing other techniques such as medical tests, anecdotal records, interviews, autobiographical reports, case histories, hypnosis, and psychoanalysis.

Various projective tests are used frequently by clinical psychologists and psychiatrists to facilitate the diagnosis and treatment of severe personality maladjustments and mental disturbances.

In 1921 the Swiss psychiatrist Hermann Rorschach (1884–1922), taking his cue from Binet's use of inkblots in 1895, devised an inkblot test similar in principle to Jung's word-association test except that the testee responds to inkblots instead of words and tells what the different designs, some in colors, suggest to him. Ten inkblots are presented in sequence printed on cards uniform in size, and the examiner notes the individual's concentration on the form, color, contents, and other aspects of the designs. The responses often disclose habits of thinking, customary speed of reaction, anxiety, depression, past mental experiences and personal values, and diverse signs of other possible maladjustments such as inability to cope with reality or with some major organic impairment. Mental depression may be revealed by responses that overemphasize the gray-black inkblots, while bizarre replies may indicate schizoid tendencies, negativism, or other personality disturbances.

At Harvard University in 1935, the clinical psychologist Henry A. Murray and his colleague Christiana D. Morgan developed their Thematic Apperception Test to diagnose the mental state and personality traits of college students. This test, which became famous, consists of a series of ten photographs portraying human relationships in lifelike situations. The student is required to explain each scene as it is presented, tell about the actions and probable motives of the characters, and indicate how the story or plot will end.* The stories made up by the student

---

*Murray's researches at the Harvard Psychological Clinic (in the period 1928 to 1937) were endangered when the eminent chemist James Bryant Conant, president of the university from 1933 to 1953, arranged for Karl S. Lashley to evaluate the work of the clinic. Lashley was not impressed by Murray's view that the human being should be judged not through laboratory experiments or piecemeal reactions but as a creative, unique whole personality continually changing throughout his lifetime. Lashley and Conant recommended that the clinic be eliminated and that Murray be discharged, but university officers ignored that recommendation and eventually promoted Murray to a full professorship.

to explain the pictures often reveal much about his own personality and mental state as he identifies with some of the characters, attempts to describe their purposes and characteristics, conceals or distorts some events or relationships, and finishes each story with an ending perhaps reflecting his own past experience and conscious or unconscious feelings. A skillful examiner may learn a great deal about the whole personality from these stories even though some traits and disturbances may remain hidden until additional information is obtained through other means. The test was revised to include twenty pictures; later again to include thirty-one pictures. It was used mainly with adults, but was eventually supplemented by a similar test for children, the Children's Apperception Test.

The American child psychologist Lauretta Bender devised the Bender Visual Motor Gestalt Test in 1938 after she noticed that the IQs of some children rose dramatically when the causes of their mental disturbances had been eliminated. The test presents nine cards in sequential order, each with a drawing to be shown to the child for several seconds and then copied or reproduced by him from memory. The drawings may reveal personality maladjustments and in some cases mental illnesses such as those caused by brain injuries.

During the 1940s, several projective tests of personality differences among individuals were developed and standardized to assist psychologists and psychiatrists in their diagnostic analyses. In 1941 the American psychologists K. Goldstein and M. Scheerer constructed the Goldstein-Scheerer Test to measure defects in abstract thinking processes, indicated when individuals are unable to handle materials or to follow instructions. They may try to cope with these difficulties in strange ways or find ingenious excuses for avoiding them, behavior often reflecting mental deterioration as in schizophrenic illnesses or in brain damage. Another projective test, the Szondi Test devised by the Hungarian biologist L. Szondi in 1949, presented forty-eight pictures of mental patients (six pictures of each of eight abnormal persons—paranoids, hysterics, etc.) and instructed the patient to choose from each set of six pictures the two he liked best and the two he disliked most in the light of their clothing, sex, and facial appearances. The examinee finally was also asked to choose the four pictures he liked best and the four he disliked most. Szondi recommended that the test be repeated six times in order to verify the results. The aim was to discover repressed motives, unconscious feelings, and forgotten experiences.

Also in 1949, the American psychiatrist Saul Rosenzweig developed his unique Picture-Frustration Test consisting of twenty-four cartoons, each portraying two persons in frustrating life situations in which one person makes an aggressive remark or an apologetic comment. The examinee writes out in the cartoon what his immediate reply would be under the circumstances. Evaluation of the replies may indicate personality traits such as aggressive or punitive tendencies; self-blame or guilt feelings; and fatalistic, indifferent, or cooperative attitudes. Another extensive test with comparable psychodramatic features was devised by E. S. Shneidman, the Make-a-Picture-Story Test, which instructed the individual to choose among sixty-seven cutout figures of men, women, children, and animals; to select a backdrop from twenty stage settings; to arrange his selected figures on the stage; and to tell a story about them. The individual's story and answers to questions about his choices often revealed his inner feelings, attitudes, and possible personality maladjustments or disturbances.

In the 1950s, J. A. Taylor constructed another popular projective test, the Manifest Anxiety Scale, which measured chronic feelings of anxiety related to educational motivation and success. Taylor reported that individuals shown by their test scores to be very anxious were in many cases superior in achievement but tended to make more responses and errors in complicated situations than calm, steady, patient individuals. In simpler situations, the latter seemed superior in performance.

ACHIEVEMENT TESTS

Four thousand years ago, candidates for public-service positions in China were required to pass competitive examinations, a practice adopted by European medieval universities. In England over a century ago, schoolmasters briefly tried expertly prepared model essays to be used as standard materials with which pupils' written work could be compared for purposes of evaluation and promotion. In Germany, Ebbinghaus devised tests of memory during the 1870s, a decade or more before similar experiments by Cattell and Farrand in America. While constructing the first sentence-completion test in 1897, Ebbinghaus noted that incomplete sentences would serve as association cues assisting the examinee to recall the specific information needed to fill in the blanks and thus complete the sentences.

Early in the twentieth century, the United States took the lead in developing standardized achievement tests, which came into use in many countries on all levels of education. Examinations today may include not only printed questions but also interviews, essays, reports, themes, drawings, dramatizations, speeches, seminar discussions, oral readings, recitations, debates, laboratory experiments and demonstrations, research projects, lectures, and the performance of specific assigned tasks. But standardized printed tests of achievement have been found to be valid and reliable through the application of statistical techniques originated by Galton, Wundt, Stern, Cattell, Pearson, Thurstone, Spearman, and others. With questions carefully selected through item analyses to ensure discriminating value, these tests have become customary means of evaluation in schools and colleges.

One of the pioneers in this development was Joseph Meyer Rice, a critic of low standards in public education. He devised an objective spelling test in 1897 and followed it with tests in arithmetic and other school subjects. Schoolmasters ridiculed his tests as a waste of time, but the results, which showed great differences in achievement among schools, proved that the quality of learning and teaching can be measured to some extent by standardized tests and scales. In 1908 C. W. Stone constructed the first new-type arithmetic test, the Stone Reasoning Test in Arithmetic. The following year, S. A. Courtis devised an objective arithmetic computation test, and also in 1909 Thorndike published a handwriting scale. In 1911 L. P. Ayres constructed a handwriting scale, and in 1912 Hillegas developed a unique scale for the measurement of English composition. In 1913 B. R. Buckingham published his popular Buckingham Spelling Scale.

William H. McCall and Thorndike constructed their McCall-Thorndike Reading Scale in 1920, thus rounding out the list of standardized tests available for use in teaching the three Rs. More and more tests were prepared and standardized in these and many other subjects, until by midcentury at least four thousand statistically reliable tests had been published.

ACHIEVEMENT TEST SERIES

Comprehensive series of school achievement tests for nation-wide use were developed during the 1920s and 1930s to measure academic accomplishments of pupils in the United States. Many of these series have been revised at frequent intervals either by the original authors or by other test specialists in order to incorporate new items, correct errors and weaknesses, and bring the norms up to date.

At Stanford University in 1922, Truman L. Kelley, Giles M. Ruch, and L. M. Terman completed work on their well-known Stanford Achievement Test Series for primary, intermediate, and upper grades, published the following year. In 1925 the Iowa Every-Pupil Tests, survey tests in high-school subjects, were completed for administration in annual Iowa State testing programs under the direction of Everet F. Lindquist of the State University of Iowa. Scores earned on Iowa examinations in English grammar and literature, history and social studies, mathematics, and science were often accepted when students applied for admission to numerous colleges. In 1928 Arthur I. Gates, Paul Mort, and Ralph Spence, of Teachers College, Columbia University, developed the Modern School Achievement Test Series for elementary grades.

In 1930 Ben D. Wood, of Teachers College, Columbia University, and John C. Flanagan prepared achievement tests for the Cooperative Test Series that was developed soon after research studies under the auspices of the Carnegie Foundation had revealed serious deficiencies in instruction, guidance, and evaluation among the high schools and colleges of Pennsylvania. Similar deficiencies were believed to be widespread throughout the nation. In 1931, tests for primary grades in the popular

Metropolitan Achievement Test Series were prepared by Gertrude H. Hildreth of Teachers College, Columbia University, while tests for the middle and upper grades were constructed for the series by R. D. Allen, H. H. Bixler, and other test specialists. Other popular series included the Unit Scales of Attainment and the Progressive Achievement Tests. In the mid-1930s, Samuel Smith and Robert K. Speer of New York University developed the National Achievement Test Series, reissued for over forty years thereafter.

The College Entrance Examination Board, founded in 1900, published achievement tests and test series annually, which were administered in many countries several times each year to measure academic qualifications of more than two million high-school students for admission to American degree-granting colleges. Thousands of colleges and secondary schools participated in the numerous testing programs of the Board, which included a two-hour Preliminary Scholastic Aptitude Test (taken by a million students) in language and mathematics; one-hour achievement tests in English composition, history, social studies, and foreign languages; a one-hour essay-writing test; and advanced-placement tests, which enabled students to apply for college credit after admission.

The General Educational Development Tests of the American Council on Education, consisting of high-school-level and college-level sets of tests prepared originally by the United States Armed Forces Institute, were administered annually to hundreds of thousands of veterans and other adults desiring to obtain high-school-equivalency diplomas or admission to cooperating colleges.

Critics charge that standardized tests are limited by their narrow scope and failure to take into account sufficiently the ever-changing mental, emotional, and physical characteristics of the individual. The immediate display of intellectual ability or recalled information in piecemeal fashion by the individual cannot replace the test of continuous life itself, evidence consisting of what he feels, says, learns, knows, and does each hour, day, and year of his life-span. They assert that test scores must be interpreted with extreme caution in attempting to evaluate creative abilities. They point out that the great men of the past—Plato, Aristotle, Mozart, da Vinci, Newton, Einstein—were not required to answer questions about bits and pieces of knowledge or display familiarity with superficial technology. Nevertheless, there is general agreement among contemporary psychologists that, if carefully constructed and properly used, standardized tests can often reveal important ideas, knowledge, personality traits, and educational needs of individuals and thus supplement other methods of psychological measurement and investigation.

6 ACTION, MOTIVATION,
AND ADJUSTMENT

Advances in the scientific investigation of human reactions, motives, and adjustments developed rapidly out of the ideas and
experiments of European and American psychologists during the
first half of the twentieth century. Wilhelm Wundt was the most
prominent and influential of these early investigators.

WUNDT

In 1796 an astronomer at the British Royal Observatory in
Greenwich was discharged because of his delay of a half-second
to a second in noting the exact time that stars crossed his transit.
His reactions were not fast enough to provide sufficiently accurate astronomical observations. For decades thereafter, scientists
discussed the causes and effects of such differences in individual
reaction times. Experiments in the 1880s showed that some differences depend upon whether the individual concentrates his
attention on the stimulus or on his own movements.

To measure sensory and motor reaction times, Wundt conducted experiments in his Leipzig University laboratory, using
for equipment a sound hammer as a stimulator; an electromag-
net connected to a battery; reaction keys for movements of fin-
gers, eyelids, lips, etc.; and a chronoscope connecting stimuli
electrically to start-and-stop clocks. He reported the average
times of reactions to light, sound, and electrical stimuli. Wundt's
findings, corroborated and refined by other investigators, including his students Titchener and Cattell, proved that sensory reaction times are very fast (about 110 to 170 thousandths of a second) for touch sensations, rapid (110 to 160 thousandths of a

second) for auditory sensations, less rapid (160 to 280 thousandths of a second) for visual sensations, and much slower (400 to 1,000 thousandths of a second) for pain sensations. Reaction times varied about 8 to 10 percent with different individuals and conditions of the experiments.

TITCHENER

Experimenting and teaching at Cornell University from 1892 to 1927, E. B. Titchener reported additional facts concerning reaction times. If an observer, for example, must choose among several stimuli for response, his reaction time increases. Muscular reaction time is greater for arm and leg movements than for finger movements. Reactions to touch are faster than reactions to light, because the latter involve time-consuming chemical effects on rods and cones of the eyes. Reactions are slower for taste and smell, which also depend upon chemical changes. Pain reactions are very slow, for they involve complex sensory organs. Simple habitual reactions occur more quickly than compound reactions affecting numerous pathways in the brain. Physical and mental fatigue can affect reaction time because of diminished attention, lack of interest or boredom, and the desire to avoid further discomfort, but the individual can rally his energy to counteract fatigue. Titchener concluded that many factors (such as practice, habit, clear judgment, suggestion, purpose, expectancy, preparation, and distractions) affect both speed and quality of reactions.

Wundt classified reactions into two parallel types: (1) responses to external stimuli; and (2) psychic processes (willing, feeling, judging, associating, and interpreting) ascertained by introspection. Titchener suggested a different classification: (1) reflexes and instincts, attributed to inherited neural mechanisms; and (2) voluntary actions, attributed to acquired neural connections. Voluntary action, he said, is based upon a substratum of inherited tendencies and equipment but also involves will, suggestion, purpose, anticipation of consequences, feelings of disappointment or success, and kinesthetic sensations. He agreed with Oswald Kuelpe's statements that unconscious incentives can determine some voluntary purposive actions and that ideas affect performance so that if the individual is prepared for what is about to happen, expectation will increase the speed, accuracy, and efficiency of his reaction to the event when it does happen.

THORNDIKE

E. L. Thorndike, observing animal and human behavior during four decades of laboratory experimentation at Columbia University, concluded that ideas may precede, suggest, and follow, but do not actually produce specific actions of the individual. He held that ideas were ineffective unless they were energized by inherited tendencies and anticipated satisfactions. Any idea could precede any action. These views were reflected in Thorndike's significant theories concerning motivation and behavior. Commenting on William James's assumption that every idea finds expression immediately in a specific motor reaction, he stated that such a reaction will often not take place if it has previously had painful consequences, whereas memory of satisfying results will favor its occurrence. He agreed with Titchener that voluntary behavior depends not only upon inherited neural mechanisms but also upon purposes, pleasant or unpleasant feelings, kinesthetic sensations, and simple or complex images.

According to Thorndike, voluntary activities obey the laws of instinct, readiness, exercise, and effect. Mental fatigue is a negligible factor. Not mental fatigue but boredom, he said, accounts for inefficiency during continuous work. He cited experiments (upon his suggestion) by his student Tsuru Arai in 1912 indicating that mental fatigue reduces efficiency less than 5 percent in an hour while efficiency often increases again about 4 percent when the individual nears the end of a burdensome task. Thorndike, William James, and Hugo Münsterberg noted that even when mental fatigue seems to intensify, the individual's interest, enthusiasm, and persistent effort may enable him to counteract weariness and regain high efficiency, a process that James called *second wind*. Thorndike suggested that practice accompanied by sustained interest and satisfying achievement is the best way to maintain high performance in mental work.

He described instincts as unlearned patterns of behavior and as the foundations of purposive action. Reflexes, he stated, are also unlearned responses, but more limited, rigid, definite, and uniform. In 1913 he listed forty-two instincts in three groups: (1) food-getting (acquiring, hoarding, eating) and self-protecting actions (as in avoiding danger); (2) reactions to other people (exemplified by gregariousness, rivalry, kindness, and the like); and (3) unlearned physical movements (as in vocalization) and unlearned mental activities (as in those motivated by curiosity). In 1940 he listed twenty desires (such as pleasant sensations) and sixteen aversions (such as bitter tastes and pain) as basic motives for behavior. His experiments in 1898 had shown that failure and frustration could sometimes serve as internal stimuli impelling the individual to redouble efforts to succeed. On the other hand, his later experiments, as in 1931, indicated that knowledge of progress toward a goal usually increased motivation, effort, and efficiency.

Thorndike's emphasis on the emotional satisfaction of success as a key element in voluntary behavior was rejected by many behaviorist psychologists, who attributed all behavior to conditioned reflexes. Similarly his assumption that each stimulus becomes attached to a specific reaction, his theory of connectionism, was rejected by Gestalt psychologists, who pointed to the factors of configuration in perceptions and of organic unity in responses as basic elements in behavior. Thorndike argued that these Gestaltist ideas were mystical, yet he himself introduced a somewhat mystical factor of belongingness in an attempt to explain connections between stimuli and reactions.

KRAEPELIN

Emil Kraepelin (1856–1926), professor of psychiatry at Heidelberg University, often called the father of modern psychiatry, studied under Wundt at the University of Leipzig. In 1882 he conducted experiments on psychological reactions involved in work and the effects of fatigue and drugs. He continued these experiments for a decade, along with investigations into perception, memory, association, judgment, and other basic processes. For over thirty years at his clinic in Munich, Kraepelin applied

Wundt's and Galton's methods of observation, case histories, laboratory experiments, and testing to the study of thousands of mental patients—their everyday habits, diet, handwriting, oral and written language, ideas and purposes, learning, and sensory and motor responses. He differentiated between organic and functional types of mental illnesses, a distinction now accepted by leading clinical psychologists and psychiatrists. The word-association tests of Kraepelin, Galton, and Wundt became a standard diagnostic technique to probe inner conflicts and severe personality maladjustments.

Kraepelin differentiated physical (sensory and motor) from mental (emotional and psychic) fatigue. Attentive practice, he asserted, should gradually improve efficiency in work performance until a decline occurs due to boredom and fatigue. Sustained activity is subject to forces of inertia (the tendency to continue the same reactions) as it approaches peak efficiency. Thereafter, to counteract mental fatigue, the individual needs a brief rest period even though his mental effort, motivated by a prospect of success, often begins and ends in a spurt. An excessively protracted period of rest, however, may sacrifice the impetus of inertia, with a consequent decline in efficiency despite elimination of fatigue. Practice, fatigue, mental attitude, habituation, ready adjustment to work, boredom, and continuous effort have a significant effect, varying somewhat with individuals, upon work efficiency and output.

Kraepelin's theories of initial and final spurts and of inertia or momentum as forces lending impetus to purposive reactions were recapitulated in the concepts of his contemporary Woodworth (of Columbia University) concerning preparatory and continuing drives involving neural mechanisms and mental adjustments. The assertion by G. W. Allport that motives impelling individuals to begin a course of action and then to carry on the same activities even after they no longer serve the original purpose restates one aspect of Kraepelin's principle of inertia.

Kraepelin agreed with Wundt that physiological and psychic elements of behavior have a parallel relationship. Patients with severe personality disorders caused by physical, organic defects, he contended, cannot be expected to make a satisfactory recovery. Others, whose difficulties are caused by environmental and social conditions, can be helped to readjust provided the causes are removed and desirable work habits and congenial activities are encouraged.

JAMES

William James (1842–1910), physiologist, philosopher, and psychologist, was born in New York City into a distinguished family of intellectual leaders. (His brother was the great novelist Henry James.) Shortly after graduation from the Harvard University Medical School in 1869, James taught anatomy and physiology at Harvard, later serving as a lecturer in psychology and philosophy. He was appointed assistant professor of philosophy in 1880, professor of philosophy in 1885, professor of psychology in 1889, and again professor of philosophy in 1897, a position he held until 1907.

James ranked as one of the great leaders in both fields, philosophy and psychology. The progress of psychology in America owes more to him than to any other individual. Beginning in the 1870s, he pioneered in laboratory experimentation and in consistent emphasis on life activities as the key to the understanding of human behavior.

In view of his training in anatomy and physiology, it is not surprising that James emphasized physical processes in his investigations of human behavior. He attributed the association of ideas mainly to repeated passage of nerve currents in the brain and nervous system, and to what he called the *laws of habit,* which favor the repetition of the same ideas. He was never able to explain satisfactorily, however, how connections in the central nervous system could account for new ideas and new associations of ideas. The structural psychologists, including Titchener, avoided this difficulty by citing only experimental and introspectional evidence concerning these mental reactions, whereas James and later functionalist psychologists attempted to find physiological, motor explanations. James, too, utilized a modern experimental approach to the study of motivation, habits, and other aspects of behavior, but always from the point of view of purposive physical activity induced by sensations.

Repetition and habit, said James, are not meaningless, automatic processes but involve understanding by the individual as he reacts to conscious sensations. His activity is based upon (1) remote sensations, like those of sight and hearing, enabling him to adjust actions in order to achieve desired results; and (2) resident sensations, the kinesthetic sensations of motor movement, enabling him to adjust his impulses and produce more accurate reactions. Thus deaf persons, in order to learn to speak, must be trained to control the voice through adjustments of their muscular, vocal equipment in response to resident, kinesthetic sensations of motor movements.

According to James, voluntary reactions are responses to the meanings of sensations. The individual reacts to sensory stimuli to fulfill a practical function. With the possible exception of reflex action, human behavior, including habits, consists of reactions directed toward a goal. This view is fundamental to the functionalist school of psychology, to which James has therefore been regarded as a most influential contributor along with his contemporaries James Rowland Angell, Harvey A. Carr, and John Dewey. (Angell, Carr, and Dewey were for some years associated with the University of Chicago, where Angell emphasized functionalist views applied to habit formation, reaction times, and auditory perception, while Carr stressed relationships among sensory, perceptual, and motor reactions, and Dewey expounded theories of perception, cognition, and methods of thinking.)

The philosophical roots of James's approach are to be found in the works of Charles Sanders Peirce (1839–1914), mathematician and logician, who taught briefly at Harvard University and later at the Johns Hopkins University. Peirce was greatly influenced by Kant's theories—for example, that thinking begins with experience but also applies a priori thought categories to experience—and by Darwin's evolutionary hypothesis. In 1878 Peirce set forth (in the *Popular Science Monthly*) arguments for his view that the practical consequences of any idea are the only valid test of its truth, a central thesis of the philosophy of pragmatism adopted by James, Dewey, and other adherents to functionalist psychology. Thinking and reactions, said Peirce, should be evaluated on the basis of their practical value for the pursuit of understanding, knowledge, and other definite goals.

James agreed with Peirce that individuals should not be content with ideas as such but should test them by analyzing their consequences and should act upon them for the sake of efficiency in the practical pursuits of life. He listed twenty-eight major instincts, defining them as unlearned activities directed toward specific goals and requiring no planning or instruction in order to serve personal interests and aims. The most useful instincts, he asserted, are manipulation and construction, innate propensities far more valuable than the concepts of idealist philosophers that do not of themselves result in action. According to James, all forms of consciousness (sensations, ideas, and feelings) produce some kind of movement—for example, changes in breathing, blood circulation, and the like—but the real power of an idea depends upon instincts and upon intended or habitual reactions, the inner driving forces of individuals.

James's experiments on memory during the 1890s helped to discredit the old established theory of mental faculties and the doctrine of formal discipline in teaching. Practice does little to improve memory, he asserted, except when a person learns by practice to utilize more efficient methods of memorizing. He agreed with Herbart, however, that memory is a most valuable means of integrating past with present mental associations so that the individual will think and act effectively in his purposive behavior.

James declared that ideas are inseparable from emotions since an individual experiences emotion only by understanding and reacting to a total situation, as in apprehending and fearing an impending danger, although some kind of motor activity precedes, accompanies, and sustains emotional reactions. He added that not only overt action but also subconscious instincts, feelings, and habits of thought profoundly affect emotion and behavior. Perfect success in life is impossible, he said, and true achievement is most unlikely when people act contrary to their professed beliefs. But even the most consistent person cannot always know all future consequences of his actions (or of events and environmental conditions) on ideas and behavior patterns of other people. He should, however, have faith in religious ideals, a will to believe, for religious beliefs and conduct are the most important functions of mankind. Every person has nothing to lose but much to gain through a belief in divinity and immortality.

McDOUGALL, WOODWORTH, DEWEY, FREUD

The views of William McDougall (1871–1938) concerning the psychology of action, motivation, and adjustment were based upon biological evidence and his own observations and experiments in the fields of normal and abnormal behavior. A native of Lancashire, England, he trained, experimented, and taught in major areas of physiology and psychology at Oxford University for many years, then served as professor of psychology at Harvard University beginning in 1920 and at Duke University from 1927 to 1938.

In an article in *Scientific Monthly* (1924), McDougall commented on the basis of his hormic school of psychology, stating that human behavior exhibits only one fundamental characteristic: a purposive and vitalistic striving toward definite goals of individuals and society. It is a mistake, he said, to describe conscious actions in terms of simple, predetermined atoms of behavior, as the behaviorists do, or to analyze organic reactions as if they were simply complex units of consciousness, the configurations of Gestalt psychologists. Sigmund Freud proved that even in dreams purposive striving toward goals plays an important role, directing buried or thwarted tendencies so as to achieve satisfactions. According to McDougall, all mental and physical reactions—including instinctive responses, inherited aptitudes and tendencies, conditioned reflexes, bodily movements, and neural mechanisms—are energized and controlled by purposive drives of the individual. Inherited instincts provide motive power for all thinking and action and form the basis for the development of human personality, interests, capacities, and habits. Instincts are not blind impulses; they direct neural energy toward goals desired by the individual as he perceives and interprets initiating stimuli. His purpose and motive determine and often even modify substantially his perceptions and interpretations. For this reason, the acts of a friend may seem quite different from identical acts of an enemy.

Although McDougall accepted Freud's view of the unconscious as a complex of basic drives, he was more optimistic than Freud about man's capacity to control or direct such forces by reason and purposive intelligence. He also accepted Jung's classification of dominant personality traits into introvert and extrovert traits. At Harvard University, he experimented with hypnosis in the treatment of epileptics. He concluded that extroverts were particularly susceptible to hypnosis, alcohol, drugs, and dissociation tendencies—characteristics probably attributable to hormonal imbalance and other physiological or chemical factors that redistribute neural energy toward the most active motor mechanisms of the body. The same factors, he suggested, stimulate overcompensatory reactions such as those of hysterical persons who fall into spells of laughter at a time of intense grief.

McDougall's *Introduction to Social Psychology* classified human behavior into four levels of reaction: (1) reactions modifiable by pain and pleasure; (2) reactions modifiable by rewards bestowed and punishments imposed by society; (3) reactions redirected by the individual in anticipation of social praise or blame, the most effective sanctions conducive to moral conduct; and (4) reactions initiated by the individual as he strives to carry out ethical convictions. Each dominant instinctive reaction is associated with concomitant emotions: flight with fear; repulsion with disgust; curiosity with wonder; pugnacity with anger; self-abasement with subjection; self-assertion with elation; and parental impulses with tenderness. Subordinate instincts include reproduction, gregariousness, acquisition, and construction. Pugnacity, is the most potent instinct, resulting in anger and aggressive action on a large scale among all human groups; rivalry (as William James had also stated) is responsible for many personal accomplishments in work, education, literature, arts, and sciences; and the sexual instinct, being attended by extremely strong desires, is the most difficult for the individual and the social forces of religion, law, and custom to control.

McDougall held that man inherits basic instinctive mechanisms upon which are built all human attributes and modes of behavior, even aesthetic aptitudes, moral sensitivity, visions, dreams, and unconscious drives. Other social psychologists, such as Floyd H. Allport of Syracuse University, refusing to go so far, believed that, except for a few major inherited types of reflex reactions, most behavior patterns in infancy and childhood develop through learning and social experience. McDougall himself often described these influences as potent factors in human growth and development.

Woodworth at Columbia University pointed out that instincts are not automatically effective. Although the individual readily expresses or reinforces some of them, he acquires through life experience habits and motives that impel him to put aside, resist, or inhibit many instinctive drives. Woodworth reiterated the statement of his renowned teacher Sherrington that the motive power in behavior is a neurophysical mechanism that produces preparatory reactions (instrumental drives) or consummatory reactions (satisfying drives). Each drive, whether it be innate and unlearned or acquired and learned, has a residual force that leads to another drive in a continuous series of actions, motivations, and behavior adjustments.

Nevertheless, Woodworth agreed with McDougall that human desires, purposes, and goals are the forces that arouse neural mechanisms and then sustain their activity. Life experience and education can modify and control inner drives, enabling the individual to pursue more useful forms of behavior than native tendencies could otherwise produce. The parental instinct, for instance, may expand in scope to include kindness toward children outside the immediate family. Innate acquisitive tendencies may, through experience and training, become subordinate to acquired habits of mutual aid and cooperation.

In *Democracy and Education* (1916), John Dewey wrote that the purpose in the mind of the individual as he pursues any course of action makes his conduct intelligent and thus different from blind impulsive behavior and also different from ideas or modes of behavior imposed upon him by others. Motives, adjustments, and habits develop out of practical experience as the individual gains better understanding of personal and social problems and greater power to cope with them. In his early writings, Dewey referred to the primacy of instinctive drives in behavior; but in *Human Nature and Conduct* (1922), he maintained that there are no separate instincts or independent psychic impulses. Organic reactions, he said, involve much more than narrow instinctive pathways or channels of expression, for they bring into play the whole living organism, which is affected and modified by each of its own multiple responses. It is therefore an error to attribute any kind of behavior to rigid, uniform, unlearned impulses or instinctive mechanisms. Moreover, the problems, conditions, and environmental forces toward which an emotion or action is directed are always changing, so that whatever the individual perceives, does, and learns differs from one instant to the next. His behavior is never merely a separate psychic element or instinct but is always a composite reaction of the whole person as he senses and reacts to further consequences of his activity. Each experience of fear, for instance, differs from all previous such experiences both in its environmental causes and conditions and in the effects on the individual's further understanding and behavior.

Dewey noted that impulsive actions of individuals may seem superficially to be blind and sudden enough to fit into the traditional concept of an instinct. However, they may also be sublimated to compensate for inhibition or to serve other definite purposes; they may be responses imposed by others and simply accepted purposely but without question; they may become habitual, or they may be submerged or repressed; and they may be initial acts in a sequence aimed at satisfying individual and social objectives. What a person does suggests his future patterns of behavior under similar conditions even though he continually grows in understanding and capacity. Since the individual depends upon others for communication, sustenance, and learning, his interests, motives, and behavior are always socially rooted, socially meaningful, and socially significant. In *How We Think* (1910), he set forth his well-known five phases or steps of thought (sensing a problem, defining it, considering possible solutions, selecting the most promising ones, and testing them in action) that enable individuals to solve intellectual problems and cope effectively with practical life situations. The meaning, truth, and value of an idea derive from its utility for action.

Sigmund Freud, in his *Introductory Lectures on Psychoanalysis* (1916), held that behavior (energized by the libido, or psychosexual energy) is motivated by two kinds of impulses: the life force or eros, manifested in sexual and ego drives; and the death force, expressed in aggressive, destructive activity. Torn between these life and death forces, the individual becomes subject to contradictory feelings and urges directed against himself or other persons. As he matures, he learns from experience to modify infantile pleasure-seeking reactions, to inhibit and readjust his attitudes, habits, and conduct in obedience to social restrictions and realities. Three factors or organized energy sources motivate behavior: (1) the unconscious id, a storehouse of instinctive, psychosexual energy utilized for self-preservation, sexual satisfaction, and propagation; (2) the conscious, intelligent ego, which recognizes the realities of social and natural conditions and requirements and adjusts overt conduct to them; and (3) the superego or conscience, which censors, guides, and checks or balances the id and the ego. All acts of the individual—thoughts, ideas, attitudes, memories, sensations, perceptions, habits, emotions, and inner conflicts—may be repressed and remain permanently in the storehouse of his unconscious; they may impel him to conform to social standards; they may induce compensatory behavior, sublimation, or other defense mechanisms; and they may produce inferiority and guilt feelings, psychoneuroses, or impulses toward self-destruction. Periodically, however, Freud modified his ideas about inner conflicts and psychoneurotic behavior, at first attributing them to infantile sexual and excretory experiences, later to Oedipus and Electra complexes, then to the full development of the superego, as well as to environmental maladjustments and conditions, and, finally, to a diversity or combination of these causes.

ADLER, LEWIN, CANNON, JUNG, PILLSBURY, ET AL.

The Viennese early Freudian psychologist Alfred Adler, best known for his theory of the will-to-power and the inferiority and superiority complexes, grew dubious about Freud's exclusive emphasis on psychosexual energy as the core of human behavior but rooted his own theories in the organic sexual experiences of infants. The child, said Adler, begins to feel inadequate and inferior because of an awareness of the smallness or absence of the sexual organ or of other organic and physical or intellectual deficiencies. As early as 1888, J. L. A. Koch had written a volume that similarly discussed normal and abnormal feelings of inferiority. In his *Practice and Theory of Individual Psychology* (1924), Adler elaborated on this kind of reaction from the point of view of Freudian concepts of repression and compensation.

For Adler, the individual's innate will-to-power, his goal of superiority to compensate for a weakness or deficiency, is even more potent than automatic sexual or other drives as a determinant of behavior patterns. Aggressive patterns of behavior include jealousy, greed, ambition, and hate, while nonaggressive behavior takes the form of anxiety, fear, and avoidance of responsibility. These defense mechanisms compensate for feelings of inferiority arising out of the individual's sense of his own weaknesses. Freud, however, had attributed inferiority feelings to the mother's excessive love for an infant handicapped by illness or other disadvantages or difficulties. Critics of Adler's view doubted the validity of his postulate that an innate will-to-power controls behavior, and cited environmental and social conditions as the key factors responsible for inferiority and superiority complexes. In his later years, Adler, too, stated that environmental difficulties encountered during both childhood and adulthood often modify or negate complexes, traits, and patterns of behavior.

The German Gestalt psychologist Kurt Lewin (1890–1947) based his topological method of investigating motivation upon analysis of the number of activities performed by the individual to fulfill his needs and objectives. The number of activities in pursuit of a goal reflects, he said, the strength of the motive and drive. As the individual attempts to satisfy inner felt needs and reacts to the environment (objects possessing for him a demand value, or valence), a feeling of tension results, accompanied by strain and stress, which can be relieved through successful efforts to overcome personal and environmental obstacles, social disapproval, and other impediments and to gain rewards and satisfactions. Each person acts within an existing social climate and life space, a psychic space or field of experience, so as to adjust his behavior to the immediate conditions confronting him until he accomplishes a fully satisfying purpose. Repeated failure, however, may produce defense mechanisms, such as rationalization, and eventually may cause neurosis or other psychic disturbances. Lewin described adjustment by escape as an attempt to ignore conflicts and difficulties by withdrawing from challenging situations, perhaps avoiding frustrations by recourse to daydreaming, repetition of infantile modes of behavior, or inconsistent, contradictory, and incompatible acts.

The physiologist Walter Bradford Cannon (1871–1945) of Harvard University emphasized the relationship between physical functions and the stimulation of internal drives such as hunger, thirst, pain, fear, and rage. He attributed the most common behavior patterns—eating, drinking, resting, and numerous other physical reactions—to the internal environment that impels the person to satisfy immediate bodily needs. Cannon's experiments demonstrated the validity of the popular assumption that psychological attitudes and emotions affect digestion. His most important works, *Bodily Changes in Pain, Hunger, Fear, and Rage* (1915, 1929) and *The Wisdom of the Body* (1932), expounded his findings on the adrenal glands and other physiological factors of emotion, motivation, and adjustment. He delineated the profound effects of emotions, such as fear, joy, grief, and anger, upon the nervous system and other organ systems. Much of human behavior, he asserted, depends upon involuntary, originally innate physical adjustments made automatically. By this process of biological homeostasis, the individual achieves inner, organic stability, the release of energy, and the maintenance of optimal living conditions. Basic motor activities depend upon internal drives, not upon rational thinking or planning. A person obsessed with rage wants to fight, and one in great fear wishes only to escape. The bodily organs automatically adjust to emergency situations by altering glandular secretions, blood circulation, muscular action, and other physical processes until internal disturbances are eliminated and a normal balance of forces has been restored. To Cannon it seemed as if the body as a whole sensed and decided things for itself and directed all its elements, including switchboards in the brain and nervous systems, to fulfill the needs of the organism, usually in advance of rational analysis or interpretation.

Numerous studies of motivation comparable to the quantitative, experimental investigations by Lewin and Cannon included the notable researches by Carl J. Warden (1890–1961) of Columbia University and those by Edward C. Tolman (1886–1959) of the University of California. Warden reported on experiments with laboratory animals (crossing an electrical obstruction to achieve a goal) that indicated the strengths of their basic drives in the following order, beginning with the strongest: maternal, thirst, hunger, sex, and exploration. Tolman, using hungry rats in similar experiments, reported that, within limits, the stronger a drive is, the faster an animal will learn to react correctly in order to gain a reward. The experiments of Robert M. Yerkes with chimpanzees and apes indicated that there is an ideal strength of drive for many types of behavior and that motives either too weak or too strong result in inefficient or erratic performance. Recently, investigators have shown experimentally that knowledge of progress toward a goal is favorable to efficient behavior; also that the desire to win praise for effort is more effective than the motive of avoiding blame, although the latter is better than being ignored.

Research studies by Julius B. Maller of Columbia University and others reported that in a competitive society competition and working for the self are stronger motivating forces than cooperation. In 1974 R. Heilbroner in *An Inquiry into the Human Prospect* concluded that social coercion agreed to by citizens is the best way to solve common social problems in any society. But the British investigators J. M. Orbell and B. Rutherford held that in the long run authoritarian governments produce many fewer benefits for the people than more democratic or mainly laissez-faire governments, which do not interfere as much with competitive enterprises and unplanned decentralized rewards. Psychologists are being challenged to investigate the genesis and development of altruism and other social attitudes, the origins and practical operations in society of individual conscience (or

Freud's superego) and the psychological aspects of submission to authority, for there is little agreement, generally no decisive evidence, in this area of research.

Carl Gustav Jung (1875–1961), the Swiss founder of the analytical school of psychology, followed Freud in attributing human behavior mainly to unconscious inherited racial memories or traces, primitive innate ideas, emotions, impulses, and capacities. Every person, said Jung, is born possessing the germs from which all future tendencies and acts, all biological, social, and spiritual reactions, develop throughout his life-span. Instead of adhering to Freud's twofold classification of the libido into life and death forces, however, Jung divided it into three basic instincts: food-getting or nutritional; sexual; and herd or collective drives. In Jungian theory, the inherited collective unconscious mind limits, corrects or readjusts, and compensates for incorrect or imperfect conscious purposes and reactions. This process is exemplified by dreams, which connect the conscious life of mystical and mythical realities with the unconscious storehouse of universal truths. The effort at compensation for weaknesses accounts for the behavior of introverts and extroverts. (The Jungian distinction between these two types of personality was accepted by the majority of contemporary and later psychologists.)

Jung's delineation of the dominant motives of human behavior included ideas remarkably similar to those expounded by the noted French social reformer and advocate of cooperatives Charles Fourier (1772–1837). In *The Passions of the Human Soul, Fourier identified the most* potent motives as (1) bodily passions (directed toward food and drink, smell, taste, and sexual or tactile sensations and satisfactions) and (2) group passions (exemplified in ambition, love, friendship, and other comparable attitudes manifested in relationships to other people).

In the 1940s and 1950s, influential American clinical psychologists and psychiatrists adhered to Freud's basic view of the unconscious mind but differed with him about other aspects of motivation and behavior. Karen Horney, Erich Fromm, Harry Stack Sullivan, Abraham Maslow, and G. W. Allport expressed greater confidence than Freud did in man's ability to counteract the conflicts and limitations imposed by inherited forces of human nature. It seemed to them that Freud had overemphasized the psychosexual libido, the id, as the determinant of motives and behavior. They believed that social and cultural influences and life experience working through the ego and superego can successfully apply ideals and rational decisions and thus readjust and improve the incentives, motives, and behavior patterns of individuals. Recently, experimental psychologists who emphasize either behaviorist or cognitive approaches and quantitative analyses of personality and behavior have tended to discount the value of Freudian psychoanalytical theories. Among others, the therapist Joseph Wolpe asserted that only conditioning provides basic readjustment of behavior. In his method of reciprocal inhibition, individuals experience pleasurable reactions in emotionally disturbing situations and thus counteract customary adverse reactions.

During the 1940s, Pillsbury at the University of Michigan summarized widely accepted conclusions concerning motivation and adjustment. He noted that frustration and conflict often produce major readjustments in an individual's behavior patterns, either through a direct attack to eliminate difficulties or through an indirect attack by means of sublimation, as suggested by Freud, or the substitution of new interests, motives, and purposes. The individual coping with conflicts or disappointments may resort to such defense mechanisms as overcompensating activities or exaggerated responses, or he may seek some means of escape from frustrating situations. Pillsbury listed nineteen methods of compensatory behavior adjustments, including rationalization, projection, repression, anxiety, regression, various psychic disturbances and disorders, and fatalistic acceptance of conflict and failure, a defense mechanism to counteract episodes of worry and fear.

Pillsbury's writings delineated the ways in which the various schools of psychology and the works of the great psychologists during the first half of the twentieth century supplemented and balanced one another, thus correcting one-sided overemphases while still defending their respective approaches and contributions. His *History of Psychology* and *Handbook of General Psychology,* and similar historical and comparative works by Edward G. Boring of Harvard University, John F. Dashiell of the University of North Carolina, Henry E. Garrett of Columbia University, and Gardner Murphy of Columbia University, Harvard University, and the University of the City of New York, familiarized students and instructors with the fundamental views of the principal schools of psychological thought.

7 EMOTIONS

Aristotle, who endorsed the theory of Hippocrates postulating (about 460 B.C.) that a balance among body fluids determines the individual's temperament, or dominant mode of emotional response, stated that both physical and mental phenomena are factors in emotion. Attributing anger, for example, to overheated blood, he also pointed out that the desire to retaliate for some personal injury or offense stimulates and sustains that emotion. His views prevailed as authoritative dicta for two thousand years in the Western world.

The seventeenth-century philosophers Descartes and Spinoza speculated about the nature and role of emotional reactions. Descartes, who believed in innate ideas and the sharp separation of mind from body, attempted unsuccessfully to locate in the nervous system a specific area as the seat of emotions. Spinoza, who regarded emotions as excessive, impulsive reactions that upset the proper balance in human life and enslave mankind, demanded rational self-control as the means to maintain equanimity and to free the self from the bondage imposed by irrational impulses. He defined emotion as a composite of physiological forces and related ideas or mental concepts. The seventeenth-century philosopher Hobbes held that man is a physical organism innately endowed with extremely aggressive impulses and emotions that should be redirected and strictly controlled by society. The revolutionary eighteenth-century educator Rousseau insisted that the infant is born with noble emotions and humane sympathies, which society inhibits and misdirects or distorts. The eighteenth-century idealist philosopher Kant mediated between the views of Hobbes and Rousseau, stating that innate dispositions are neither good nor bad, that they need to be guided, reinforced, or modified through life experience and free self-expression in order to develop rational control of one's emotions and effective self-discipline. Early in the nineteenth century, the pioneering educational psychologist J. F. Herbart expounded new ideas about the genesis and role of emotions as determinants of behavior.

HERBART, HENLE, FECHNER, RIBOT

Herbart, in his textbook of psychology published in 1816, described the human mind as a unified aggregate of psychic states arising from ideas interacting with one another in a dynamic system of conflict or reinforcement. The individual, said Herbart, attempts to achieve a balance or equilibrium never fully realized in his conscious feelings, thoughts, and emotions. The conflicts between his present and past ideas bring some of them into consciousness but suppress others, which remain in the unconscious mind. The conscious ideas strengthen connections among new and past thoughts and awaken or intensify feelings, emotions, and desires. According to Herbart, the individual is always fluctuating from one emotional state to another. The intensity of each emotion depends upon the environment, his bodily state, reactions of the nervous system, and past experience. Herbart noted that a person may be optimistic or joyful, then sad and irritable, evincing sudden emotional changes without apparent cause.

His views gained wide acceptance among nineteenth-century psychologists. John Dewey and other twentieth-century functionalist psychologists, however, charged that Herbart had overemphasized ideas or mental states as static determinants of emotions. Dewey asserted that ideas are not static but inseparable from motor activity, that reactions to stimuli initiate further activities, purposes, ideas, and emotions. But the Herbartians regarded emotion-inducing ideas as dynamic forces moving from unconscious to conscious realms of the ego, a view that antedated by many decades the similar conclusion of Freudian psychoanalysts. Herbart's doctrine, integrating interacting ideas, overt activity, and emotions, helped to destroy the traditional concept of the mind as a mere collection of separate faculties. For Herbartians, the mind is an organic unity that reacts to the physical and social world on interrelated conscious and unconscious levels, a view consistent with the conclusions of Gestalt psychologists in the twentieth century.

F. G. J. Henle, the German anatomist and assistant to Johannes Müller, published a two-volume *Handbook of Rational Pathology* (1846, 1852) that emphasized the connections between physical and psychic activity in human behavior. Henle associated the expression of emotions with the condition of the nervous system; with the rate, force, and duration of the individual's reactions to stimuli and to environmental influences; and with ideas that initiate emotional responses such as joy and sadness. Individuals differ widely in the degree of excitability, some being generally quick to react; others slow, quiet, or reserved; some tending to be cheerful or sanguine; others morose or melancholy. He noted that emotions consist of ideas in association with resulting physical changes that take the form of conscious sensations in the nervous system combined with motor impulses.

In 1871 G. T. Fechner, an admirer of Herbartian theories, reported on his experiments in aesthetics. He explored effects of curved lines, balanced and symmetrical figures, and contrasting colors upon emotions of observers examining beautiful objects. Fechner's experiments, although they encouraged subsequent investigations, were limited in scope and results, for he could not demonstrate precise quantitative relationships between given designs and sensations or emotional reactions of individuals. He noticed that individuals differed markedly in their judgments of beauty and in the intensity of their emotions. It seemed evident to other investigators that feelings of pleasure and displeasure depended not merely upon sensory reactions quantitatively measurable in the laboratory but also upon the observer's attention, experiential background and training, temperament, mood, and acquired tastes and habits. In his *Principles of Psychology* (1872), Herbert Spencer held that reactions to beautiful things depend largely upon the observer's conscious sympathy for feelings implied in them. Pleasurable emotions are inhibited by any excessive strain on the senses, tension in eye muscles, monotony, or sudden breaks in continuity. The observer should rise above immediate superficial impressions and everyday pedestrian considerations as he interprets and responds to harmonious designs.

The French psychologist Théodule A. Ribot, in *The Psychology of the Emotions* (1897), rejected Herbart's concept of interconnected ideas as the core of emotions. Ribot held that emotions are rooted in the individual's innate physical structures and inborn, unconscious impulses, feelings, and dominant attitudes. These innate forces explain why some people are more sensitive and deeply thoughtful but less energetic or expressive emotionally than others. According to Ribot, however, individuals may still counteract these innate tendencies and change their habitual emotional patterns by constantly imitating the majority of people in the community or by forming a habit of shifting rapidly from one mood to another contrasting emotion. Moreover, said Ribot, individuals differ greatly in the ability to recall emotions, and only a few can always remember clearly past emotions along with the ideas, causes, sensations, and feelings associated with the emotions. He had a high regard for the introspectionist and experimental methods of Wundt, whose structuralist psychology he introduced to French students. A contemporary French psychologist, F. Paulhan, emphasized reactions to environmental influences much more than did Ribot, a point of view eventually adopted by the behaviorist psychologist Watson and his followers.

DARWINIAN SCIENTISTS

In 1872 Charles Darwin published *Expressions of Emotions in Man and Animals,* a treatise designed to clarify the relationships between emotions and the appearance, disappearance, and modification of animal species. He contended that not only physical attributes but also patterns of emotional reaction have evolved in order to assist organisms in their struggle for survival. Natural selection of the fittest competing individuals operates so that those with superior strength, speed, intelligence, endurance, aggressiveness, and useful emotions win the struggle for existence. Thus a strong emotion of fear in the face of danger enabled some to withdraw and escape with their lives; similarly, at times the emotion of intense anger motivated some to advance, attack their enemies vigorously, and survive. Like physical weaknesses, indifference to danger often made survival impossible. Those patterns of intense emotion that have survival value persist and are inherited. Eventually, succeeding generations that no longer need to fear dangerous enemies will still tend to experience and express the same old emotion, but in a modified, weaker form. Man, for instance, does not have to bite enemies to death, as his ancestors may have done for self-protection or self-preservation, but he still grits or shows his teeth in anger. In his discussion of the biological significance of emotions, Darwin's friend Herbert Spencer, ardent proponent of Darwinian theories, concluded that simple, primitive patterns of overt behavior and concomitant emotions are in due time replaced (through inheritance and learning from experience) by multiple, highly complex modes of reaction.

G. S. Hall, in his two-volume work *Adolescence,* agreed with Spencer that many instinctive feelings, such as love, pride, hunger, pleasure, and pain, originated in invertebrate species and persisted as psychic reactions in gradually evolving higher vertebrate species. Emotions, said Hall, express themselves efficiently at the most favorable psychological moments. Emotions of joy, sadness, fear, and anger tend to express themselves most frequently and intensely in childhood and youth. The adolescent's sensations, physical maturation, imagination, impulses, and emotions reach a high level of stress and strain, recapitulating later stages of human evolution in an outburst of growth and energy. In 1915, applying Freudian ideas to the analysis of anger, Hall stated that when this potent emotion is repressed by social institutions and customs, the adolescent often takes refuge in sublimation. He may find satisfaction from winning a contest against some hated rival, or from dreams and reveries about acts of revenge. Repression of this emotion may produce disturbances in the unconscious mind, accompanied by explosions of temper, inordinate ambition, overt violence, morbid complexes, or other compensatory mechanisms.

In *Essentials of Psychology,* Pillsbury agreed with Hall concerning the undesirable consequences of an excessive repression of emotions, with the added comment that certain reasonable curbs on instinctive impulses and related expressions of emotions are nevertheless unavoidable or imperative. Training and experience can help the individual to develop self-control.

McDOUGALL

Nineteenth-century psychologists connected emotions such as love, fear, and anger and related physical reactions with inherited instincts. Thus H. Maudsley in *The Physiology of Mind* (1867) and G. H. Schneider in *The Will of Animals* (1880) associated emotive and neural processes with specific corresponding instincts, views elaborated later by William McDougall. But McDougall encountered difficulty in his attempt to pair each emotion with a corresponding instinct, as, for example, the emotion of fear with the instinct to escape. Fear can arise without any instinctive impulse to escape; anger can be felt without any desire to attack; and joy can be experienced for any of innumerable reasons. One can stand still in fright or turn the other cheek in anger. Individuals differ in emotional responses to identical situations, some being indifferent to events that arouse deep emotions in others. Nevertheless, psychologists generally accepted McDougall's thesis that emotions arise and tend to persist because of inherited unlearned instinctive tendencies. McDougall held that changes in motivation and emotions cause shifts in the distribution of neural energy and motor responses. A person who is at first fearful, then abruptly becomes angry, redistributes and redirects energy so that, instead of withdrawing in fear, he advances and attacks, perhaps with teeth gritted and face flushed, manifesting angry emotion.

JAMES, LANGE

William James and the Danish physician Karl G. Lange at about the same time during the 1880s developed independently the James-Lange theory that emotion consists of the feeling or

perception of changes occurring in bodily organs.* The theory
assumes the following sequence: (1) sensory perception of an exciting object or situation; (2) instinctive or habitual reactions,
including overt bodily movements and internal visceral changes;
(3) emotion, an organic feeling or perception of the bodily reactions by means of nerve messages sent to and interpreted by the
brain. According to the James-Lange theory, an individual sees
a dangerous object, begins to tremble or run, and then experiences the emotion of fear. His awareness or perception of his
own trembling and running constitutes the emotion. Physical
processes engender and direct emotional activity. This theory
was contrary to the traditional view that the individual sees a
dangerous object, immediately experiences fear, and only then
trembles or runs away.

Critics of the James-Lange theory objected that people make
the same movements when they run to catch a train as they do
when they run to escape danger. James explained that, although
several emotions involve some identical reflex movements, each
emotion also involves movements of special sense organs, muscles, or neural structures that differentiate one emotion from
others. Intense fear and deep joy, for example, may both be attended by increased rates of the heartbeat and respiration, but in
fear the facial and skeletal muscles contract and become tense,
whereas in joy they tend to relax.

When the objection was made that the sight of a dangerous
object does not always produce immediate physical reactions,
James modified his view, stating that the individual reacts to a
meaningful situation in which the object is only one element.
This modified view was regarded as a concession to the traditional concept, which emphasized ideas and judgment as potent
factors preceding and causing emotion. Moreover, physical reactions, such as trembling, may persist after the danger has passed,
indicating that ideas and a disturbed mental state can dominate
the entire emotional experience.

Critics of the James-Lange theory included the physiologists

* James expounded his view in the article "What Is An Emotion," in *Mind*,
1884; Lange set forth the same theory in the volume *Om Sindsbevaegelser (Concerning the Emotions)* published in 1885.

Sherrington and Cannon. In experiments on dogs, Sherrington removed connections from the spine and central nervous system to visceral organs and discovered that emotions were still being experienced, a result that, while it did not altogether disprove the James-Lange hypothesis, weakened the argument that motor and internal visceral reactions not only precede but also constitute the indispensable basis for emotions. James contended that the dogs experienced emotion despite severed neural connections only because their brains still retained consciousness of past movements of the face and limbs. In 1915, however, Cannon published a different analysis, the widely accepted Cannon-Dana theory of emotions.

CANNON, DANA, BARD, CRILE, CARLSON

Walter B. Cannon, Charles Dana, and Philip Bard at Harvard University developed experimental evidence that bodily changes do not precede (as James had assumed) or follow but accompany emotions. They associated strong emotions with a high degree of feeling, perception, and excitement in the central nervous system. Emotions depend upon neural activity in the brain cortex and in thalamic processes of the diencephalon, the area between the midbrain and the cerebral hemispheres. When stimuli from sense organs arouse emotional feelings in the brain cortex and thalamic processes, the latter discharge impulses into motor nerves, thus producing changes in muscles and in digestive and other visceral organs. The assumption was made that bodily changes are sensed by brain centers that sustain and reinforce the emotional state. Cannon, Bard, and their associates reported that they had eliminated anger reactions in a cat by removing tissue in the thalamic processes, and they therefore concluded that the hypothalamus is necessary for emotions. But experiments during the 1930s and 1940s by Lashley and others indicated that, although thalamic areas apparently participate in organizing emotional reactions, the removal of hypothalamic areas does not prevent or materially alter strong emotions.

Cannon investigated relationships between emotions and the two divisions of the autonomic nervous system, which function in opposite directions to regulate involuntary activities of circulation, respiration, and digestion and thus maintain a balanced condition (homeostasis) of the internal environment. He noted that the sympathetic division (along the middle area of the spinal cord) raises blood pressure and augments emotions, whereas the parasympathetic division (along the upper and lower areas of the cord) reduces blood pressure and moderates emotions. Nevertheless, when he cut away the sympathetic segments in animals, they continued to exhibit the same intense emotional responses to stimuli. This result supported Sherrington's experimental finding that bodily changes are not necessary for emotional experience.

Cannon noted further that the autonomic nervous system activates the medulla of the adrenal glands to secrete adrenaline, which profoundly affects bodily functions and the individual's ability to meet emergency situations. Deep emotions disturb major organ systems and cause the adrenal glands to discharge more adrenaline into the bloodstream. Individuals differ in their susceptibility to glandular changes. He discovered that the injection of adrenaline did not produce specific emotional reactions but merely increased general tension and nervousness, indicating that bodily changes influence emotions but are not necessary for a particular emotional experience.

Similar conclusions resulted from investigations by the surgeon George Washington Crile at Western Reserve University and the physiologist Julius Carlson at the University of Chicago. Crile's laboratory experiments disclosed that strong emotions are accompanied by an increase in the number of Nissl bodies (clumps of granules in the cytoplasm of nerve cells); increases in adrenaline and in thyroid secretions, in oxidation of muscles, and in glycogen released or stored by the liver; increased rates of circulation and respiration; changes in metabolism, and inhibition of various digestive functions. In his *Origin and Nature of the Emotions* (1915), Crile emphasized that these bodily changes contribute to the efficiency of the motor reactions stimulated by deep emotions. Intense fear, he stated, is an extremely primitive instinctive emotion in all animals, one that affects every organ and tissue. Man has learned to control fear only to a limited extent, now reacting even to minor dangers or superficial annoyances with physical manifestations, somewhat modified, like those of his ancestors during their fierce struggle for existence. Carlson and Cannon analyzed the effects of unpleasant hunger sensations on the rate of contractions in muscles of the stomach walls, a rate that increases with reduced blood sugar but decreases with brisk exercise and emotions of fear and anger. Emotional disturbances affect appetite and food intake, effects related to neural centers in the hypothalamus. Carlson and Cannon described the impact of strong emotions on gastric secretions, digestion, heart action, blood pressure, and circulation.

The experiments and theories of James, Lange, Cannon, Crile, and Carlson paved the way for several decades of researches designed to clarify the reciprocal relationships between mental states or operations and bodily changes. These investigations proved that emotions profoundly affect organic functions and health, and that organic functioning and health influence emotions and moods. Their work gave impetus to the psychosomatic approach in the diagnosis and treatment of physical illnesses, including peptic ulcer, cardiac neuroses, certain respiratory ailments, and sexual dysfunctions, which are often associated with mental stress and emotional disturbance. Investigators used X rays to photograph changes in stomach tissues of animals affected by intense emotion; sphygmomanometers and sphygmographs to measure and record changes in pulse rates and blood pressure under conditions of anxiety and stress; pneumographs to record respiratory movements at times of deep emotional reaction; galvanometers to measure changes in skin resistance to electric currents during perspiration caused by intense emotions; electrocardiographs to record dysfunctions of the heart during strong emotions and emergency situations; and cathode-ray oscillographs to produce electroencephalograms (EEGs), graphic records of alpha, beta, delta, and gamma brain waves associated with epilepsy, brain tumors, and extreme emotional tension.

PSYCHOSOMATIC DISORDERS

Hippocrates associated the emotion of intense fear with conditions in the brain, a view modern psychologists could accept.

The eighteenth-century German poet and philosopher Friedrich von Schiller, when he was a medical student at Stuttgart, declared in a statement virtually identical with the basic premise of psychosomatic medicine that emotions have a drastic effect upon the nervous system and physical health just as physical disorders have a drastic effect upon mental and emotional reactions. Systematic scientific study of psychosomatic ailments made rapid progress during the middle decades of the twentieth century. Among the most prominent early contributors were Cannon, Freud, Alexander, French, English, Bittelman, Wolff, Abramson, Dunbar, and Selye.

Experiments by Cannon and his colleagues indicated that strong emotions, which may occur without apparent organic causes, can produce physical symptoms and psychosomatic disorders. Laboratory experiments by Donald B. Lindsley and other investigators of brain waves in emotionally disturbed individuals demonstrated close relationships between emotions and cortical brain functions. Wide acceptance of Cannon's conclusions stimulated research programs emphasizing ideas of Freud who in psychoanalytical investigations applied the same concept that physical and psychical abnormalities may be caused by unconscious inner conflicts and repressed emotions.

Franz Alexander and Thomas M. French, founders of the Chicago Institute for Psychoanalysis, who differed with Freud about the genesis of unconscious emotional conflicts, set forth their concepts in *Studies in Psychosomatic Medicine* (1948). O. Spurgeon English and E. Weiss expounded the central themes and research findings of the psychosomatic movement in their influential pioneering text *Psychosomatic Medicine* (1943). Béla Mittelmann, Harold G. Wolff, Stewart Wolf, M. P. Scharf, S. Morrison, and M. Feldman explored the impact of deep emotions of fear and anger on the digestive system, reporting research data and applications useful in the diagnosis and therapy of gastritis and ulcers. Harold A. Abramson similarly reported on psychosomatic aspects of asthma and allergies. In the 1940s, Helen Flanders Dunbar of Columbia University published comprehensive reviews of the psychosomatic field. The Canadian endocrinologist Hans Selye suggested new concepts about mechanisms involved in traumatic experiences, emotional stress, and subsequent symptoms of organic and psychosomatic illnesses. These and many other physiologists, endocrinologists, psychoanalysts, psychiatrists, and psychologists contributed to the early rapid development of the psychosomatic approach in medicine.

WUNDT AND TITCHENER

Wundt and Titchener depended upon introspection, including introspective reports of subjects in laboratory experiments, to investigate the genesis and expression of emotions from the structural point of view. Emotion was assumed to be a complex form of consciousness involving pleasant and unpleasant feelings, a dominant stirred-up organic and mental state resulting from reactions of the individual to an affecting situation or difficulty. Emotions, they asserted, are associated but not identical with organic sensations and bodily changes. The latter are regarded as possible causes, accompaniments, or consequences of emotion.

Wundt considered emotions and feelings to be similar in many respects, but critics objected that feeling is a passive experience, very different from emotion, which is an active response to a stimulus. According to Wundt, whether an emotion will be pleasant or unpleasant depends upon (1) intensity of the emotion-inducing stimulus, (2) its quality, and (3) its sequence and time of presentation. A stimulus of moderate intensity induces a pleasant emotion, whereas very strong or very weak stimuli initiate unpleasant emotions. Thus a moderately loud sound may arouse a pleasant reaction, but sound that is either extremely loud or almost inaudible excites an unpleasant reaction. A hopeful stimulus, such as good news, may cause elation, while one presenting bad news may produce depression.

Analyzing the duration of emotions on the basis of introspectional reports by individuals in his laboratory, Wundt delineated four time sequences in emotional reactions: Emotion may (1) begin suddenly and decline slowly; (2) develop gradually to a peak of intensity, then decline rapidly; (3) develop and disappear but recur repeatedly; or (4) alternate if it is pleasant with an opposite emotion that is unpleasant. Waiting for a stimulus may cause emotional tension, and the end of waiting may produce emotional relaxation. According to Wundt, emotions often arise out of a general organic state of excitement, agitation, and tension, a theory that other psychologists were unable to verify by introspectional reports of individuals participating in their laboratory experiments.

Titchener held that emotions and feelings belong to the same general category of conscious experience based upon both instinctive and acquired tendencies. Emotions and feelings are so closely related that an emotion sometimes passes over into a feeling, and vice versa. Emotion is not merely an aspect of sensation, for sensations can continue over a long period despite an indifferent emotional state, nor is it necessarily dependent upon attention to a specific stimulus. An instinctive disposition to be afraid of a situation may result in trembling or other organic reactions, which are not the emotion but only its expressions. Moreover, said Titchener, unlike emotion, a particular sensation may be both pleasant and painful, as, for example, a tickling or scratching sensation. On the other hand, an emotion may become attached to a specific sensation. Emotions are more stable and enduring than sensations, for the latter often succeed one another rapidly, being subject to such forces as adaptation to sense organs, contrast with other sensations, and attention by the individual. Psychologists disagree as to whether there are any real composite emotions—for example, loathing as a compound of fear and disgust. According to Titchener, a person's mood is a relatively weak temporary emotion, while passion refers to a more lasting interest and emotional response, and temperament denotes the individual's typical emotional patterns of reaction.

WOODWORTH, CARR, DEWEY

At Columbia University, Woodworth not only disagreed with the structural, introspectionist approach of Wundt and Titchener but also postulated a sequence of reactions differing from the one postulated by James and Lange. Woodworth maintained that higher brain centers perceive and interpret a stimulus, which then induces emotion, such as fear in response to danger.

The interpreted perception impels the individual to react purposefully (for example, to escape or attack) and simultaneously initiates organic changes that prepare him for the reaction. The mental attitude of the person determines the significance attached to the stimulus, the feeling of fear, the concomitant bodily changes, and the reaction. All the emotional and physical reactions involve both divisions (sympathetic and parasympathetic) of the autonomic nervous system. As Cannon had shown in laboratory experiments, the middle (sympathetic) division creates and intensifies bodily changes in heartbeat, secretions, and the like, characteristic of the fear emotion, while the other (parasympathetic or cranial-sacral) division acts as a check and promotes relaxation and similar opposing bodily changes. The higher brain centers control the entire reaction process. Every organ is subjected to opposing neural connections, some of which reinforce organic reactions while others diminish or inhibit such reactions. The mental attitude, goal, and emotional responses to stimuli depend upon innate instinctive equipment and neural connections; training and experience merely help the individual to connect his emotions with particular familiar objects or situations. Thus people are afraid instinctively, but they also learn from experience which things should be feared. The emotion itself is inborn and unchangeable, but the associations and applications are learned.

Harvey A. Carr at the University of Chicago suggested that emotions may not be innate or unchangeable, as Woodworth claimed, but the results of the individual's intellectual judgments and interpretations based upon his experience with the same kinds of life situations, which had previously caused similar pleasant or unpleasant emotions. The emotion of fear may reappear whenever the individual judges a new impending danger to be similar to a previous one that led to fearful consequences. Laboratory experiments did not, however, prove or disprove Carr's hypothesis.

But John Dewey maintained consistently that the intellect and emotions work in unison, not as separate forces. It is a mistake, he said, to regard emotions as private whims or subjective impulses disconnected from the intellect or reason. Sensation, perception, reasoning, feeling, and emotion and bodily changes are all integrated activities cooperating to achieve the purposes and fulfill the needs of the organism. For Dewey, the brain and all other bodily structures function in reciprocal adjustment to each other and to the natural and social environment, creating one series of feelings and activities after another and enabling the individual to cope with new life situations by means of successful, satisfying thoughts, purposes, and actions.

WATSON AND COGHILL

In agreement with Pavlov's theory of conditioning and Dewey's view of sensory perception as activity involving inherent motor reaction, John B. Watson at The Johns Hopkins University (1908–1920) applied an objective approach in experiments with animals and infants to analyze emotions. (Watson attended Furman University in South Carolina before pursuing graduate studies in psychology under the direction of the functionalist psychologist Angell at the University of Chicago.) Initially, Watson held that human behavior depended primarily upon speech and social communication. Later, however, he modified this view with references to subvocal movements involved in trial-and-error learning, reasoning, and overt responses. Rejecting Wundt's introspectionist method, he thought that the functionalist approach was also inadequate. Beginning in 1913, he advocated resort to objective physiological data derivable through experimentation and observation of overt responses to stimuli, the technique employed in Pavlov's laboratory.

Pavlov had attributed emotions to neural conduction and connections affecting the central, peripheral, and autonomic nervous systems, glands, and effector organs of the body. He maintained that inborn reflexes are purely conductive, whereas subsequent reflexes depend upon new connections within the nervous systems, especially within the brain cortex, as the individual interprets and reacts to stimuli.

Following extensive observations and experiments with infants (in a Baltimore, Maryland, hospital), Watson concluded that fear, rage, and love are either inherited or developed very shortly after birth as emotional responses to environmental stimuli. All other emotions are learned later through the ongoing neural connections postulated by Pavlov as the chief mechanisms of conditioning. The original three emotions serve as a nucleus of numerous subsequent emotions. At first the newborn fears only loud noises and a sudden loss of support, but he soon learns to connect his sensations and fears with other things, such as dark places, solitude, strangers, furry animals, and various partly familiar, partly unfamiliar objects and dangers.

In 1930, however, K. C. Pratt, A. K. Nelson, and K. H. Sun reported experiments indicating that an infant's entire situation, including bodily needs, determines his emotional responses to stimuli. Thus a hungry infant may react with fear or anger to certain stimuli, whereas a well-fed infant may ignore them. Mary C. Jones demonstrated that a child can be gradually conditioned through repeated experience with feared objects to reduce or eliminate many of his fears. Studies by E. R. Guthrie and by K. M. B. Bridges proved that the earliest emotions are more generalized and complex than Watson had assumed, beginning as undifferentiated excitement. According to Bridges, specific emotions of fear, anger, and love usually begin to function within six to twelve months after birth as a result of normal physical and mental growth and learning from experience. Operant conditioning experiments on rodents by B. F. Skinner at Harvard University showed how the individual's decisions, emotions, and purposive actions determine his subsequent abilities and reactions.

In experiments from 1925 to 1935, G. E. Coghill at the Wister Institute of Anatomy in Philadelphia traced the formation of neural connections and overt reactions in a species of salamander and discovered that mass action of the embryo as a whole precedes and directs specific reflexes. He referred to the gradual transition from general to specific reactions as a process of *individuation*. Coghill's findings were cited by Gestalt psychologists as evidence that the individual reacts to an entire pattern of stimuli, not to separate, successive stimuli but first of all to a total situation.

Watson, Skinner, and other behaviorists experimented with

the technique of unconditioning or reconditioning, the converse of Pavlov's initial method of conditioning. When the emotion of fear is being caused by a single stimulus, such as a loud noise, for example, one can often counteract or eliminate the emotion rather soon either by removing the stimulus or by associating it with another, more pleasant experience. If the emotion arises out of previous similar life situations, attempts to eliminate it by reasoning or reassurance alone will rarely succeed. More effective is reconditioning through repeated association of the emotion-inducing situation with pleasant consequences. Thus a child who receives a gift whenever a fear animal approaches may eventually associate the animal with satisfying experiences and cease to fear it.

JANET, BREUER, FREUD, RANK, ERIKSON, FROMM

Jean Martin Charcot (1825–1893), the French neuropsychiatrist and teacher of Sigmund Freud, followed the examples of Franz Anton Mesmer (1734–1815) and James Braid (1795–1860) in using hypnosis as therapy for hysteria (which he attributed to inherited neural degeneracy and only secondarily to inner conflicts of the individual). Pierre Janet (1859–1947) agreed about a hereditary organic etiology and continued Charcot's methods of treatment, but he placed much more emphasis on unconscious and conscious psychological causes of such disorders. Janet believed that emotion was an elementary feeling that caused definite organic symptoms in the individual, who might later remember and thus experience again similar but less intense feelings. Memories of unpleasant emotions might profoundly disturb him. Constant inner conflicts might produce hysteria, the phobias and obsessions of psychasthenia, and a state of chronic anxiety or neurasthenia. Unconscious motives might be the root causes of these psychoneuroses. Often the disturbed individuals displayed no emotion even while complaining about their "unbearable" illnesses. These inconsistent reactions, said Janet, indicated dissociation within the psyche, resulting from the individual's lack of adequate tension-creating energy needed to integrate his feelings, emotions, and ideas.

The Austrian physiologist and psychiatrist Josef Breuer (1842–1925) was known for research into functions of the inner ear to control the sense of equilibrium and for his discovery that the vagus nerve is involved in the control and disturbances (neuroses) of the respiratory system. In 1880 Breuer was using hypnosis to treat hysterics, including Anna O., a twenty-one-year-old woman ill with severe respiratory and muscular disabilities and mental disorders. Breuer helped her adjust to reality (although he did not cure her illness), and she subsequently achieved worldwide renown as a feminist and social reformer. From this patient's recollections under hypnosis, Breuer had discovered that her neurosis was rooted in emotional conflicts, feelings of guilt and fear, arising from circumstances of her father's death. Instead of merely suggesting to such patients during hypnosis (as Janet had done) that they should inhibit symptoms of their illness, he advised them during their normal posthypnotic state to describe in detail their previous disturbances, a method of catharsis that often seemed to diminish their tensions.

Because of Anna O.'s sexual fantasies toward him (a process later defined by Freud as transference to the psychoanalyst of the patient's unconscious sexual attachments) and to consequent friction in his family, Breuer became reluctant to treat hysterical women. However, he confided in and collaborated with Freud, who persisted in exploring among patients the genesis of emotional conflicts and symptoms. At first, Freud stressed the factor of psychological trauma resulting from early instinctive sexual drives and experience as causes of hysteria, but later he broadened his analysis to include complexes, the struggle for moral self-censorship and self-control, and environmental influences. He formulated concepts about the preconscious and unconscious mind, repressed memories of emotional conflicts, feelings of guilt and fear, compensation, introjection, displacement, sublimation, ambivalence toward others, free association, and the interpretation of dreams. His numerous hypotheses and therapeutic techniques constituted the foundations of psychoanalysis. Freud never abandoned his central premise that emotions buried deep in the unconscious mind determine the basic motives and behavior patterns of human beings. In 1980 psychiatrists and psychoanalysts from many countries met in New York City to celebrate the centenary of the psychoanalytic discoveries and therapeutic techniques developed in 1880 through the cooperation of Josef Breuer and Freud.

At first, Freud had traced intense fear and anxiety in adults to unconscious apprehensions of infants at the time of birth, a concept elaborated by his Viennese student Otto Rank in complex theories of birth trauma. Rank, however, gave the mother-child relationship during the birth process much greater importance than had Freud, who had maintained that sexual and excretory functions and difficulties were the primary factors in emotional conflicts. Freud later rejected Rank's view and also pointed out that the difference between emotional disturbances or other neuroses in normal persons and schizophrenic reactions in psychotics is one only of degree—an individual difference in basic libido, in sexual drives, affected secondarily by training and nurture. Unconscious conflict is shown by normal individuals in trivial forgetfulness and minor mistakes, contrasted with severe, lasting emotional upsets and disorganized behavior patterns among schizophrenics. Erik Erikson of Harvard University, mediating between Freud and Rank, held that emotional disorders, though rooted in experience during infancy, especially in libidinal, genital, and motor maturation processes, may continue to develop during early childhood as a result of mother-child contacts and other social relationships.

The psychoanalyst Erich Fromm attributed emotional conflicts not merely to unconscious desires but mainly to moral dilemmas of the individual as he attempts to cope with deep feelings and drives, to solve problems arising from his relations to other people in a defective social order, and to gain personal freedom and integrity.

ADLER, JUNG, PILLSBURY, AND OTHERS

Another dissent from Freud's analysis of emotional disturbances was elaborated by Alfred Adler. He held that the urge to gain power and to dominate or become superior was more potent than libidinal drives in the genesis of emotional conflicts. He agreed with Freud that the individual very early in life becomes aware of his inherited organic weaknesses and has difficulty facing reality, but he attributed the development of major psychic disturbances to inability to achieve domination and superiority. This failure is accompanied by repression and compensation. Thus women are more submissive than men and try to compensate for their submissive role by acting in an aggressive manner; men tend to display or exaggerate their masculinity, a defense mechanism to conceal any tendency toward femininity and submissiveness. Thwarted desire to become superior may result either in aggressiveness, greed, hate, and jealousy, or in fear, loneliness, anxiety, and repressed antagonism toward others. In this way, individuals develop inferiority and superiority complexes, exaggerated self-assertion, habitual expression of fixed ideas, and other neurotic reactions.

Jung held that the mechanisms of emotion depended mainly upon the degree of an individual's extroversion and introversion, the process of balancing his tendency to respond to the outside world against the tendency to concentrate on his inner needs and desires. This process involved conscious energy and also unconscious energy that was subdivided into personal and racial drives. The racially inherited unconscious drives were those patterns of feeling and thinking that had been formed and fixed through continual repetition and handed down from ancestors to successive generations. Repression of either personal or racial unconscious impulses was responsible for emotional conflicts and maladjustments. Since the individual's emotions and ideas became inadequate, unsatisfactory, and frequently contradictory, he unconsciously reacted with dreams, unusual responses in word-association tests, slips of the tongue, mystic visions, and myths as forms of compensation. In the 1950s, Jung urged that individuals should choose freely and boldly a moral purpose that would fulfill them as persons despite any disapproving group or social conventions. This free choice, said Jung, would enable them to direct unconscious psychic energy and help them integrate their behavior and eliminate inner conflicts or uncertainties, such as doubts about their masculinity or femininity.

Pillsbury classified adjustments to emotional stress and conflicts into four types: (1) direct or indirect attack (as in aggression, sublimation, and substitution of acceptable reactions for traumatic ones); (2) defense (as in evasion, compensation, rationalization, and projection to conceal or counteract dangers, deficiencies, or difficulties); (3) escape (as in withdrawal or flight, daydreaming, repression, acceptance of sympathy from others, and dissociation of ideas); and (4) surrender (as in failure to react, the ostrich complex, or in fatalistic resignation, often accompanied by fear and worry). Pillsbury pointed out that Pavlov, Jules Masserman, and Norman R. F. Maier, experimenting with dogs, cats, and rats, respectively, had induced neuroses by repeatedly subjecting the animals to stressful situations and had reported methods of adjustment comparable to those among human beings but on a less sophisticated level.

Recently, in another scientific approach to the study of emotions, thousands of investigators have explored effects of chemicals and pharmaceutical drugs upon brain chemistry and emotional and other psychic reactions in animals and man. Research into the influence of such compounds as adrenaline, serotonin, LSD, acetylcholine, hormones, tranquilizers, and peptides, for example, upon human moods and emotions is nevertheless still in its infancy. A promising beginning was made in the 1970s by R. C. Gur, M. Reivich, M. E. Phelps, and other researchers in the use of positron emission tomography (PET) techniques to trace blood flow and metabolic processes in the brain as a concomitant of intellectual and emotional reactions of organisms under varying conditions of health, disease, and internal physical and chemical environments. The value and limitations of these physiological researches, reminiscent of the early investigations by Cannon and Crile, remain to be determined. At the same time, genetic studies of animal strains by J. R. Royce, R. H. Smith, and J. L. Connor explored the influence of genetic and environmental factors on moods and emotions. Optimistic behaviorists continue to predict that physiological researches will eventually explain all major aspects of emotional behavior.

8 MEMORY, IMAGINATION, AND DREAMS

Significant theories about memory, imagination, and dreams can be traced as far back as the classical works of Plato and Aristotle, both of whom in the fourth century B.C. formulated hypotheses accepted by many psychologists in the nineteenth and twentieth centuries.

PLATO AND ARISTOTLE

To Plato must be accorded credit for the earliest known systematic analysis of memory, which he attributed to the association of past forgotten ideas with new similar or contrasting ones. In *Phaedo,* a dialogue about the death of Socrates and immortality, he noted that the sight of an object is quickly associated with its owner. If two things have been linked in past experience, thinking about one may recall the other. When the individual has seen an object, he may later recall it together with similar or dissimilar forgotten objects or related experiences. Sensations and communication with others act as stimuli or cues that enable a person to reproduce information and ideas already known but submerged in his unconscious mind. Every idea is real, everlasting, in a universe of interrelated ideas, whereas things seen or heard are ephemeral appearances, shadows, partial copies of the real eternal ideas known to man's immortal soul. Gestalt psychologists today regard percepts and ideas as parts of composite, interrelated wholes greater than the sum of their parts, a concept in some respects comparable to Plato's theory.

Plato associated the brain with perception, the heart with will and spirit, and the liver with appetite and desire. He held that these organs function together under the direction of rational thoughts created in the mind. The individual interprets images and perceptions, associating them with ideal eternal truths, the realities he must have known in past experience extending back into infinity.

Plato's introspectional analysis of dreams may be regarded as anticipating the researches of Sigmund Freud, who emphasized dynamic principles in his interpretations of dreams. According to Plato, when a person dreams, he loses rational control over impulses, desires, and distorted thoughts, allowing low instincts and false notions to prevail until correct thoughts appear in his reawakened mind, which thereupon rejects the dream's erroneous impulses and unreal images.

Aristotle attributed reality to concrete objects and events as well as ideas. He advocated scientific observation and experimentation to ascertain how and why things happen, how and why perception, memory, and logical thinking function as they do. Many of his own conclusions, however, were based upon ingenious speculations rather than experimental procedures. He delineated four laws governing the association of ideas as the primary factor in memory: (1) similarity, whereby one idea reminds us of similar ideas; (2) contrast, whereby one idea reminds us of contrary ideas; (3) spatial contiguity, whereby ideas of things related in space are recalled together; and (4) temporal contiguity, whereby ideas related in time are recalled together. Memory depends upon the fact that the perception of an object always leaves an impression (like the impression of a ring on one's finger), which, if we attend to it, impels us to think about the same object again and to identify it as something in our past experience. Impressions remain in the unconscious mind until they are brought into consciousness in accordance with the four laws. He noted that afterimages (positive, like the original, or negative, unlike the original) may occur after the stimuli causing the original images to disappear. In dreams the imagination rearranges impressions and images resulting from past sensations but without exercising logical control or correcting errors; therefore, dreams cannot accurately predict future events. Aristotle associated images during sleep with transmission of psychophysical energy by blood to the heart, which he mistakenly identified as the chief sense organ.

Modern psychologists attempted to reduce Aristotle's four laws of association to a single law of contiguity because contrary ideas are similar in some respects (just as blue and red are different in appearance but alike in being colors) and because objects contiguous in space are also contiguous in time. Investigations have disclosed that memory, imagination, and dreams depend not only upon the association of ideas but also upon specific stimuli, purposes, meanings, attitudes, attention, emotions, physical structures, repetition, and a great variety of genetic and social influences. None of the modern theories, however, has invalidated basic concepts of Plato and Aristotle concerning the association of ideas.

QUINTILIAN, SAINT AUGUSTINE, MAIMONIDES, AQUINAS

Some of the factors emphasized in recent investigations of memory were well known in ancient and medieval times. The famous Roman educator Quintilian in the first century A.D. taught that repetition, practice, and intrinsic interest were necessary for effective learning and recall. In the fourth century, Saint Augustine held that ideas encountered together in past experience tended to reappear together in memory. The philosopher Maimonides (1135-1204) stressed the important role of physical structures for memory, stating that individuals born with relatively dry brains find it easier to remember information than do people burdened with excessive internal humidity. He commented, however, that the right attitude, education, repetition, practice, and effort can improve learning and recall. Saint Thomas Aquinas (1225-1274) associated brain injuries with loss of memory, reiterating the view of Hippocrates that many disorders of memory, thought, and emotion are caused by organic injuries and by physiological maladjustments.

BRITISH ASSOCIATIONISTS

The associationist doctrines formulated by Plato and Aristotle became central principles of the British empiricist philosophers during the seventeenth and eighteenth centuries. Leaders among these philosophers were Hobbes, Locke, Berkeley, Hume, Hartley, Brown, James Mill, John Stuart Mill, Hamilton, Bain, and Spencer.

Thomas Hobbes, author of *Leviathan* (1651), attributed the association of ideas to an inertial psychic force that causes images to be retained after objects seen have disappeared. Sensations decay in imagination and fade in memory, while in dreams the same kinds of images and ideas are distorted into absurdities because in sleep the brain and nerves are numbed and therefore do not introduce corrective ideas. Ideas are recalled together because of their past spatial or temporal coexistence. Connections among previous ideas produced by sensations are reproduced in memory, imagination, and dreams.

John Locke in 1690 held that intuition enables the individual to compare ideas and reproduce them in memory in various combinations, contrasting, separating, abstracting, and mixing them. Ideas derive from sensations imposed by external objects or by internal mental operations that integrate and associate them, making them consistent. Ideas created and connected in perception and reasoning are imperfect copies of real objects, which have solidity, extension, form, and motion. Individuals differ in the vividness and accuracy of their memories, qualities greatly affected by repetition and by careful thinking about logical relationships among successive ideas.

George Berkeley in 1710 declared that only mind can detect and associate ideas; that despite qualitative differences (for example, between real pain and the idea of pain), all feelings, images, and thoughts are alike in being interrelated mental experiences. It is a mistake to associate ideas with matter; they are connected only with other ideas, essences originating in the mind of God. (In 1677 Spinoza had described ideas and matter as two appearances of one real, divine substance that is neither mind nor matter.) Ideas, said Berkeley, are created by God and, imprinted on human senses, then perceived and compared by the mind. Ideas become associated by means of motion, time, extension in space, color, and shape. (In 1709 his *New Theory of Vision* stated that three-dimensional vision depends upon associations between visual and kinesthetic sensations.)

In 1748 David Hume wrote that ideas are associated because the mind has observed repeated connections between them, so that, for instance, a picture of a person impels us to think again about the original. In memory, past impressions are recalled through such associations, but the ideas copying or reproducing them are then weaker than the first impressions. In memory, imagination, and dreams, ideas become associated as the result of their similarity, contiguity in time and space, and cause-effect relationships. Nothing else really exists except a succession of impressions formed into ideas created and interrelated by the mind.

David Hartley in the mid-eighteenth century attributed the association of ideas to simultaneous and successive contiguity in past experience, and he proposed a physiological explanation inspired by Isaac Newton's comments on perception. Sensations activated by a flexible substance, or ether, produce corresponding fainter vibrations in the brain, creating ideas and images in memory, as well as afterimages that may persist briefly following the impact of sensory stimuli. Because sensations are frequently connected with other sensations, corresponding ideas similarly become associated in memory and imagination. Hartley agreed with Locke that ideas are not innate but originate in experience. He emphasized the functions of neurological structures and the brain in perception and thought processes. His theory of neural vibrations, though eventually rejected by psychologists, gave impetus to scientific investigation of relationships between physical structures and mental functions of memory and imagination.

Thomas Brown (1778–1820) identified temporal succession and contrast as the principal factors in perception, association of ideas, memory, learning, and imagination. Even spatial contiguity, he said, arises out of mental extension of time inasmuch as the divisibility of space and feelings of movement depend upon slow or rapid passage of successive time intervals. Recency, duration, and repetition are effective elements in the association of ideas. Contrast is as important as similarity: For example, a cold, wet climate may remind us of warm, sunny days, and out-of-tune music may bring to mind images of beautiful harmony.

James Mill and John Stuart Mill, portraying the mind as a composite of sensations, feelings and ideas, regarded similarity and temporal contiguity as essential bonds connecting ideas. They suggested the principle of *oblivescence* whereby associated ideas that no longer receive our attention simply drop out of consciousness as if eradicated by new ideas. Attention and interest must therefore be primary elements in perception and memory. The mind attends to ideas repeatedly associated together, but afterward (because of the onset of new ideas and loss of interest in old ones) tends to forget many ideas in the original group. Thus old ideas disappear in oblivescence. (Recent experiments by Donald B. Lindsley of the University of California and other investigators indicate that an antecedent stimulus, such as a light about to be seen, can sometimes be wiped out of consciousness, perhaps on a marginal level, by a subsequent more intense stimulus even though the light has already produced a slight reaction—the phenomenon of backward masking. Moreover, while many perceptions seem to occur instantaneously, they actually develop in a succession of very brief time intervals.) John Stuart Mill later modified his associationist approach and adopted a Kantian analysis of the mind not as a composite of associated ideas but as an integrated self with inherited powers of thought.

Sir William Hamilton, opposing the Millses, stated that any perception or idea may reawaken memory of an entire group of related perceptions and ideas. In certain mental disorders involving fragmentation of personality, integration and recovery can often be achieved if correct associations are repeatedly restored.

Alexander Bain and Herbert Spencer adhered to a biological analysis to explain the effects of interest, repetition, contiguity, and past experience upon memory and imagination. In their view, all mental reactions, including ideas and images, occur when stimuli repeatedly energize the individual's inherited nervous structures and thereby help him adjust better to his environment. Mental operations involve interrelated concomitant activities, movements, and efforts of body and mind. When these reactions are successfully repeated, they strengthen pleasurable associations so that the individual recalls the experiences readily.

Monotonous, unsuccessful, or painful experiences retard memory and learning.

Bain and Spencer agreed that sensations, perceptions, images, thoughts, and emotions appear in a temporal succession or transition from one psychophysical state to another. They predicted that detailed scientific investigation of the association and recall of ideas would lead to improvement of human character, capacities, and conduct. Their confidence was soon partly justified by new concepts and discoveries of the German psychologist Ebbinghaus and American psychologists (such as William James, Thorndike, Watson, and Skinner) concerning habit, repetition, attitudes, attention, interest, effort, interference, and reinforcement as factors involved in memory, imagination, and learning.

Bain, who for two decades taught philosophy at Aberdeen University, eventually modified his early physiological approach and mechanistic theories of associationism, adhering instead to a conception of the mind as an integrated, purposive, unitary, spontaneous force. Spencer also qualified his associationist sympathies, emphasizing instead the role of the whole person as an inheritor, accumulator, and transmitter of progress in the process of racial, moral, social, and cultural evolution.

EBBINGHAUS

Traditional theories about memory, formulated by ancient philosophers and modern associationists, were based largely upon theological dogmas, speculations, random introspectional impressions, and unsystematic observations of human behavior. Aristotelian theories prevailed for two thousand years as authoritative dicta, never subjected to testing by scientific criteria although Aristotle had advocated inductive observation and experimentation. Even Francis Bacon failed to appreciate the revolutionary hypotheses of his great contemporaries Galileo and Harvey that were based upon the experimental procedures that Bacon himself espoused in his epochal *Novum Organum* (1620). For two hundred years afterward, there were noteworthy experiments and discoveries in anatomy and physiology about the brain and nervous system and extraordinary progress in the physical sciences, but psychology, including the study of memory, lagged behind.

During the nineteenth century, leading scientists from Thomas Young to Sherrington, completing hundreds of fruitful experiments on sensation and perception, established a new emphasis in major fields of psychology upon experimentation, observation, and measurement. In 1816 Herbart elaborated in detail on the traditional view that the individual remembers ideas by connecting new experience with accumulated past experience as an apperceptive base. In 1885 Ebbinghaus, an adherent to Wundt's structural school of psychology, reported significant findings resulting from his unique experiments on memory. He did not reject the associationist ideas of the Herbartians, but he pioneered in the use of meaningless nonsense syllables (for example, *rit, bam, nef*) that eliminated the distorting effects of the associations engendered by meaningful words. In this way he succeeded in measuring basic processes of learning and memory.

For his experiments with himself as subject, Ebbinghaus devised about two thousand nonsense syllables, each consisting of a pair of consonants with one vowel between them. Selecting syllables at random, he arranged them on cards in series of different sizes. He found that he could reproduce perfectly from memory a line of three or four syllables read once, but that a series of more than seven syllables generally required rereading in order to recall it without errors. The number of needed repetitions increased more rapidly than the number of syllables. Thus a series of twelve syllables required about sixteen repetitions for mastery, whereas one consisting of thirty-five syllables required at least fifty-five repetitions. In these experiments, a single perfect reproduction from memory was accepted as proof that he had learned the series.

In other experiments designed to determine the percentage of information remembered and the percentage forgotten, Ebbinghaus applied a standard of two perfect reproductions from memory. In these experiments, he relearned the lists of syllables after various intervals. The time required for relearning after each interval (compared with the time required for the original learning) enabled him to calculate the amount of information forgotten. He learned twelve lists of thirteen syllables, for example, and at the end of one hour relearned them in 56 percent less time than had been required for the original learning, a saving in time of 44 percent. Other savings were 28 percent after two days, 25 percent after six days, and 21 percent after thirty-one days. It took only one hour to forget 56 percent of the learned information, but thirty-one days to forget an additional 23 percent. These experiments proved (1) that as time passes more of the learned material is forgotten and the number of repetitions needed for relearning increases, but (2) that the rate of forgetting, which is very rapid at first, slows down. Ebbinghaus was the first investigator to construct a curve showing the changes that occur over time in rates of forgetting.

He also measured the relationship between repetition and the time needed for relearning. Thus he learned a series of syllables in eight repetitions, and after twenty-four hours relearned it. Then he learned a series in sixteen repetitions and similarly relearned it, and he continued in the same way with additional series. The times needed for relearning decreased in proportion to the repetitions. Reading a series sixty-four times brought a saving of about 64 percent in the time needed for relearning. These calculations proved that overlearning (extra or unnecessary repetitions) within limits set by fatigue improves retention. (In 1929–1930, however, W. C. F. Kreuger's experiments showed that additional repetitions after much overlearning improve recall at a diminishing rate.)

Ebbinghaus used a telling method to determine the amount of information that can be immediately recalled. In this method, he learned a series of syllables in pairs, examined the first syllable in each pair, and attempted to give the next syllable from memory. This method measured accuracy of learning and rate of forgetting; it proved (1) that some associations are formed even in the learning of nonsense syllables and (2) that information is forgotten very rapidly during the first day or two after being learned. Moreover, connections formed among syllables in a series being learned persist so that the learner saves time even when relearning the series in reverse order.

In experiments using both the savings method and the telling method, A. Jost, a contemporary of Ebbinghaus, found that recently learned associations are subject to an immediate rapid rate of forgetting, whereas older associations are forgotten at a much slower rate. Several repetitions right after learning help reduce the rate of forgetting. Immediate repetitions followed by frequent repetitions during long periods of time enable the individual to recall promptly without effort the words of his native language, innumerable practical associations, and habitual reactions. Numerous experiments have been conducted that confirm the slow rate of forgetting of old, thoroughly learned and long-retained materials. In 1952 the noted investigator of children's vocabulary Madorah E. Smith reported her own experience of recalling more than half of biblical questions and answers two decades after having memorized them, and then, after another interval of sixteen years, still being able to recall almost as much of the original information.

In 1956 the cognitive psychologist George A. Miller asserted that, whereas usually no more than seven separate bits of information can be recalled at once, grouping into large units allows data to be recalled readily in immediate memory; in 1963 G. Sperling, studying visual memory, claimed to have identified a short-term immediate memory lasting only several seconds; and in 1966 J. L. McGaugh, reviewing numerous experiments, distinguished between a short-interval memory ranging from several seconds to a few hours and a long-term memory that persists perhaps a few days and then may become permanent memory.

Early experiments by Ebbinghaus, Jost, George Müller, and Alfons Pilzecker explored the effectiveness of recognition in reviving old associations. Apparently owing to a complex process of long-term assimilation, recognition of old learned materials is more efficient than outright recall. The learner can recognize and identify such materials when he sees them even though he was initially unable to recall or reproduce them from memory.

GEORGE ELIAS MÜLLER

In 1900 George Elias Müller (1850–1934), noted professor of philosophy at the University of Göttingen, and his associate Alfons Pilzecker, in their *Experimental Contributions to Theories of Memory,* described the process whereby new learning and mental activity interfere with the recall of prior learned information. They formulated a theory of perseveration and consolidation of neural action. After learning has taken place through adequate repetition, they explained, interruptions at about that time or soon thereafter have an adverse effect of retroactive inhibition upon recall. Following a given longer interval, without further disruptive associations, however, there is consolidation of the learned materials and no further impairment of memory develops.

In experiments, Müller and Pilzecker discovered that, on the average, individuals could recall only about 26 percent of learned materials after a period of mental activity, but about 50 to 56 percent after a period of rest and mental inactivity. They verified Ebbinghaus's conclusion that distributed practice is a more effective learning method than cramming or massed repetitions. They noted that grouping items to be memorized and rhythmic repetition of grouped materials improve perseveration, consolidation, retention, and recall. Müller invented a memory drum to control information presented in experiments. (A number of such devices were used at the turn of the century; one consisted of a cardboard disk on which syllables were printed and viewed through a slit, a metronome to control disk movements, and an electrical battery and wires to turn the disk and make successive syllables visible.)

Müller's theory that memory depends mainly upon preserving and consolidating functions of the nervous system received support from numerous investigations in the 1950s to the 1980s concerning effects of electroconvulsive shock treatments and chemicals upon the brain and the processes of perseveration and consolidation, which Müller regarded as central factors in retention and recall.

McGEOCH

In 1931 the American psychologist John A. McGeoch reported his experimental finding that the successive study of similar subjects interferes much more than the successive study of dissimilar subjects with the task of relearning. Thus the study of science followed immediately by the study of history inhibits memory much less than is the case with the successive study of two rather similar branches of history. In 1931 also, McGeoch's experiments revealed that the more intelligent and mature an individual is, the greater is his recall if he learns material as a whole instead of in parts. During several decades of research, he corroborated and supplemented with quantitative data many of Ebbinghaus's conclusions about repetition, overlearning, and rates of forgetting. One conclusion, that recall of meaningful information is necessarily superior to the recall of nonsense syllables, was widely accepted despite conflicting evidence from other investigators, who attributed the results merely to more effective methods of associating and learning meaningful materials. McGeoch attributed better retention and recall of motor skills, compared with mainly verbal learning, to the more thorough mastery and overlearning usually involved in motor responses.

JAMES, DEWEY, ANGELL, SEASHORE, WOODROW

In 1890 at Harvard University, William James performed laboratory experiments which convinced him that practice in memorizing does not improve the general ability to retain or recall. Practice develops more efficient habits of learning, association, and memorization, which facilitate retention and recall of subject matter similar to the practice materials; it does not improve recall of altogether different kinds of subject matter. According to James, a few days of practice in learning a series of nonsense syllables may save as much as 50 percent of the time and repetitions needed to learn and recall another similar series of syllables, but will not help in learning or recall of prose, poetry, or other meaningful kinds of material. For most purposes, not practice but better thinking produces better understanding, retention, and recall.

James described the mind as a storehouse of memories, ideas, and interests. Every new experience becomes associated with stored elements and incorporated into its ready-made stock. This view recapitulated Herbart's theory that an apperceptive base (apperceptive mass) receives new impressions from the external world and thereby forms a new field of consciousness. Associations between old and new experiences reawaken and invigorate the individual's past interests and stimulate him to pay attention to new, similar information. James agreed with Herbart's principle of preparation for learning, which stated that the recall of old lessons prepares the student for the next steps and facilitates mastery and recollection of new lessons, including related but supplementary or enriched subject matter. James concluded that the process of learning and memory through association obeys the laws of coalescence and syncretism in accordance with which old and new associations are fused as harmonious parts of a whole interrelated and assimilated activity, a conception similar to the Gestalt psychologists' view of perception and of thought as unified, integrated, structured experiences. He attributed all mental phenomena to purposive efforts of individuals to achieve goals by choosing, comparing, analyzing, and organizing past experiences and applying them to present situations. This pragmatic interpretation of behavior became a basic concept of the functionalist psychologists Dewey and Angell.

John Dewey, in *How We Think* (1910), reiterated James's emphasis on purposive action as a factor in memory. He stated that the awareness and recall of past experiences enable the individual to overcome doubt or inertia, to coordinate selected previous knowledge with new information, and thus to make judgments required for meeting similar life situations and solving problems. Angell agreed with James that habit, the flywheel of society, depends upon a process whereby ideas formulated in the past suggest similar ideas applicable to present experiences and needs. He declared that efficiency of recall depends upon frequency, intensity, and recency of past associations and experiences, all coordinated and directed toward the individual's immediate practical needs. Associations involving contiguity in space and time, similarity, contrast, and cause and effect provide originality and orderly sequences in human thought, and even ideas that are similar but not closely joined in past experience may be recalled by means of deliberate purposive action, a subtle use of associations that distinguish man from other animals.

In 1927 Herbert H. Woodrow arrived at the same conclusion as James, based on similar experiments. He reported one experiment with three groups of students: a control group, a practice group, and a training group. The control group read miscellaneous materials (poetry, dates, and nonsense syllables) just once and repeated them; the practice group learned the same materials but had additional practice in memorizing poetry and nonsense syllables during a period of four weeks; the training group devoted 101 minutes to memorizing the miscellaneous materials plus 76 minutes to learning the best ways to memorize. The practice group benefited slightly in ability to memorize dates and vocabulary, but only the training group improved significantly in ability to learn and recall all kinds of materials learned by these three groups. (In 1933 the British psychologist J. W. Cox and in 1934 the American psychologist Woodworth arrived at the same conclusion in regard to motor skills.) In training his third group, Woodrow instructed them to learn material in wholes, to test themselves after several repetitions, to interpret meanings and associations, to center all attention in their practice, and to assume confidently that they would recall the material.

Carl E. Seashore at Iowa University adhered to the general view of functional, purposive memory expounded by James, Dewey, and Angell. An authority on music education, Seashore pointed out that improvement in memorizing music depends upon interest in a particular composition, its similarity to other familiar compositions, sustained attention, vigorous energy and health, and native physiological equipment. Rejecting James's conception of the mind as a storehouse of past experiences, Seashore emphasized the role of neural connections in retention, asserting that any normal person possesses innate brain capacity for memorizing far in excess of the ability he puts to use. He contended that memory consists of several inborn capacities, and that students can increase their memory at least tenfold through proper training in skills of memorizing.

WOODWORTH AND THORNDIKE

Interpretations of retention and recall, expounded by Sherrington and James in the 1890s, stated that synaptic neural connections and the activation of nerve centers by external stimuli account for transmission of nerve impulses, which are strengthened by use, as in recall, but weakened by disuse, as in forgetting. Also in the 1890s, Ewald Hering at the University of Leipzig formulated a theory of primary memory (retention and recall after a single repetition) stating that every perception creates a neural pathway in the brain, thus facilitating the passage of new impulses along the pathway and resulting in retention and recall of the original perception. Hering attributed memory to the special, unique organization of organic matter.

Woodworth, student of Sherrington, and Thorndike, student of James, constructed diagrams showing the sensory nerve endings, nerve currents, nerve-cell structures, and effects of repetition and disuse upon neural conduction and responses in movement, learning and memory. Their stimulus-response (S-R bond) theory was accepted by many American psychologists early in the twentieth century. Woodworth and Thorndike held that in memory the S-R bonds are stamped in and reinforced, that in forgetting they are stamped out or weakened. Contiguity does not necessarily join ideas firmly enough for subsequent retrieval, but, after adequate repetition, identical or similar elements in ideas and information control attention and stimulate recall. Their experiments at Columbia University indicated that if students are given training in estimating areas of rectangles, they soon greatly improve their estimates; but if the shapes of the areas are changed, much less improvement results.

Thorndike's interpretation of the stimulus-response theory and his laws of learning—the laws of readiness, exercise, and effect—became widely disseminated principles of education. Learning in accordance with these laws depended upon effective functioning of memory. Interest and readiness for new learning, purposive, meaningful repetition or practice, and successful effort, encouraging expectations and renewed attempts to succeed, are all based upon ability to recall past experience. Thorndike contended that practice in addition improves the ability to multiply, but only to the extent that addition elements are identical with the elements required for multiplication. Critics objected that it is not separate identical elements that are recalled but a total situation. Thorndike explained that any state of affairs in-side or outside an organism is a potential stimulus; that response follows stimulus when the individual becomes interested enough to unite identical and other elements in learning and memory. He conceded, however, that repetition is of little use without insight, attention, and purpose; that painful as well as pleasurable experiences or recollections and expectations often strengthen the bonds of memory.

Woodworth, too, admitted that memory improves (irrespective of the number of identical elements involved) when the individual systematizes and interrelates information and experience into a coherent whole which stimulates recall of specific items. As early as 1908, C. H. Judd had emphasized generalization and application of information as aids to retention and recall. Gestalt psychologists objected to Thorndike's theories of identical elements on the ground that recall depends upon situations and experiences as meaningful wholes requiring insight into configurations, the entire framework and functions of information being recalled.

PILLSBURY

At the University of Michigan, Pillsbury described retention as that persistence of activity which characterizes all human organic tissue. This quality of persistence enables man to have memories and thereby to acquire information, knowledge, and ideas about past and present experiences. The sense organs function in such a manner that whatever is sensed persists very briefly as sensory afterimages, traces left behind by stimuli; the reactions of the sensory areas of the brain cortex similarly persist as somewhat longer memory afterimages; and true memory images persist much longer, often reappearing after many years of life experience.

Individuals differ greatly, said Pillsbury, in the extent of their use of various types of imagery. Many persons depend primarily upon visual images, others upon verbal, auditory, or kinesthetic images, as dominant aids to memory. In memorizing words, only one of every three persons tends to reproduce visual images of them; the majority reproduces slight muscle movements of speech. Children with photographic memories (eidetic imagery) may have images of objects known in past experience that are so vivid as to make them seem to be real, present objects. Musicians tend to depend upon auditory images, artists upon vivid color images. On the other hand, a visual-minded person, owing to the extra effort involved, may sometimes remember better the words he hears than the words he reads.

Pillsbury noted that in old age many individuals who cannot easily recall recent events can vividly recall events of early childhood. Among the aged particularly, and to a lesser extent among younger persons, general principles tend to be remembered better than specific information because frequent recall and applications of principles strengthen associations. For all age groups, the basic factors in memory, said Pillsbury, are threefold: (1) the nature and intensity of stimuli and the condition of each sense organ affected; (2) attention and emotional reactions, which depend upon the purposive activity of the individual as he reorganizes and reproduces past experiences; and (3) the strength of connections and integrating mechanisms in the nervous system.

According to Pillsbury, a complex process of assimilation and integration is involved in recall of information. The individual's attitude and interpretation of situations affect what he attempts to recall and also when and how vividly he recalls it. The social environment, customs, and human relationships influence his choices of things to remember. Events of the past do not always recur as images in their original order. Some individuals may even organize and recall sensory experiences arising from two or more senses. An example is colored hearing, wherein colors are sometimes recalled at once whenever particular musical sounds are heard. The work of creative artists may depend upon casual or unusual images rather than recollections of integrated past experiences. (In dreams, images of recent events tend to persist, often in a bizarre form, sometimes initiated or modified by noises or other drastic changes in the immediate environment.) In examinations, students may vaguely recognize old information, then suddenly recall related facts that clarify their vague associations. Mistakes in recognition, which is generally more accurate than recall, occur more often in associating recent events with old ones than vice versa.

TITCHENER

In his *Physiological Psychology* (1903), Wundt stated that complete ideas are too fluid, variable, and unstable to be directly associated in memory. Ideas become connected indirectly, through their partial elements, which fuse and supplement one another, stimulate brain reactions, and in memory are either blended into similar impressions or attached as supplements to dissimilar impressions. Titchener agreed with this theory but noted that introspection cannot discover such fusion of elements in ideas. Elements must therefore be controlled by purely physiological processes. In memory as one impression is reinstated or duplicated along a neural pathway, the excitation of new, similar impressions and their progress along the same pathway are facilitated and thus make possible the association, retention, and recall of ideas.

This explanation is quite different from that of the British associationists and rather similar to Hering's theory of neural impulses and neural pathways in primary memory. Titchener often objected to Wundt's disregard for integrated organic sensations in formulating physiological explanations of behavior, but he adhered faithfully to Wundtian confidence in the value of introspection as a method of exploring conscious experiences. His conclusions concerning the psychology of recognition in memory were based upon thousands of introspectional reports that he analyzed during his long tenure at Cornell University. Noting that external stimuli produce not only diverse sensations and organic reactions, but also feelings, he pinpointed the feeling of familiarity as the key factor in recognition. He described this feeling as warm, comfortable, and diffused. The association of ideas, he held, is not necessary for recognition to occur; in fact, objects or events may arouse numerous correct associations of ideas but still remain unrecognized. Feelings of familiarity may alternate with feelings of strangeness until additional associations result in either recognition or definite nonrecognition. Thus a person met on the street may suddenly after much uncertainty and hesitation be identified as an old friend in recognition or as a total stranger in nonrecognition. Failure to recognize an object does not indicate passivity or inaction but rather a positive activity that creates feelings of strangeness, unpleasant anxiety, and restlessness. If an object has become very familiar, however, any special effort to recognize it is unnecessary. The owner of a favorite pen constantly in use, for instance, ordinarily needs no attempt to recognize it, but if its setting is changed, if it is missing or has been placed among less familiar pens, the need for recognition recurs and the feeling of familiarity revives. Visual perception and the association of ideas do not constitute recognition but help it to become clear and definite.

Titchener's experiments demonstrated differences between memory images and images of imagination. The memory image, even though it represents past experiences while the image of imagination has no such associations, tends to be less stable and less colorful, to change more suddenly, to last a shorter time, and to produce more restlessness and movement and a greater sense of pleasant familiarity. Some images associated with everyday objects may exhibit characteristics of both types of image, or pass from one type to the other. In memory the individual recalls past experience that has receded or decayed and needs to be retrieved, whereas in imagination each image remains strong and vivid and if it vanishes must be reconstructed or be recalled as a memory image. Memory is limited in character and scope by the original past experience. A feeling of strangeness is basic, however, in images of the imagination, which, in contrast to memory, has no definite limits except the individual's mental capacity.

PAVLOV

Conditioned response mechanisms depend upon retention, recall, and recognition. In conditioning, the individual remembers and associates two unlike stimuli that are relatively contiguous. It will be recalled that in Pavlov's classical conditioning experiments a dog that receives food repeatedly while hearing or shortly after hearing a bell learns to associate the sound with food and then salivates whenever he hears the bell even though food is being withheld. If the food continues to be withheld, the dog soon forgets the association, ignores the bell, and stops salivating. Pavlov described this repression of memory as extinction through inhibition spreading within the nervous system, affecting particularly the cortical cells in the brain. In 1930 E. R. Guthrie at the University of Washington attributed inhibition of the dog's salivary reaction to the number of repetitions of the sound without food and to various organic motor movements and other stimuli absorbing the animal's attention. Pavlov, however, declared that the time element is decisive; that cortical brain cells, being highly reactive, rapidly become exhausted and must rest before they can revive old associations and respond to them again when the bell rings, thus achieving spontaneous recovery and disinhibition.

Even prior to 1900, Pavlov expounded his view of forgetting as an aspect of physiological repression and inhibition, just when Freud was beginning to analyze the roles of forgetfulness and repressed memories in abnormal behavior. Freud attributed these processes to dynamic motives, emotions, and submerged inner conflicts that affect the nervous system. Pavlov attributed forgetting and also sleep to active inhibitory functions spreading through cerebral areas in which, he said, sleep originates. Hypnotized persons, he asserted, lose the power to make voluntary skeletal movements because motor areas of the cerebral cortex are inhibited, but in hypnosis inhibition does not spread to certain sensory areas. Pavlov's conclusions about memory and conditioning were eventually verified in experiments by Watson, Skinner, and many other behaviorists.

WATSON AND SKINNER

The celebrated Russian physiologist and neuropathologist Vladimir Mikhailovich Bekhterev (1857–1927) applied Pavlov's research methods in numerous conditioned-reflex experiments. He concluded that, whereas instinctive reflexes are direct, immediate reactions induced by external stimuli, voluntary overt responses must be attributed to internal forces and neural traces (of past experience) operating in retention, recall, and recognition. Unaware of specific causes of his voluntary behavior, the individual imagines he is acting of his own free will, but all his emotional, cognitive, moral, social, and aesthetic responses are actually produced and controlled by physiological processes and physicochemical activity. Bekhterev's writings, especially his *Objective Psychology* (translated into French and English in 1913), helped to disseminate Pavlov's methods and views widely among Continental, British, and American psychologists.

At the University of Chicago and later (1908–1920) at The Johns Hopkins University, J. B. Watson, enthusiastic about the views of Pavlov and Bekhterev, applied their conditioning procedures in experiments with animals and infants, concentrating on the genesis of emotional reactions, learning, and personality development. In his experiments, rejecting introspection, he depended upon S-R bond theories of Thorndike and Woodworth and conditioned-reflex theories of Pavlov and Bekhterev. Watson's conclusions became the basis for American behaviorist psychology, which emphasized the role of spatial and temporal associations and repetition in organic behavior.

At about the same time, Thorndike introduced the concept of reinforcement in formulating his law of effect, which states that a successful reaction made during past attempts to cope with a situation is remembered and tends to be repeated, while an unsuccessful or annoying effort tends to be avoided. The individual recalls his feeling of satisfaction derived from previous actions and repeats them in anticipation of the same results. (Eventually Thorndike modified his law of effect in an attempt to explain why individuals often remember best their most painful experiences. At first he attributed such recall to the fact that the recollection itself was not painful. Later, however, he postulated belongingness—a relationship between past and present experience—in addition to understanding and insight as factors affecting learning and memory.)

In experiments of Thorndike, Pavlov, and Watson, reinforcement of any pattern of reaction by the individual seemed to result from the individual's awareness of his past successful responses to specific stimuli (for example, food or sounds). At Harvard University, however, B. F. Skinner (1904–) postulated two kinds of conditioning: (1) the classical or respondent type in which a stimulus directly elicits an automatic reaction, as in innately grounded reflexes, and (2) the operant or instrumental type in which the stimulus may be unknown, disregarded, indirect, or irrelevant. In operant conditioning (regarded by some psychologists as trial-and-error learning), the individual attempting to cope with a task, situation, or problem performs a series of reactions directed toward his goal. If each successive step in the series is or appears to be successful and emotionally satisfying, reinforcing his self-confidence and efforts, he will not need additional specific stimuli but will continue with the next steps in a schedule or orderly sequence of satisfying voluntary responses. Thus he builds habitual patterns of reaction. Each response acts as a reinforcing factor until he achieves his final goal or end result. In operant conditioning, as in classical conditioning, recall, recognition, and expectancy are contributing forces. In any form of conditioning, as Thorndike noted, disappointments, errors, and annoyances may fail to inhibit incorrect responses if the individual, still hoping to succeed, persists until he surrenders to recollection of cumulative failures and his expectations evaporate.

GESTALT PSYCHOLOGISTS

Behaviorism dominated the American psychological arena for several decades, into the 1950s, and still attracts numerous adherents. Behaviorists regarded contiguity of experience as a basic factor in memory and behavior. Their postulates changed the old theory of the association of ideas into concepts of neural connections and stimulus-response mechanisms. These concepts were, however, rejected by Gestalt psychologists as atomistic approaches that ignored the patterns and integrated character of perception, memory, and cognition.

During the First World War when he was interned as an alien in a German experiment station at Tenerife in the Canary Islands, Wolfgang Köhler in his unique experiments with chimpanzees discovered that they reacted not to specific or isolated stimuli but to a perception of the entire situation confronting them. Adapting means to ends, they deliberately changed their patterns of response into other reactions deemed most likely to succeed in the light of their past experiences (just as human beings do when they suddenly acquire new insight into relationships of objects to each other and to them). They selected the most promising tools to use in getting food, for example, often rejecting less suitable tools, because they understood the relationships between the tools and the whole situation. In opposition to Pavlov, Köhler maintained that a unified, insightful idea, recollection, or pattern of reaction could never be fully described or explained by tracing millions of individual connections and operations in the brain and nervous system.

The Gestalt psychologists Kurt Koffka and Max Wertheimer, who, like Köhler, taught in American universities, similarly rejected the views of behaviorists, as well as those of Wundtian structuralist introspectionists. They contended that every organism undergoes change with each function it performs; recall of past events is simply another reaction of the changing organism as a whole in relationship to its entire changing environment. Memory and true introspection, wrote Koffka, reflect interactions between the whole individual and his entire integrated situation.

PIAGET

Behaviorist critics replied that Gestalt psychologists underemphasized stimulus-response connections and that they offered no adequate explanation or description of the mechanisms that produce and direct integrated perceptions and patterns of thought and reaction. In the 1920s through the 1960s, Jean Piaget, though he did not solve this problem, pioneered in analyzing the way in which mechanisms of mental operations develop in the individual as he thinks and acts in order to utilize and control his natural, cultural, and social environment. In this process, said Piaget, the individual gains concepts about quantitative, spatial, temporal, and cause-effect relationships, step by step, remembering his successfully used concepts and organizing and applying them to new situations and tasks, thereby mastering structures or categories of logical thinking. His general ideas and intellectual capacities therefore grow out of the memory of past experience and efforts.

Critics of this view, including the linguist Noam Chomsky (who joined Piaget in rejecting basic concepts of behaviorists), attributed mental structures and functions less to specific reactions than to capacities and modes of behavior inherited from the entire race. The individual possesses an inherited long-term memory that enables him to develop ideas and knowledge about language, space, and time. As he matures, he will, for example, learn to speak and read by grasping meanings in words as wholes without having to build up meanings by interpreting individual letters in words.

BARTLETT, ZEIGARNIK, BALLARD, JOHN, HUBEL, ET AL.

Experiments, reports, and conclusions by Frederic C. Bartlett of Cambridge University in the 1930s through the 1950s shed new light upon memory processes. Bartlett found that errors in remembering often occur because the individual subconsciously simplifies or otherwise modifies and distorts his recollections of events and information to fit them into his point of view, expectations, and previous patterns of ideas and attitudes. Memory gaps tend to be filled in with imaginary episodes. He noted that auditory memorizing depends more upon patterns or grouping of information than does visual memorizing, but that both types of memorizing used together reinforce each other and make organization of diverse facts more definite and complete. Recall of one part of a poem reminds the reader about the next part because both parts belong to a unified pattern being reconstructed. Difficult, dubious, disliked, or unfamiliar material tends to be forgotten.

Experiments by Kurt Lewin and Bluma Zeigarnik at Berlin University indicated that unfinished tasks are remembered better than finished ones because of tensions created by incomplete work. These tensions persist until the individual completes each task, and he often thereafter readily forgets the entire experience.

An experiment with London schoolchildren in 1913 by P. B. Ballard showed that individuals sometimes can recall more information after the lapse of brief periods of time (such as a few hours or several days) than they can immediately recall. This tendency of memory traces to become stronger after an interval (the Ballard reminiscence effect) was found most apparent among children, less effective among adults, and more effective for meaningful information than for nonsense syllables. Warner Brown at the University of California and Thorndike at Columbia University concluded from their similar experiments that the passage of time may help to stimulate repetition and strengthen verbal memory because the information desired to be recalled fits readily into the individual's lasting interests, significant patterns of thought, and attitudes.

During the 1960s and 1970s, neurophysiological investigations, consistent with but not definitely proving theories of Sherrington and Pavlov about neural and cortical mechanisms, were undertaken by scores of American psychologists. Utilizing sophisticated apparatus to measure electrical currents in brain cells and cortical areas, E. Roy John, Z. S. Khachaturian, D. H. Hubel, N. W. Wiesel, and W. Freeman attempted to correlate patterns of neural activity with integrated reactions of animal and human subjects during conditioning, learning, recall, and recognition.

In 1980 John and his colleagues at New York University reported relationships between atypical brain-wave patterns of children and learning disabilities attributed to brain damage or disorders. Although many such relationships were found between neurophysiological electrical activity and attention, insight, motor reactions, and memory, not enough data became available either to prove or to disprove the diverse views of leading psychologists. Impressive cognitive theories of E. Roy John, D. Kleinman, and other investigators about mechanisms of memory compared them either to a neural switchboard making connections throughout the brain or to a statistical, geometric arrangement of stimuli in various areas of the brain with consid-

erable overlapping. None of the experiments shed much light
upon the basic characteristics of attention, expectancy, and understanding. Many psychologists adhered to the psychoanalytical
hypotheses of Freud and his disciples, who discovered a great
deal about submerged or repressed mechanisms of learning and
behavior.

FREUD ET AL.

In *The Interpretation of Dreams* (1900), a basic document of
the psychoanalytic movement, Freud defined dreams as highly
organized activities of imagination, and as mental functions that
construct meaningful images representing the individual's past
life situations and experiences, unconscious conflicts, emotions,
and problems of adjustment. He held that unpleasant experiences and unacceptable ideas or actions are repressed or forgotten, submerged in the unconscious mind and often reactivated in
the form of dreams. Information about the individual's dreams is
derived from his oral reports of dreamed events, which he remembers and reveals either under hypnosis or during conscious
recall.

For Freud and his associates, it seemed clear that the descrip-
tive theories and experiments of the behaviorists dealt with
merely superficial overt, observable reactions instead of the fundamental psychosexual forces persisting as submerged roots of
maladjustment or readjustment. According to Freud, dreams
condense, simplify, and distort events of past experience to conceal guilt feelings and unacceptable thoughts and to fulfill infantile wishes. A neurotic person may be able to relieve severe psychological tensions by revealing the contents of his dreams,
bringing to the surface and gaining insight into repressed impulses, unpleasant memories or ideas, and inner conflicts.

Freud's view of forgetting, sleep, imagination, and dreams
emphasized libidinal psychosexual forces of the unconscious
mind, not the exclusively physiological mechanisms of Pavlov
that stimulate or inhibit behavior. (Sexual reactions, in Freud's
theory, however, do involve purposes, ideas, cognition, and imagination as well as inherited instincts and physiological struc-

tures and processes.) Sleep, said Freud, makes possible dreams that relieve somewhat the impact of anxieties, disturbing memories, or painful experiences and contribute to powers of self-assertion and ego fulfillment. He noted that in severe neurosis temporary amnesia may result from the inability to withstand the stress of remembering adversity.

From his interpretations of the dreams reported by patients, Freud derived clues to the existence and probable contents of their unconscious minds. But his famous associate in Vienna, Alfred Adler, rejected Freud's conclusion that dreams function usually as a means of satisfying forbidden impulses. Adler asserted that dreams serve chiefly as trial balloons or proposed solutions that the individual formulates in imagination, strategies that might help him to cope with difficult or critical life situations.

Beginning during the 1950s and continuing at a steadily increasing rate during the 1960s and 1970s, psychologists conducted hundreds of experimental investigations into the conditions and characteristics of animal sleep, human sleep, and human dreams. In 1957 N. Kleitman and W. C. Dement reported on their use of electroencephalograms (records of electrical brain waves) to measure the structure of sleep and trace the relationship between rapid eye movements (REM) during sleep and concomitant dream activity. They devised a scoring system to measure sleep patterns related to rapid eye movements and dreams. Numerous investigators plotted stages and schedules of sleep. During the 1970s, studies by R. Greenberg and C. Pearlman supported Freud's assertion that dreams often help the individual reduce the level of his anxieties and adjust to stressful life situations. From their laboratory experiments in 1975, I. Lewin and H. Glaubman concluded that, compared with other types of sleep, highly active sleep involving rapid eye movements is more beneficial to subsequent intellectual creativity and performance.

Hundreds of researchers have explored the effects of chemicals and drugs, such as serotonin, vasopressin, strychnine sulfate, and LSD, upon animal and human sleep, sleep deprivation, and functions and disturbances of perception, memory, and sleep.

Repeatedly there were indications consistent with or supportive of the Freudian hypotheses concerning the therapeutic values of sleep and dreams. It should be noted that Freud himself predicted that progress in the sciences of biology and chemistry as related to neurological and psychosexual processes would eventually illuminate these aspects of human experience and help to alleviate or cope with sources of unhappiness. Recently, R. Ursin, H. Zepelin, A. Rechtschaffen, E. S. Tauber, and other experimental psychologists explored the sleep activities and patterns of animals with indications that these phenomena are species-related, supporting to some extent Freud's theory that instinctive inherited evolutionary structures and forces have shaped and controlled major aspects of memory, sleep, imagination, dreams, and overt behavior.

The existentialist psychoanalytical theorists Jean-Paul Sartre and Rollo May, though critical of Freud's approach in some respects, nevertheless agreed with his optimistic prediction that man will be able to acquire sufficient self-knowledge to choose freely and control efficiently his own total life experience. It must be admitted, however, that despite the numerous experimental (mainly behavioristic) recent investigations into phenomena of memory, imagination, and dreams, the basic problems about their genesis and interrelationships as well as their psychological functions and their effects upon overt organic behavior remain to be solved.

9 LEARNING AND REASONING

The Greek philosophers in ancient times expounded a new point of view concerning education and knowledge, a new approach that laid the foundations for the intellectual, cultural, and social achievements of the modern world. Their teachings marked a turning point in the history of mankind, the beginnings of a method of learning and system of thought that today dominate the institutions and enterprises of Western civilization.

SOCRATES, PLATO, ARISTOTLE

Socrates (470?–399 B.C.) held that through careful reasoning individuals could correct incorrect ideas about man and nature, and achieve self-knowledge, self-discipline, and universal truths. For Plato, loyal disciple of Socrates, universal truths constitute the sole reality, the real world in contrast to the unreality of material things. Ideas, recollected from past experience, associated, and organized as indestructible mental and spiritual functions, arise from unconscious depths of the immortal soul and reveal to the mind truths about the self and the universe. (Socrates and Plato rejected the doctrine of the Sophist philosopher Protagoras of Abdera that truth is relative, that the individual is the measure of all things; for if Protagoras were right, knowledge would be impossible since any belief would then be as valid as a contradictory belief.)

Aristotle, who had been for twenty years a student in Plato's Academy, taught that learning through communication of ideas is most useful and adequate if applied to concrete objects and specific facts. They constitute the indispensable ground for discovery of truth and achievement of the highest good, the rational life of the mind. Aristotle described two forms of reasoning: (1) deduction from general ideas to particular facts; and (2) induction from particular facts to general ideas. Both forms of reasoning are valid, essential means to discover realities of experience and nature. His analysis of logic (the science that he founded and called *analytics*) delineated principles of correct reasoning to eliminate fallacies or contradictions and to discover and verify truths.

Plato and Aristotle agreed upon the importance of the association of ideas and the role of individual differences in learning, reasoning, and behavior. But only Aristotle, regarding universal truths as inseparable from individual objects and events, advocated scientific observation, experimentation, and induction as the primary bases for learning specific facts as well as general principles or laws of nature.

To Plato and Aristotle may be traced the roots of virtually all the major approaches and even many of the basic theories of the various schools of psychology concerning education. They discussed with amazing discernment such things as the association of ideas; innate powers; perception, cognition, opinion, imagination, belief, generalization, introspection, and self-knowledge; motivation, sublimation, and catharsis; physical structures and functions; emotions; memory, dreams, and the unconscious; habits and repetition; human relationships and social communication; work experience and duties of men and women; aesthetic and ethical goals and experiences; personality, free will, and self-discipline; mental health and adjustment—the entire panorama of themes and theses emphasized in present-day educational literature.

CICERO, LUCRETIUS, QUINTILIAN

Although they admired Greek thought and culture, Roman philosophers and educators were less profound and less speculative than the Greeks, more interested in everyday problems and immediate tasks. Cicero in the first century B.C. advocated Aristotle's doctrine of moderation, the golden mean, in education and human relationships. He wrote eloquently about self-discipline, careful reasoning about all points of view, and candid but prudent oral communication as standards of learning and civic enterprises. At the same time, the Epicurean philosopher Lucretius declared that learning and knowledge are based upon sensory perceptions as sources of information about man and nature. He believed the universe to be entirely materialistic, a reality consisting of indestructible atoms finite in quantity and energy. He urged men to use their powers of reasoning, to achieve not a Platonic ideal or life of contemplation but immediate pleasures and happiness. In *The Education of an Orator* (about A.D. 88), Quintilian advocated theories of learning that have been implemented in many schools today. For example, he asserted that educational methods should emphasize logical reasoning from premises to conclusions, emulation of ideal personalities, systematic repetition and recall of facts, mastery of subject matter from simple to complex elements, rewards such as praise for intellectual achievements, practice in free self-expression, and adaptation of instruction to the interests and differing capacities of pupils.

CHRISTIAN CHURCH LEADERS

Some early leaders of the Christian Church (Plantaenus, Clement, and Origen) admired Plato's views, but others (Tertullian, Saint Jerome, and Saint Augustine of Numidia) gave up their early devotion to classical Greek learning and subordinated intellectual conclusions to religious faith. Augustine adhered to Plato's use of introspection to describe inner mental experiences, asserted that the teacher can only stimulate the learner to search out truths already existing in the mind, and formulated the theory of separate mental faculties (such as memory, will, and imagination) in control of the learning process.

Throughout the Middle Ages, the Church faced the task of reconciling Aristotelian ideas about the primary value of logic for the study of man and nature with the Augustinian belief in pure faith. Saint Thomas Aquinas solved this problem by accepting Aristotle as the final authority concerning logical thinking and natural laws, but held that faith goes beyond reason in arriving at ultimate truths.

HUMANISTS

Petrarch (1304–1374), the leading humanist of the early Renaissance, condemned Scholasticism and rejected Aristotle. He insisted that individuals should be free to form their own beliefs with the help of ancient Greek and Roman teachings and works of literature that would actually strengthen Christian faith. Other European scholars and humanist educators shared Petrarch's admiration of Greek classical works and belief in individual freedom. Among them were Boccaccio, Filelfo (who taught that girls as well as boys could learn the classics), and Pico della Mirandola in Italy; Villon, Lefèvre d'Étaples, and Budaeus in France; Groote, Agricola, and Erasmus in Germany; and Colet (founder of Saint Paul's School), Sir Thomas More, Sir Thomas Elyot, and Roger Ascham in England. Vittorino da Feltre in a famous "court school" at Mantua, Italy, and the humanist scholar Guarino da Verona in a similar school at Ferrara, Italy, implemented many of Quintilian's ideas concerning the psychology of learning. A comparable but more narrowly humanist school organized by Johannes Sturm (1507–1589) in Germany placed greater emphasis on formal methods of learning—drill work and practice, examinations to measure achievement, immediate correction of errors, and classification of pupils on the basis of age and academic progress.

LOYOLA, MULCASTER, BACON, LOCKE

The Spanish educator Ignatius Loyola, founder of the Jesuit order in 1540, insisted upon rigid disciplinary teaching, drill, and especially memorization of theological doctrines, but he also included formalized study of classical languages and literature, history, mathematics, rhetoric, logic, philosophy, mathematics, and science. His Jesuit secondary schools employed (and still employ to this day) the same methods of systematic repetition and practice, examinations, and closely supervised drill work being used at that time in the secondary schools (the *Gymnasia*) of Germany, which implemented the pedagogical ideas advocated by Johannes Sturm.

Richard Mulcaster (1530–1611), headmaster of the famous Merchant Taylors' School in London, adhered to earlier humanist views and implemented educational policies altogether different from those of the Jesuit schools. Mulcaster advocated that instruction be adapted to the interests and mental abilities of pupils, that universal education be provided for girls as well as for boys, and that the study of specialized subjects be restricted to pupils adequately prepared to master them (a principle similar to laws of readiness and success formulated by twentieth-century psychologists).

In England, too, Francis Bacon urged that learning could be advanced only through inductive study of nature by means of sense experience and observation, collection of facts, and careful experimentation to test the validity of conclusions. In his antipathy to the deductive method of reasoning, however, Bacon went so far as to discourage reliance upon mathematics, and he condemned the reasonable hypotheses of Copernicus, Galileo, and Harvey that were later verified by observations and experiments. Bacon wrote eloquently about the value of reading and literature to broaden the intellectual horizons of learners and familiarize them with possible truths anticipated by great thinkers in their literary works.

Bacon's emphasis on observation, experience, and induction had considerable influence on the contemporary educator Wolfgang Ratke in Germany, who in turn influenced the great Moravian bishop and educator John Amos Comenius. Thus pedagogical ideas about the value of teaching useful information, nature study, and graded materials adapted to pupils's interests and capacities, and encouraging self-direction in learning, were widely disseminated. In England, John Milton (1608–1674) adopted views similar to Bacon's about the usefulness of reading and literature. Unlike Bacon, however, he valued mathematics and deductive logic as part of a broad, practical curriculum.

Among leading British associationists, John Locke contributed most to psychological theories of learning and reasoning. According to Locke, a child at birth has no ideas but thereafter gradually develops them through experience. The mind of the neonate is like a blank tablet upon which impressions are made that eventually enable the individual to interpret and compare perceptions, the raw materials of thought. (Other philosophers, such as Descartes and Leibniz, assumed that a person could never begin to understand truths of mathematics or logical reasoning without the assistance of innate ideas.) Locke held that learning depends upon sensory experience and the association of ideas; the learner needs practice in correct reasoning and in comparing and evaluating ideas in order to develop his faculties, skills, interests, and behavior. Even laws of logic and principles of morality are not inborn; they are learned from experience and serve as the basis for knowledge about real objects in the universe.

Locke's theory of learning as a process of discovering connections among sensations, memories, and ideas (similar to Platonic and Aristotelian statements about the association of ideas as the key elements in memory) became a fundamental doctrine of early twentieth-century behavioristic psychology. Behaviorist and functionalist psychologists agreed with his thesis that experience in the form of reactions to stimuli—that is, constant physical and mental activity—is the foundation of learning, growth, and development.

Rousseau, Pestalozzi, and Froebel were among the great educators who adhered to Locke's concept of learning through purposive, enjoyable activities; contacts with nature; life experience; pursuit of individual interests; habits of careful observation and reasoning; progress from simple, concrete ideas to more complex, abstract ideas; and adaptation of teaching to the capacities and emotional and social needs of children.

Herbart constructed a formal scheme of instruction based upon Locke's association of ideas as a twofold method of learning: (1) absorption of new ideas; (2) assimilation of new ideas through recall of past ideas from unconscious levels of the mind and reflection about their similarity or dissimilarity. However, he rejected the concept of innate, separate mental faculties, asserting that the mind functions as a unified, single entity. Herbart's reference to integrated associative learning anticipated in some respects Freud's conclusions about the unconscious, Thorndike's principle of readiness for learning, and Pavlov's theories of conditioning.

WUNDT, JUDD, JAMES, McDOUGALL

Wundt at the University of Leipzig wrote in 1903 that thinking of any kind requires mental symbols, including language symbols. He held that speech grew out of gesture and other bodily movements during the evolution of mankind, being used at a very early stage to express ideas as well as feelings. Man gradually broadened his mental powers, especially the power to form abstract ideas, with the aid of language and communication. An abstract idea, said Wundt, is a composite resulting from numerous simple ideas, memories, and images and unified by a central meaning applied to a life situation.

C. H. Judd, who studied with Wundt in Leipzig, then taught at New York University (1898–1901) and at the University of Chicago (1909–1938), held that generalization in learning and reasoning is achieved by noting similarities among ideas or situations, eliminating irrelevancies, and constructing logical conclusions from valid premises. Any sound, relevant generalization can be applied as needed to a variety of problems and learning tasks. Most types of learning depend upon social communication, whereby the individual ascertains that society expects him to acquire specific skills, knowledge, and behavior patterns. Stimuli, sensations, and perceptions are tools that enable the learner to solve immediate problems and develop general principles transferable to future life situations. It is therefore necessary to teach children to think abstractly and correctly through guided self-activity.

Numerous investigators supported Judd's point of view about the transfer of training; for example, in the 1950s and 1960s, experiments by I. Maltzman, H. R. Entwisle, W. H. Huggins, and others showed that learning which emphasizes generalizations is superior to learning restricted mainly to disconnected facts.

William James asserted that persistent effort to accomplish a purpose as well as intrinsic interest in an activity are necessary for optimum learning—that is, the formation of habits of thought and behavior that can be utilized throughout the individual's lifetime. Ideas, images, and purposes have an impact upon neural connections, muscle movements, and reaction patterns of the learner. The mind works as an integrated composite so that the individual who concentrates on a definite purpose can most often overcome obstacles and succeed in his educational and vocational career.

William McDougall emphasized the role of purposive activity in the learning process. He cited, for example, experiments showing that, despite the potency for insects of instinctive patterns, certain wasps learn from experience and try out new methods of feeding their young when the experimenter blocks their customary rigid methods. Organic purposive action involves an awareness of a whole situation. But it is not any Gestalt mental configuration, nor mechanistic conditioned reactions, but rather a process of trial-and-error learning from experience that brings optimum growth and individual and social progress.

THORNDIKE

E. L. Thorndike achieved fame for his experimental studies of animal and human learning, beginning at Harvard University in James's laboratory during the late 1890s and thereafter continuing at Columbia University for several decades. He held the rank of professor of educational psychology at Teachers College of Columbia University for forty-five years (1904–1949), inspiring thousands of students who disseminated his findings and views widely in American and foreign schools, colleges, and universities. He contributed significantly to major fields of experimental and educational psychology, including individual differences, tests and measurements, animal learning and behavior, learning among children and adults, transfer of training, fatigue, memory, heredity and instincts, habit formation, and psychology of the gifted.

For his animal experiments, Thorndike used mazes and puzzle boxes containing obstacles that chicks, dogs, and cats learned to manipulate correctly in order to obtain food. In this trial-and-error process, the animals began with random reactions, soon learned to give up futile responses, and repeated successful reactions (recalled from past similar situations) until they could easily and promptly reach the food. Thorndike recorded the time devoted to trials and the number of successful and unsuccessful efforts, and constructed learning curves showing rates and trends of learning graphically. He observed that the rate of learning varies with different species, individual animals, tasks, and conditions. Although rates of learning tended often to be more rapid at the start, then to become slower, in other cases the learning process was slow at first, then more rapid, and finally slow again. Periods of little or no progress were shown as plateaus in the learning curves.

Similar experiments were performed by N. Harter and W. L. Bryan with students learning codes for telegraphic messages, and by E. J. Swift, J. H. Bair, and W. F. Book with individuals learning to typewrite. Their experiments indicated that learning generally takes place in lower and higher stages of difficulty and is subject to plateaus in difficult stages, to loss of interest, and to monotony, requiring new approaches or intensified efforts. In learning familiar types of material, students tend to begin quite rapidly, then progress more slowly, whereas in learning unfamiliar kinds of material, they tend to begin slowly, then increase their rate, and finally slow down again. Thorndike attributed diminishing rates not mainly to mental fatigue but to boredom. Inadequate stimulation and lack of motivation reduce learning efficiency to a much greater extent than do common adverse conditions of learning. Rates of learning motor skills are limited mainly by physiological capacities, while rates of learning academic subject matter depend mainly upon innate mental ability.

Experiments by Thorndike's student Tsuru Arai (1912), by Isaac Emery Ash (1914), and by Hugo Münsterberg (1916) indicated that, although attitudes, motivation, and intense effort help to counteract boredom and subjective mental fatigue, continuous learning of a task eventually slows down and ceases because of the need for rest, diversion, or sleep. Kraepelin had attributed reduced efficiency in learning and work performance not only to boredom, poor attitudes, organic defects, and personality maladjustments, but also to excessively long rest periods that diminish inertia and momentum. Pillsbury and Titchener reported that, just as physical fatigue slows work performance, mental fatigue retards learning, reduces attention, impairs discrimination, inhibits new ideas and self-direction, increases the number of mistakes made, and induces lassitude or discomfort.

Commenting on the transfer of knowledge gained from learning one task to the learning of another, Thorndike declared that transfer depends upon identical elements in both tasks. Thus a learner studying a foreign language is helped when he encounters many words very similar to those he has already learned in his native or another language. Identical elements in such words affect his attitudes, stimulating self-confidence and progress. Experiments by L. J. Postman in 1962 and by others showed also that the study of materials altogether unfamiliar or very different from previous information tends to interfere with new learning and results in negative transfer.

Thorndike urged teachers to evaluate all major conditions of learning before reinforcing any of them, and to encourage pupils to make their own plans for satisfying activities. Such advice is often difficult for teachers to implement, as indicated during the 1970s by the researches of P. V. Gump, R. G. Barker, R. Ross, R. E. Traub, and others who attempted to evaluate the effects of open or flexible classrooms. Despite numerous analyses of unpartitioned space, informal settings and projects, noise, crowding, privacy, small schools, large schools, segregated and desegregated groupings, public and private, religious and secular environments and the like, findings were often inconclusive due to the complexity of human relationships, wide variations in instructional equipment and programs, pupils' diverse and unknown past experiences, and interests and attitudes of teachers and parents. Many psychological effects of these factors upon the learner remained largely unexplored or controversial.

Thorndike accepted James's assumption that neural connections and conduction constitute the physical mechanism of learning and habit formation. He elaborated on this view in formulating his own theory of stimulus-response bonds to explain the nature of learning. He held that the formation and modification of neural paths of conduction account for the learner's abstract ideas and generalizations as well as his specific reactions to stimuli. In 1913 he postulated his own laws of readiness, exercise, and effect, which he applied to trial-and-error learning.

The law of readiness states that the learner progresses in learning when his neural connections favor it and he can therefore act so as to achieve a feeling of satisfaction or self-expression, whereas not to act would prevent new connections and cause annoyance or displeasure. This principle is rather similar to Herbart's theory of the apperceptive mass as preparation for learning, and also to theories of McDougall and Woodworth about purposes, interests, drives, and mind-sets as essential conditions of efficient learning. Thorndike asserted that the better prepared an individual becomes to learn correctly, the greater will be the likelihood of satisfaction and success.

The law of exercise (or use and disuse) extended James's theory that learning results mainly from purposive activity. Thorndike's law states that if a response to a stimulus (or situation) is repeated often enough, repetition will strengthen neural connections and the bond between them. Conversely, lack of repetition during a given time period will tend to weaken neural connections and the bond. Thorndike revised his original law of exercise to take into account the criticism that in some instances practice may be useless or worse in the absence of understanding or insight. He concluded, however, that repetition is generally helpful provided that the materials and data being repeated belong together and the learner perceives the meaningful relationships involved in them.

Thorndike's law of effect states that a response that gives the learner satisfaction strengthens the neural bond between the stimulus and the response, but dissatisfaction or an unpleasant result tends to weaken the connection. He eventually modified this law because of his realization that annoying results and the learner's need to correct serious mistakes do not always retard but in fact often improve learning. He concluded that learning depends not only upon satisfying results of effort but also upon a factor of belongingness in materials being learned, a factor regarded by many psychologists as too obscure to explain why learners frequently learn best from their most distasteful or painful experiences.

Thorndike formulated the following five supplementary laws of learning. (1) The law of multiple reactions states that the learner must weigh and consider which of several possible responses to a situation is likely to be most successful and satisfying. (2) The law of mental set or attitude states that the learner's situation, interest, and enthusiastic effort affect the amount of voluntary practice, the strength of new neural connections, and learning progress. (3) The law of partial activity states that learning involves discrimination among diverse approaches to a problem and choice of the most promising one. (4) The law of analogy states that the individual learns by comparing past and present problems and applying similar responses to similar problems. (5) Finally, the law of associative shifting states that the learner can associate any reaction to a stimulus with any other stimulus affecting him; in this way information, ideas, or skills previously learned in one situation can be used again in coping with other situations.

PAVLOV, WATSON, SKINNER

Pavlov's classical theory of conditioning emphasized physical stimuli and reactions to them as the basis for learning. For Pavlov, learning meant that a specific natural physical stimulus had become associated with a new artificial physical stimulus. In simultaneous conditioning, artificial and natural stimuli appear together, while in delayed conditioning, the natural stimulus follows shortly after the artificial one. In his classical experiments, the relationship between the natural stimulus (the sight of meat) and the artificial stimulus (the sound of a bell) had to be understood by the animals, but no assumptions were required about their inner psychic attitudes. (Although Thorndike's law of associative shifting stated a central theme in Pavlov's theories—that what has been learned in one situation is remembered and then used effectively in another situation—Thorndike felt that Pavlov had neglected vital factors of meaning and insight involved in slowly working, gradual processes of memory, forgetting and learning.)

John B. Watson was influenced mainly by Pavlov's experiments on conditioning, Jacques Loeb's physiological studies of behavior (elucidated at the University of Chicago), and Thorndike's connectionist ideas. Although he respected some of Thorndike's reservations about Pavlov's theories, Watson adhered firmly to an extreme behaviorist position, attributing not only the learning of information and skills but also every other aspect of behavior to conditioning of physiological reactions. He rejected introspectional research, psychoanalysis, Gestaltist concepts regarding insight, and functionalist doctrines based upon the innate tendencies or dispositions enumerated by James and McDougall. He declared, citing among other evidence his Baltimore hospital observations of infants, that from the earliest moments of life the child acquires patterns of feeling, thought, and behavior through intraorganic stimulation and contacts, the mother's voice and various auditory, tactile, visual, and olfactory stimuli. Thus he gradually learns about the external world through his own observable physiological responses to physical events, objects, and forces. Despite his advocacy of thoroughly mechanistic techniques and concepts, however, Watson held that the individual always reacts to the environment as an integrated, unified organism.

At Harvard University, B. F. Skinner in his early experiments with rodents utilized boxes containing food trays, depression levers, flashing lights, and release keys, equipment arranged so that the animals could learn to manipulate objects in order to obtain food. For experiments on the conditioning of infants, he constructed an enclosed crib that provided a wholesome environment in which the infant, unhampered by excessive clothing or restraints, spent much of his time. The air crib facilitated the application of stimuli and positive reinforcing rewards under controlled conditions. It was used effectively (in Skinner's family and other households) to help children form desirable behavior patterns and excel in learning achievements.

Skinners's theory of operant (or instrumental) conditioning stated that the individual's reactions to his own activity reinforce his purposive voluntary responses and even his accidental responses. The reward earned and its satisfying effects, including knowledge of results, are the operant forces that elicit and reinforce activity. Thus food obtained and accompanying satisfaction reinforce further actions performed to obtain nourishment. If the results of the individual's activity are not satisfying to him, the activity will not serve as a reinforcer and will therefore not be repeated. (E. R. Guthrie at the University of Washington pointed out that reinforcement works because the satisfied learner, having succeeded, no longer needs to search for competing or alternative methods of getting his reward.)

Describing the characteristics of operant conditioning, Skinner noted that an initially neutral stimulus may be paired repeatedly with a reinforcing stimulus and thus itself become a reinforcer. A positive reinforcer, such as a reward or knowledge of success, elicits the desired response, while a negative reinforcer, such as punishment or awareness of failure, tends to negate the response. Similarly, verbal communication (praise or blame) may provide positive or negative reinforcement. The precise effects of a positive or negative reinforcer, or of an overabundance of reinforcement, vary with individuals. A reward serves most effectively as a positive reinforcer if it follows immediately after the response being reinforced. Continuous reinforcement tends to be effective more promptly than intermittent or interrupted reinforcement, but is more subject to eventual extinction. If reinforcements repeatedly applied as rewards fail to elicit precisely the desired response, they will in such cases often result in a response approximating the desired response. An entire series of reactions may be elicited by one positive reinforcer or even by a single accidental reinforcer. Reinforcers may be applied either in accordance with a fixed ratio or irregularly, or they may be scheduled on the basis of the average number of repetitions regarded as necessary for adequate reinforcement of a desired response.

Autoinstruction with teaching machines exemplifies the value of self-knowledge and rewards in learning. About 1920 S. L.

Pressey of Ohio State University invented a teaching machine that accepted or rejected the learner's answers to questions arranged in a graded sequence. Similar devices were made available during the 1940s in the form of self-teaching or programmed textbooks. In the 1950s, Skinner devised a linear type of programmed material broken down into detailed units in an orderly sequence so that mastery of one unit leads to the next. The learner answers each question correctly before attempting the next question, thus obtaining knowledge of success as positive reinforcement and avoiding reinforcement of errors. In a branching system of programmed learning materials devised by N. A. Crowder during the 1960s, the learner answers multiple-choice questions in one frame (set of questions) correctly before attempting the next frame. If he answers any question incorrectly, however, he must study explanations in a preliminary frame before returning to answer the failed question again.

Used most frequently in vocational and commercial education, teaching machines and programmed textbooks have been praised for helping to adjust instruction to the needs of individual students. They have, however, been criticized for wasting time on teaching facts already known to the learner; for weakening his ability to plan, to create new ideas, and to make his own decisions; and for impeding his opportunity to choose and develop enthusiasm for selected aspects of a subject.

E. C. Tolman at the University of California asserted that both the overt reactions of the learner and his thinking (cognitive) process and expectations (recalled by him through introspection and revealed to observers) should be taken into account. At Harvard University, W. K. Estes, editor of a six-volume reference work on learning experiments, similarly emphasized the need for utilizing introspectional methods as well as behavioristic approaches in the study of learning and reasoning. At the University of California Ernest R. Hilgard, whose researches, articles, and textbooks were highly influential from the 1930s into the 1980s, applied an eclectic point of view to the problems of psychology. Hilgard's prefatory essay on consciousness in contemporary psychology (published in *Annual Reviews of Psychology,* 1980) reviewed brilliantly the basic behaviorist, functionalist, experimentalist, new introspectionist, and cognitive approaches of psychologists to the study of learning, motivation, growth, and personality.

The behaviorist theories of Watson and Skinner and the functionalist theories of John Dewey were widely accepted by educators during several decades prior to 1950. Thereafter, Gestaltist and cognitive theories about insight, including particularly Piaget's concepts, became highly influential in educational psychology. (Freudian psychoanalytic approaches continued to influence mainly the psychology of emotions, mental disturbances, and personality development.)

DEWEY

Beginning in the 1930s and 1940s, Dewey's philosophical and psychological theories had a profound effect upon pedagogical thought and practice in Western countries. In theories of Froebel, Montessori, and Dewey, sense experience and spontaneous activities are fundamental elements in learning and growth— mainly as symbols for Froebel, formal training materials for Montessori, and inseparable parts of a reflex arc or single unit of stimulus, response, and awareness for Dewey. Education, said Dewey, is a social function whereby individuals are not only trained by conditioned reflexes or automatic reactions to stimuli but also educated by activities and experiences from which they learn to understand meanings in language, objects, and events and to share efficiently in the common interests, practices, goals, and values of society. Educative experiences help the individual to solve problems arising out of natural or planned environments so that learning becomes a rational process for the continuous experimental reconstruction of shared experience. Reasoning, habit formation, and integrated psychophysical voluntary reactions of the whole person to whole situations characterize effective learning and constitute the most promising pragmatic method of solving increasingly complex problems. Teaching methods should guide the learner to apply inductive and deductive reasoning correctly in five steps to his recalled past and present experience so that (1) he becomes seriously interested in a problem or situation, (2) defines the difficulties and issues, (3) collects and arranges relevant information, (4) considers possible solutions, and (5) tests them in everyday living.

Dewey's five steps, emphasizing problem-solving and purposive activity, differed from the Herbartians' five steps for the mastery of ideas as such, but were similarly formal and theoretical despite Dewey's advocacy of spontaneous projects. He applied his concepts during a brief period of experimentation at the University of Chicago, but subsequently at Columbia University disseminated his pedagogic theories mainly through writings and lectures, even though he derogated traditional lecture methods as artificial and isolated from life experience. Proponents of the progressive-education movement applied Dewey's theories extensively and attempted to test them by results in school situations; but, notwithstanding some impressive successes, their findings were not convincing enough to disprove adverse conclusions. Idealist critics, among them Herman Harrel Horne of New York University, regarded inspiring teacher-pupil relationships, deductive reasoning, insight, and ideals as the most desirable ingredients of the learning process.

GESTALT PSYCHOLOGISTS

In 1912, the German Gestaltist pioneer Max Wertheimer, active in Frankfurt, Berlin, and New York City, published *Experimental Studies in Visual Perception of Movement,* an exposition of the Gestalt principle of integrated perception. The German psychologist Kurt Koffka, who worked in Frankfurt and in the 1930s at Smith College, rejected mechanistic stimulus-response theories and emphasized the role of discovery, imagination, and creative thinking in the learning process. The Estonian Wolfgang Köhler worked in Frankfurt, Berlin, Southeast Africa (where he carried on his famous experiments on the mentality of chimpanzees and apes), and at Swarthmore College, publishing *The Mentality of Apes* in 1925 and *Gestalt Psychology* in 1929.

Gestalt psychologists maintained that the learner responds to a whole situation (as Dewey had suggested), not merely to isolated or successively perceived parts. The parts are interrelated so that every part contributes to the organization and pattern of the learning situation. Configuration makes any complex problem, task, or material more than the sum of its parts. Every part depends upon the whole organized system as well as upon all the other parts for its own characteristics and functions.

Methods of learning in the fine arts of painting and music illustrate the educational implications of the Gestalt principle of pattern or organization. The student develops insight into the effects of each line or note upon the whole painting or composition to which it contributes. He plans, shapes, and introduces or modifies individual colors or phrases; he eliminates excessive or unsuitable elements; and he adjusts and tests his work as he notices its results, meanings, functions, and purposes in relation to the production as a whole. Thus self-criticism, self-direction, and effective self-expression become basic factors of self-instruction. Changing perceptions of his creative work as a whole motivate him to continue efforts and to gain new insights and skills.

PIAGET

In Switzerland, where he was professor of science at the University of Geneva and director of the Jean Jacques Rousseau Institute, Piaget, who was active in research until his death in 1980, delineated his views concerning the learning and reasoning processes in numerous publications, including *The Language and Thought of the Child* (English translation, 1926); *The Child's Development of Intelligence* (1936); *The Psychology of Intelligence* (1947); and *The Early Growth of Logic in the Child* (with B. Inhelder, 1964).

Piaget analyzed the reciprocal functions of perception and reasoning as intertwined activities responsible for the child's slowly growing concepts and powers to cope with the environment. Intellectual development, he said, involves the feedback effects of emotions, attitudes, sensory perceptions, thinking, motives, and actions. The child, even when apparently imitating others, learns by interpreting and applying his own new perceptions, nonverbal and verbal thoughts, insights, feelings, and reactions. He thereby corrects and improves his interpretations of space, time, number, and cause-effect relationships. Learning is a process of assimilation and continuous intellectual development through satisfying self-direction, action, and conceptual growth based upon consequences of experience. Thus the learner builds a lasting intellectual system of knowledge, ideas, judgments, and logical thought, achieving not merely behavior patterns but also productive cognitive attitudes and mastery of permanent meaningful concepts.

Researches during the 1960s and 1970s to refine or extend some of Piaget's conclusions were reported by S. Glucksberg, H. Beilin, M. Shatz, and others concerning children's cognitive growth in speech and communication, and by R. Gelman, P. E. Bryant, J. Baron, C. J. Brainerd, L. Siegel, B. Schaeffer, P. H. Miller, T. Trabasso, and others concerning children's development of number concepts, inferences, memory, and spatial relationships. Many of these researches corroborated Piaget's findings about the limited range and depth of cognitive reactions among preschool children and the very gradual development of their logical thought processes. In the Sapir-Whorf theory of language and reality, Edward Sapir and Benjamin L. Whorf emphasized the central role of language in guiding children to form and refine their logical thinking and interpretation of the environment, for language and communication shape thought itself and thus control the child's understanding of reality.

10 PERSONALITY AND CHARACTER

Research findings and concepts on personality and character have been developed by sociologists, philosophers, theologians, educators, and psychologists. These groups are often in agreement on basic matters but differ in emphasis on various factors. Psychologists, for example, emphasize the physical and mental patterns of individuals; sociologists emphasize the role of social institutions, social interaction, collective behavior, and group relationships.

Psychologists define *personality* as the sum total of one's integrated traits and reaction tendencies, a composite of characteristics expressed in habits, attitudes, ideas, motives, and behavior patterns. Observable personality traits reflect the individual's distinctive ways of relating to the social environment and differentiate him from others.

Character refers to those qualities of personality that account for the individual's significant purposes and conduct. What he says and does in life situations reveals inner motives, inhibitions, attitudes, and principles, which may be consistent with or contrary to moral values widely accepted in the community. Character develops and changes as the result of interpersonal relationships and other experience.

HIPPOCRATES, PLATO, ARISTOTLE, THEOPHRASTUS

Popular modern ideas about personality and character can be traced as far back as Hippocrates and other great thinkers of ancient times. It will be recalled that Hippocrates in expounding a theory of four temperaments (phlegmatic, sanguine, melancholic, and choleric) attributed these to the dominance of phlegm, blood, black bile, or yellow bile in the human body. Galen supplemented the Hippocratic theory, increasing the number of temperaments from four to nine and relating them to conditions of cold and humidity. These views dominated medical science until they were negated by the researches of Albrecht von Haller and other physiologists in the eighteenth century. Nevertheless, the hypothesis of causal relationship between physical factors and psychological dispositions has found support in genetic researches associating genes and chromosomes with personality traits, and also in biological, endocrinological, and experimental psychological investigations of the nervous system and organic behavior. The problem of determining precise relationships among physical qualities and personality traits remains largely unsolved.

Plato formulated concepts of personality that in some respects resemble those of twentieth-century psychoanalysts. His assumption of an inner driving force, *eros*, foreshadowed the Freudian postulate of libidinal and ego impulses. Plato classified motivating drives and personality traits into a threefold hierarchy of appetitive impulses, spirited impulses, and rational impulses, all of which he held should be directed toward the good, the wise, and the beautiful. Individuals differ in the degree and rate of progress from the lowest appetitive to the highest rational impulses. Plato agreed with Socrates that all aspects of personality involve cognition and are subject to control by ideas, knowledge, and logical reasoning. He accepted the Socratic doctrine that anyone who knows what is really good will do it, that the normal mind can master and direct voluntary actions.

While not rejecting the Platonic view of knowledge as a decisive influence, Aristotle gave equal prominence to concrete experiences, physical factors, habits, emotions such as love and hate, and unreasoning desires, impulses, and ambitions. Evil is not a necessary part of reality but indicates only the individual's failure, often because of physiological deficiencies or acquired distortions of character, to practice the highest standards of rational conduct. Ideals and eternal truths exist inseparably from concrete things and practical experience. Just as nature functions to

produce unconscious results, individuals can act to fulfill unconscious motives. Furthermore, the body, especially the condition
of the blood, affects the individual's emotions and personality.

According to Aristotle, good character is developed through
good deeds in the same way that builders develop skill through
experience in building, but with the difference that what a man
does will reflect good character only if he means to do good regardless of the consequences and puts his purpose into practice
in the right ways at the right times. Right actions are moderate,
rational actions that avoid evil impulses promising extreme pleasures. Aristotle deplored the fact that individuals tend to take
credit for good conduct but to avoid responsibility for miscon-
duct. The ideal character is one that impels man to act with true
courage for a noble purpose, with temperance, fairness and justice, good taste, respect for truth, self-restraint, and self-respect.

The Greek philosopher Theophrastus was a student of Aristotle, whom he succeeded as head of the Academy in Athens. He
wrote thirty unique sketches describing the personalities of
Athenians, such types as flatterers, grumblers, skeptics, fools,
gossips, boasters, garrulous fellows and others having character
flaws. He was puzzled by the wide range of individual differences in personality among Athenians who had nearly identical
social and educational backgrounds. But instead of theorizing as
Plato and Aristotle had done, he merely described in detail the
mannerisms and behavior of typical characters, setting a precedent followed by essayists throughout medieval and modern
times. His character writing was emulated, for example by John
Hall (*Characterismes of Vertues and Vices,* 1608); Sir Thomas
Overbury *(Characters,* 1614); John Earle (*Microcosmographie,*
1628); and Samuel Butler (*Characters,* 1667–1669). The French
moral philosopher Jean de La Bruyère (1645–1696) wrote
many similar character sketches portraying introverts, extroverts, and other personality types. Masterpieces of world literature from Chaucer and Shakespeare to the present have applied
the same approach effectively, though more indirectly, to illuminate universal personality types and common traits of human
character.

BACON, LOCKE, ROUSSEAU, FOURIER, OWEN, KANT

In ancient Rome, Cicero, admiring Platonic and Aristotelian views, held that the ideal personality reflects qualities of moderation, friendliness, self-discipline, prudence, tolerance, generosity, and integrity; mankind is unique in prizing such qualities while sharing lower instincts with brutish animals. According to the foremost Roman educator, Quintilian, good character is developed through emulation of admirable personalities and guided formation of desirable habits, producing qualities of modesty, self-restraint, integrity, and respect for others. Saint Augustine in the fourth century, pioneering in the use of introspection, reported on his own experiences and sins of his youth. Evil character can be reformed, he said, only through confession, knowledge of truth, and conversion to Christianity.

Little progress was made in the investigation of personality during medieval and early modern times. The philosophers Moses Maimonides in the twelfth century and Saint Thomas Aquinas in the thirteenth century adhered to theories of Hippocrates and Aristotle, supplementing them with their own interpretations of relevant biblical doctrines. For Maimonides, the desire to do good reflected a higher moral character than the mere desire to inhibit one's evil impulses. For Aquinas as for Maimonides, good character meant a way of life guided by principles of justice, temperance, courage, prudence, kindness, and obedience to divine law.

Francis Bacon, the apostle of inductive scientific method, rejected Platonic and Aristotelian abstractions and suggested that the facts of personality and character should be collected and summarized by observers so as to disclose the causes and consequences of good and evil traits. Bacon's descriptions and theories about character were, however, based upon his reading of history and literature and his everyday unverified impressions, not upon scientific methods. He described human types as basically either honorable or deceptive, humorous or solemn, narrow-minded or magnanimous, prudent or bold. He attributed personality traits to a complex of physical factors (sex, age, beauty, and health), social status, accidents of birth, conditions of wealth or poverty, and specific life experiences. He pointed out that many people have a tendency to compensate for their shortcomings, weaknesses, or even deformities by ignoring them, by pretending superiority, by minimizing the importance of deficiencies, or by citing the same undesirable traits in others.

Locke, while noting in his *Some Thoughts Concerning Education* (1693) the importance of a healthy physical constitution, advocated training of children through reasonable, moderate discipline, good models to emulate, praise and approval of ethical conduct, and gradually enlarged opportunities for free activities, including enjoyable reading and study. According to Locke, children can readily be trained to form habits and qualities of diligence, prudence, tact, and consideration for others, provided only that parents and tutors carefully observe their behavior and then provide them with adequate guidance. The nineteenth-century German psychologist Herbart (rejecting Locke's view of the mind as a composite of separate powers or faculties, such as memory, perception, and reasoning) contended that systematic study of social sciences and literature would foster ethical character.

Rousseau in his classic on education, *Émile* (1762), agreed with Locke about the development of personality and character through free activities and respect for individual differences. But he rejected the idea of disciplining children, maintaining that they should be allowed to follow their natural interests, learning from experience and the consequences of their decisions and behavior. Thus they will learn to accept parental authority as a natural state of affairs. Rousseau denied the assertion of Hobbes that human beings are innately aggressive, corrupt, and greedy. Children, in Rousseau's view, are born good, capable of sympathetic feelings toward others. Through self-expression and free choice of activities, they will develop fine, outgoing personalities as well as high moral character and achieve Locke's ideal of a sound mind in a sound body.

Modern pragmatist psychologists, such as William James, concluded that every child should be persuaded to form desirable interests, attitudes, and habits that adults have found necessary for successful everyday living. Habits provide stability in personality; and desirable, efficient habits of thinking, willing, and acting should be encouraged and guided so that they will become permanent traits of character.

The utopian socialist French reformer Charles Fourier (1772–1837) agreed with Rousseau that social institutions have corrupted human nature. He maintained that natural innate impulses should be encouraged and sustained by a new society providing freedom and justice so that people having differing personalities will live together in harmony and happiness. Fourier described and classified hundreds of character traits representing distinct types. At about the same time, the British socialist reformer Robert Owen advocated a similar planned transformation of society. Owen held that the individual is born neither good nor bad, that moral standards and behavior are molded by the social environment, and that new cooperative economic, political, and educational institutions would produce a healthy, virtuous, enlightened, prosperous, and happy society. Although a number of cooperative communities were established along lines advocated by Fourier and Owen, none succeeded in its primary goals. Nevertheless, socialist theories about the impact of institutions and competitive behavior upon character attracted wide attention among educators and social psychologists.

Despite numerous research studies during recent decades to evaluate the effects of competition and cooperation upon personality, character, and achievement, the findings and conclusions remain in dispute among psychologists. In the 1970s, for example, investigations into school programs by D. W. Johnson, R. T. Johnson, and others found individualistic competitive programs to be more successful than cooperative programs. Studies of pupils' performance by G. W. Lucker, D. Rosenfield, and J. Sikes attributed a slight advantage to cooperative group programs of learning. Evaluative reports of such factors by G. J. Coles and A. B. Chalupsky indicated little difference in achievement. In 1979 S. B. Crockenberg reported that, compared with individualistic competitive methods, cooperative learning tends to produce greater conformity of individuals to the group.

MÜLLER, HENLE, MEUMANN, FOUILLÉE

The nineteenth-century German psychologists Johannes Müller, Friedrich Henle, and Ernst Meumann developed rather similar analyses of physiological factors affecting personality traits. Müller emphasized the effects of balance among sensory impressions, motor responses, and psychosexual impulses of reproduction as determinants of dominant phlegmatic, sanguine, choleric, or melancholy dispositions. These temperaments, he said, reflect the individual's weakness or strength in emotional and purposive reactions. Henle pointed out that ideas and reasoning often stimulate inner feelings and motor responses, but that introverted and extroverted temperaments and vigor of behavior depend upon the sensitivity of the nervous system. Meumann similarly postulated that the physical elements and structures of the nervous system affect the strength of inner feelings and motor reactions, reflecting the persistence of the will, the decisiveness of attitudes, and the stable or erratic moods of individuals.

The French philosopher and educator Alfred Jules Émile Fouillée (1838–1912) formulated a theory that physiological mechanisms determine personality. Later he modified this theory by his idealist concept that the mind creates ideas and goals that act upon passive matter to control sense impressions and physical reactions. In the natural world, he declared, human thought, aims, and character are unique elements. He classified personality traits into three types according to the relative intensity of the individual's willpower, sensitivity, and mental power.

JOHN STUART MILL, BAIN, McDOUGALL

John Stuart Mill denied the possibility of ever obtaining experimental or other scientific knowledge about the roots of personality and character. Nevertheless, he suggested that it might be useful if theories about personality were subjected to the test of common experience and also to careful observations and judgments by competent and objective psychologists. Mill defended the liberty of each person to act as he wishes, subject only to the right of others not to be harmed by his acts.

Mill's friend and associate Alexander Bain at Aberdeen University expounded a hypothesis that physiological structures in the brain and connecting motor mechanisms account for the development of individual differences in personality, but he later agreed with Mill that scientific investigations could never fully explain human willpower, emotions, ideas, and purposive actions.

William McDougall in his *Introduction to Social Psychology* (1908) identified fourteen instincts that enable individuals to control or modify acquired qualities of personality and character. He classified human purposes into two types: self-regarding (or self-satisfying) and self-denying (or inhibiting) sentiments. Self-regarding sentiments included pride and self-assertion stimulated by praise and respect from others. Self-denying sentiments often develop from rejection and blame. Moral attributes can be brought under a person's control if he will apply his ideals so as to make them and expression of them habitual in relation to other people despite possible adverse consequences. McDougall noted further that the effect of a personality trait, such as prolonged anxiety or self-confidence, varies greatly depending upon the individual's intensity of feeling, his conative persistence in expression and action, and his sensitivity to consequences. Abraham A. Roback, McDougall's assistant at Harvard University, condemned Watsonian behaviorist ideas as excessively mechanistic, and Freudian and neo-Freudian psychoanalytic analyses as unverifiable assumptions of causal relationships between sexual or excretory functions and the development of character.

STERN, SCHELER

William Stern, the German pioneer in the psychology of individual differences, expressed views consistent with McDougall's hormic psychology. From 1934 to 1938 (the year when both men died), he served with McDougall on the faculty of Duke University. Stern agreed with McDougall's classification of personality into self-regarding and self-denying types. He noted that individuals differ in their application of these types of reactions to others; that each individual experiences an inner conflict between the two types; and that this conflict may cause or intensify physical and mental disturbances.

The views of Max Scheler (1874–1928) exemplified how philosophers of various schools analyze personality and character on the basis of their own metaphysical doctrines. For Scheler, pleasure, beauty, truth, goodness, nobility, and holiness exist as real things known intuitively and directly by the individual. Every person's character changes as a result of experience, but he remains essentially and permanently the same integrated self who recognizes and knows truth, beauty, and goodness even though his reasoning cannot satisfactorily explain them. Ideally, the individual feels intuitively that his love and sympathy for others is a source not of weakness but of strength. Scheler accepted the Freudian hypothesis that man shares with other animals certain low instincts as the foundation of higher aspects and values of human nature.

JAMES

William James at Harvard University in the 1890s held that each person's philosophy, emotions, and sympathies depend for development and expression upon structures and connections in his nervous system and also upon practical activity and learning from experience. The personality and character of individuals can best be judged by analyzing effects of this mixture of physical and social elements, especially the extent to which they have become sympathetic and tender-minded or aggressive and tough-minded persons. Sympathy exemplifies some natural characteristics common to man and certain other animals. Just as a mother cares for her child, so a dog will often come to the aid of a child or another dog in time of illness or danger. Aggressiveness, too, is a natural tendency in animals, frequently essential to self-preservation.

Human beings are sufficiently flexible in nature, said James, that they can learn to control in some degree their undesirable or excessive tendencies or impulses. In fact, some people have developed the noble quality of loving their enemies. Manifestations of an admirable personality trait or quality of character can become habitual through positive experience and repeated activity; in turn, habits strengthen the particular trait or quality. Even mannerisms, intellectual attitudes, and modes of speech and behavior may become habitual enough to reinforce desirable personality characteristics, such as self-confidence, self-control, and self-direction, in contrast to inconsistency, daydreaming, and self-indulgence. Bad habits form a bad personality; good habits form a good personality. James agreed with Alexander Bain that ideas, knowledge of facts, and self-knowledge enable the individual to improve his habits, personality, and character, provided he possesses enough initiative to do what is right, and enough persistence to hold steadfast to his right actions without exceptions. At the City College of New York, the personality psychologist Gardner Murphy, elaborating on this concept, asserted that desirable personality traits depend upon the biological equipment, habits, and social experiences, especially in intimate family relationships, of the individual.

LOMBROSO, KRETSCHMER, SHELDON

During the 1830s, the German physiologists Friedrich Eduard Beneke and Carl Gustav Carus classified individuals into constitutional types, such as the long-legged type with thin blood vessels and small heart and liver and the short-legged type with thicker blood vessels and large heart and liver. The Italian criminologist Cesare Lombroso went a step further and offered quite dubious evidence for his conclusion that inherited physical, neural, and mental abnormalities are the primary causes of a criminal personality. He claimed that criminal types could be identified through their unusual physical characteristics or stigmata—that is, partially atavistic defects representing primitive stages of human evolution, as, for example, crooked noses, slanted eyes, and misshapen ears. When one of Lombroso's students reported that a majority of noncriminals in a typical mixed group exhibited the stigmata, Lombroso claimed that all such individuals would eventually be found to be criminals.

He formulated an equally unproved hypothesis that men of genius tend to be immoral or mentally abnormal. Some twentieth-century psychoanalysts, observing that often the genius is indeed egocentric, withdrawn, and unorthodox, ascribed these personality traits to repressed, sublimated sexual impulses. Most psychologists today suggest that the special attributes of geniuses are the results of hereditary abilities and favorable internal and external environmental influences during infancy and maturation.

The German psychiatrist Ernst Kretschmer classified mentally ill patients into three body types: (1) the *pyknic,* with a plump, short-limbed, stocky, rounded physique; (2) the *asthenic,* with a thin, long-limbed, underdeveloped physique; and (3) the *athletic,* with a muscular, sturdy physique. (He also found a number of individuals in a special *dysplastic* fourth group possessing undersized bodies with some very small parts.) Later Kretschmer observed numerous normal as well as abnormal people and classified them according to body types. He concluded that pyknics are extroverts exhibiting volatile moods and emotions, and also that the mentally ill among them tend to be manic-depressives. Schizophrenia was most common among asthenic patients, paranoia among athletics. Kretschmer classified the general population into (1) the introspective, mild, quiet, serious-minded type, the schizothymes, and (2) the lively, enthusiastic, energetic type, the cyclothymes, to which most pyknics belong. There seemed to be some validity in his classification of mentally ill patients, but his method of grouping the entire population was never widely endorsed by psychologists although his schizothymes and cyclothymes appeared similar to the introverts and extroverts postulated by Jung. Jung's theory was based, however, not upon physical measurements but upon the inward and outward direction of psychosexual energy. (Jung eventually realized that introvert and extrovert tendencies coexist and the individual is an ambivert who usually tends more in one direction than the other but may from time to time shift between them.)

The American psychologist William H. Sheldon, reporting on

his analysis of several thousands of photographs of young adults during the 1930s, concluded that the individual's body type (somatotype) is determined by the dominance in his physique of one of the following three kinds of structural forms: (1) endomorphy, characterized by various rounded soft parts and fleshy digestive tissue that have developed from the endoderm in the embryo and indicate a relaxed, cheerful, submissive, luxury-loving temperament; (2) mesomorphy, in which strong muscles, bones, and connective tissues are most prominent, features associated with endurance and an aggressive personality; and (3) ectomorphy, marked by a large brain area; long, fragile bones; and elongated skin and vessels in the central nervous system, structures derived from the embryonic ectoderm and indicative of a serious, sensitive, reserved character. Later Sheldon speculated that the individual's internal chemical environment affects his personality type and character, and further that sexual differences determine the intensity of certain expressions of personality in men and women.

Investigations into the disintegration of personality among addicts (whose drug habits are often attributable to preexisting personality maladjustments) tend to reinforce Sheldon's theory about the drastic influence of the internal chemical environment on the individual. Research studies by leading psychologists and psychiatrists (Carl Ransom Rogers, Adolf Meyer, and others) have pointed to other factors, especially cognitive self-concepts and interactions between the person and his social environment, as decisive influences upon personality.

JAENSCH, SPRANGER, G. W. ALLPORT, GOLDSTEIN

During the 1920s, the German psychologist Erich Rudolf Jaensch and his colleagues at Marburg University investigated the extremely vivid (eidetic) memory images of many children. Some of the children possessed B-type vivid imagery that reproduced the original objects at any desired time as if they were perfect photographic replicas. Other children possessed T-type, mainly uncontrollable, hit-or-miss vivid imagery similarly far superior to ordinary memory images. Both for children and for adults, Jaensch attributed introspectional supersensitivity, strong, inflexible character, and artistic interests to the B-type and a more flexible, outgoing, volatile personality to the T-type children. Eidetic imagery appeared to weaken beginning at about fourteen years of age. Jaensch suggested that chemical secretions of endocrine glands may account for individual differences in eidetic imagery and related personality traits. This hypothesis seemed borne out to some extent by physiological data: For example, underproduction of hormones by the thyroid gland may cause sluggish temperament, while overproduction may result in irritability and nervousness. Nevertheless, no causal relationships among physical abnormalities, eidetic imagery, and personality traits have been definitely established.

Eduard Spranger, another renowned German psychologist and a contemporary of Jaensch, expounded a broader view of personality. He classified individuals on the basis of their ethical beliefs and philosophy of life. According to Spranger, the kinds of things a person most prizes determine which of six types he belongs to: (1) theoretical-minded; (2) economic-minded; (3) religious-minded; (4) aesthetic-minded; (5) social-minded; and (6) political-minded. These types are not mutually exclusive, but the individual tends to attach most importance to some one of them and to keep the other kinds of values subordinate to it. One's dominant type of personality is therefore a matter of degree of interest and motivation. The individual who usually places the greatest value on material possessions and economic success, for instance, may also pursue artistic, political, or other interests, but his economic motives will remain paramount and dominate his personality.

At Harvard University, G. W. Allport discerned considerable merit in the concepts of Jaensch and Spranger. His experiments verified Jaensch's reports concerning eidetic imagery, but he found no evidence of a causal relationship to personality traits. Allport listed on a psychographic chart fourteen qualities of personality related to physique, mental ability, emotional reactions and moods, introversion, extroversion, aggressiveness, submissiveness, self-understanding, self-confidence, socialized behavior, and social intelligence and participation. He maintained that the seeds of every personality are formed during infancy out of the turmoil of experience and training, but that they can be made to develop in any of several directions. The resulting personality traits will always depend upon a person's comulative life experience as he gradually achieves full independence—freedom to follow either an old or an entirely new path toward self-realization. Home and family, sexual factors, culture and learning, and dynamic activities of adjustment to stresses and life situations all have an influence on the individual's prime values and goals. His overall personality is a composite of the fourteen basic qualities, including social, ethical, religious, and aesthetic values, goals, and attitudes, each measurable on Allport's rating scale of 1 to 100 points.

In opposition to McDougall's thesis that instincts are rigidly fixed, and also to the Freudians' emphasis on libidinal drives, Allport held that the individual modifies his basic goals, interests, and values, thus repeatedly achieving a new balance in qualities of personality. Although the psychologist can use the fourteen traits as a convenient reference, conclusions must be tentative, since the influence of each trait will vary with the life situation, behavior pattern, and human relationships prevailing at any one time. An individual may thus, for example, become aggressive on one occasion, but submissive on another, and either quality may become more or less consistently characteristic of him. Although he may sometimes rationalize his motives or deceive himself about them, he will usually reveal them in responding to the psychologist's direct questions, and his responses deserve full credence unless there is definite reason to distrust them.

From a similar point of view, the German psychiatrist Kurt Goldstein (1878–1965) emphasized the fact that, whereas psychologists can identify and measure some of the physical and chemical factors affecting personality development, they can actually investigate very few reactions and behavior patterns, a tiny fraction of an individual's complex experiences. Each person acts continuously as an integrated self with a past and present background of interrelated attitudes, purposes, emotions, and thoughts. A dominant need of the normal individual is to sustain desirable, moderate tension and healthful activity as he copes with changing impulses, conflicts, problems, and environments in order to achieve self-realization, satisfactions, fulfillment. Ideals and abstract thinking are essential dynamic elements in the normal person, directing or modifying his purposes, attitudes, temperament, habits, and other aspects of personality.

Goldstein pointed out that, in some cases of brain injury, patients lose much of their ability to think abstractly, to form generalizations about specific information, problems, or tasks. They become entirely absorbed in efforts to avoid stress and tension. Owing to the feedback of experience and continuous purposive striving, the human personality involves much more than any conceivable, measurable combination of physical and chemical elements. There are really no separate drives, just as there are no separate faculties, but only tendencies of the individual single, unified organism to act in useful ways in order to fulfill his purposes. The individual chooses his purposes, on some occasions even ignoring urgent physical needs for the sake of some activity he considers more important for his self-realization.

BEHAVIORISTS

The behaviorist view, based upon Pavlov's concept of conditioning and represented most effectively in the early writings of Watson and Skinner, attributed the development of the individual's personality and character mainly to his overt behavior, including automatic responses and purposive activities. As early as the 1890s, William James noted, for example, that people who make a habit of drinking and always find excuses for it become alcoholics, incurable unless they admit their addiction and act to eliminate it. John Dewey pointed out that the formation of specific habits involves intellectual functions of memory, imagination, and reasoning. These inseparable ingredients of overt behavior cooperate in shaping character, human nature, and standards of conduct. The French psychologist Bernard Pérez classified personality traits on the basis of physical movements, characterizing individuals as slow, intense, volatile, and the like. Soon thereafter, Pavlov's investigations of conditioned reflexes paved the way for Watson's experiments with infants (see p. 53) and his conclusion that enduring qualities of personality and character are cumulative results of conditioning as individuals react to environmental stimuli throughout their life-span.

PSYCHOANALYSTS

Freud described personality as the composite result of activity by three forces: (1) libidinal psychic energy or the id, which functions to satisfy instinctive needs and aggressive impulses; (2) the conscious self, the ego, which develops through sequential stages of human growth and learns to act as a control to inhibit extreme or antisocial tendencies and to hold libidinal energy in abeyance (submerged in the unconscious mind) when necessary to achieve ultimate satisfactions; and (3) the superego or conscience, developed through social experience and education, which attempts to adjust behavior of the ego to standards and expectations of the community. Freud was never able to explain to his own satisfaction the origins of psychic energy, or *eros,* but he speculated that evolutionary processes, such as Darwinian natural selection, produced biological alterations in bodily structures and modifications in sexual instincts and reactions. He noted that biological changes so far known do not account for the transmission of culture, logical thought, language, art, poetry, and ideals to succeeding generations.

Freud was convinced, however, that personality traits and ethical values are rooted in the very early experiences of the infant, especially in erotic and excretory functions and inhibitions. The libidinal energies of the child from birth to four or five years of age, expressed during the oral, anal, and phallic stages of maturation, produce the Oedipus complex of boys (libidinally related to mothers) and the Electra complex of girls (libidinally attached to fathers). According to Freud, the child thereafter minimizes sexual drives until adolescence, when such impulses are awakened from the unconscious realm and usually directed toward individuals of the opposite sex in accordance with society's expectations. The individual's character is gradually modified by early inhibitions, guilt feelings, persistent repressions of wishes,

especially sexual desires, and inner conflicts arising from unconscious life and death instincts, causing him to reinforce personality traits of various kinds.

A number of Freud's disciples and other psychoanalysts and
psychiatrists, while endorsing his general point of view, attributed personality development to divergent forces: (1) Alfred Adler
to feelings of inferiority and superiority, social restraints, and
the struggle of the ego to compensate for personal weaknesses
through aggressive behavior—factors often causing reactions of
doubt, uncertainty, withdrawal, or anxiety; (2) Carl Gustav
Jung to introvert, extrovert, or ambivert reactions (to environmental conditions, sensory experience, and life situations), intel-
lectualization of behavior, perfectionist fantasies and dreams, or
extreme attempts to obtain immediate gratifications; (3) Otto
Rank to the drastic birth experience and abrupt separation of
the infant from his mother's protective womb, eventually producing overdependence, feelings of inadequacy, and perhaps
greedy, parasitic, or ingratiating qualities; (4) Karl Abraham to
erotic and other biological experiences of infants, but also to racial, social, and economic forces affecting personality traits; (5)
Otto Fenichel mainly to anxieties created by stressful life situations; (6) Erich Fromm, Karen Horney, and Harry Stack Sullivan to social, cultural, and interpersonal influences; and (7)
Theodor Reik to extrasensory perceptions in the vestigial unconscious depths of the mind, narcissistic tendencies, and the influence of respected adult models.

EXISTENTIALISTS

The Danish philosopher Sören Kierkegaard (1813–1855) believed that personality and character develop from inner feelings,
strivings, perceptions, and conflicting relationships to nature, to
other people, and to the unique self. Each individual passes
through three stages of experience: (1) a pleasure-seeking or,
alternatively, an intellectualist aesthetic stage; (2) an ethical
stage of self-awareness and deliberate choice of obligations to
fulfill and ways to live, with hopes for the future despite anticipation of eventual, inevitable death; and (3) a religious stage,

during which the person becomes intuitively more conscious of his own existence as a continually changing self, loving, indifferent, cruel, or even hateful toward others, anxiously facing possible disappointment and annihilation, realizing his complete dependence on God.

The German philosopher Martin Heidegger, influenced by Kierkegaard's works, postulated four aspects of personality development; (1) concern about, and fear of, the world; (2) awareness of human mortality; (3) awareness of one's own immediate, continuing existence as a unique self; and (4) adjustment to inner conflicting moods while resolutely confronting the future. In another existentialist approach, the French atheistic philosopher Jean-Paul Sartre (1905–1980) associated personality development mainly with relationships to other people as objects of perception. He insisted that every person must freely make his own life and should feel responsible only to himself for the consequences. Sartre, rejecting the Freudian idea of unconscious experience, expressed faith in intelligent self-direction and concluded that the fantasy of becoming an eternal absolute reality is only the self-delusion of a lonely soul yearning for a nonexistent God. Man can only create more order in the things and experiences he possesses or uses that become part of himself.

For many psychologists and psychiatrists, there seemed some truth in the existentialist reference to human personality as a disorderly world of inner conflicting forces, doubts, and contradictions pervading the individual's thoughts about, and attitudes toward, the self and relationships to fellow human beings. Psychiatrists have found therapeutic value in a patient's achievement of insight into his own nature and the realities of nature and society.

PILLSBURY

At the University of Michigan, Walter B. Pillsbury commented on the following techniques and tests used in the investigation of personality and character: (1) questionnaires in which the individual's answers to printed questions reveal some of his beliefs, behavior patterns, ethical standards, and social attitudes, the resuits of which are not absolute measurements but assessments varying with the group in which he is a member; (2) rating scales used by a group of experienced observers (or self-rating scales used by the person himself) to assess characteristics such as attitudes, honesty, interests, and the like; (3) a sampling of the individual's behavior in controlled situations, the method used by Hugh Hartshorne and Mark A. May in 1928 to measure certain qualities of character among schoolchildren (see p. 123); (4) specially designed clinical materials, such as Jung's word-association test, Rorschach inkblots, and photographs, which evoke reactions serving as clues to the individual's patterns of thinking, past experiences, and personality traits—Jung's test being less useful, according to Pillsbury, because of the conventional meanings attached to his stimulus words; and (5) interviews during which an examiner will ask standard questions or converse informally with the individual to identify his behavior patterns, habits, motives, beliefs, moods, and attitudes.

Pillsbury warned that personality tests should be evaluated carefully as to validity and reliability, that precautions should be taken to discourage the individual from innocently or deliberately giving false information, and that the scores should be interpreted with great care and only by trained psychologists. During the 1960s and 1970s, personality tests were severely criticized as subject to inadequacy in contents, to racial and other biases, and to misuse for unjustified stigmatization of individuals or minority groups. In 1974 the American Psychological Association published a list of standards for the construction and use of educational and psychological tests. N. D. Sundberg of the University of Oregon (in *Assessment of Persons,* 1977) and other leading personality psychologists during the 1970s emphasized the need for improvement of instruments, materials, techniques, and applications in this field.

Pillsbury classified the factors affecting the development of personality and character into three groups: (1) cultural factors, including educational institutions, natural environmental conditions, and the traditional beliefs and customs of the society; (2) hereditary and physiological factors (for example, functions of the endocrine, thyroid, pituitary, and adrenal glands); and (3) psychological factors proper, most particularly the habits and behavior patterns formed through reactions to stimuli, the processes of conditioning and cognition. The relative importance and roles of the individual's inner psychic forces and his lifelong reactions to environmental influences became the subject of spirited debate in recent decades, especially in the 1970s, among American personality psychologists, such as N. S. Endler, D. Magnusson, and C. J. Krauskopf, without, however, achieving any definite resolution of the issues.

11 MENTAL ILLNESS

The psychology of abnormal behavior explores the nature, causes, diagnosis, and treatment of irrational reaction patterns of individuals, devoting special attention to severe emotional and mental disturbances, deficiencies, and diseases. Psychological abnormalities range in severity from temporary psychoneurotic disorders and adverse psychosomatic conditions to major organic or functional mental illnesses.

HIPPOCRATES, PLATO, ASCLEPIADES, CELSUS, ARETAEUS, GALEN

Little is definitely known about concepts of mental illness in ancient times. In Egypt and Babylonia as early as seven thousand years ago, the priests referred in their religious incantations to evil spirits as causes of insanity, and trephining may have been intended to drive evil spirits out of holes made in the skull. The Hebrews regarded insanity as divine punishment for transgressions and urged the afflicted to atone for sins. In India and China, physicians discussed symptoms of insanity and advocated humane treatment, including the establishment of special hospitals or regimens. Pythagoras about 500 B.C. attributed insanity to brain disturbances and prescribed the therapeutic use of massage, restricted diets, and recreation.

Hippocrates, with whom ancient Greek medical science reached its highest level about 400 B.C., attributed mental illnesses to specific organic causes, especially bile disorders affecting the temperaments. Carefully observing and recording the symptoms of depression, hysteria, and epilepsy, he concluded that hereditary factors predispose some individuals to develop these abnormal conditions. He prescribed baths, special diets, moderate exercise, massages, bleeding, and various drugs, including enemas and purgatives. These procedures, he asserted, would help nature to restore harmony among body fluids and thus ameliorate symptoms of mental disease. He predicted that the interpretation of dreams could shed light upon the roots and progress of many psychological ailments.

Plato agreed with his elder contemporary Hippocrates that mental diseases could be caused by physical factors, but he also believed in moral and divine causes. He held that the decisive factor producing a healthy personality was harmony in the rational, spirited, and appetitive forces of life energy, or *eros*. He noted that some persons become predominantly intellectual in outlook, others intensely practical and ambitious, and still others mainly sensualist in motives and behavior. The life of reason centers in the brain, but all parts of the body are interrelated and work together to maintain a wholesome personality. Individuals differ in mental capacities, intensity of spirit, and sensory reactions and feelings. Plato agreed with Hippocrates about the significance of dreams, which he attributed to attempts to compensate for unsatisfied desires of the waking state. He associated crime with mental instability and disturbances, as well as with adverse social and cultural forces. Plato's disciple Aristotle discussed psychological factors but concluded that only the physical factors cited by Hippocrates were primary causes of mental disorders.

The ancient Romans added little to Greek concepts of mental illness. Worthy of mention is Asclepiades (124–40 B.C.), who differentiated acute from chronic psychological ailments, noted the differences between hallucinations and delusions, condemned the use of bleeding and physical restraints, and advocated a pleasant therapeutic environment for the relief of tension in mental patients. Medical treatises by the celebrated Roman physician Aulus Cornelius Celsus (first century A.D.) described symptoms of brain injury, epilepsy, convulsions, mental confusion, and paralysis. The Greek physician Aretaeus of Cappadocia set forth the theory, shared by some modern psychologists, that abnormal personality traits are mainly exaggerations of normal traits. He speculated about a possible hereditary predisposition to develop abnormal patterns of behavior. Although he did not dispute the popular idea that the heart is the center of the soul, he held that malfunctions in the brain and in abdominal organs contribute to the onset of mental illness.

Galen, the influential Roman disciple of Hippocrates, combined data obtained through dissections of animals and inspections of parts (often accompanied by inaccurate analogies to human beings) with metaphysical and theological speculations so widely adopted by medieval peoples as to retard for centuries progress in the scientific study of abnormal behavior. Nevertheless, he identified many organs and functions of the nervous system and brain and described causes of mental illness, such as brain injuries, alcoholism, psychic disturbances of adolescence and the menopause, and emotional upsets resulting from frustrations of everyday living.

ALEXANDER OF TRALLES, AVICENNA, AVERRHOËS

The Greek physician Alexander of Tralles, practicing in Rome during the eighth century, referred to brain injuries as causes of mental disorders and to inflammation of the brain as the cause of delirium, but his medical treatises recommended fantastic remedies (for example, carving a picture of Hercules in action on a stone to be applied to patients).

Arabian and Iranian physicians in medieval times accepted Galen as their medical authority. The Arabian philosopher Avicenna (980–1037) wrote a medical treatise (*The Canon*) that was used as a basic textbook in European universities for more than five centuries. The Arabs practiced humane treatment of insane persons in special hospitals as early as the eighth century. They used sedatives such as hashish to calm mental patients. Philosophical and scientific medical works by the Cordovan philosopher Averrhoës (1126–1198), though condemned as heretical by Moslems, were endorsed by Albertus Magnus (1193–1280) and other medieval Scholastics despite their own firm opposition to scientific methods of research.

Throughout the Middle Ages, demonology and witchcraft were associated with mental illness. During the tenth to fifteenth centuries, a type of mass madness, a dancing mania, repeatedly afflicted large numbers of people in various German and Italian provinces. Possibly due to mass suggestion, their reactions consisted of wild dancing and contortions to the point of exhaustion. Many victims journeyed to chapels of Saint Vitus to be cured of their malady, hence the name Saint Vitus's dance. (There is no evidence that the epidemics were related to the neurological disease of the same name described by the English physician Thomas Sydenham in 1686.)

PARACELSUS, AGRIPPA, WEIER, SCOTT, SAINT VINCENT DE PAUL, SYDENHAM

Widespread ignorance among medieval peoples concerning mental disorders was reflected in the common belief in witchcraft, in the practice of flogging to cast out demons from the minds of the insane, and in therapeutic pilgrimages to religious shrines. Pope Innocent VIII approved a handbook published in 1484 that advocated torture and execution of "witches" (often these were persons who exhibited mental abnormalities).

In the seventeenth and eighteenth centuries, fantastic therapies were common: for example, dragging mental patients back and forth in cold water to calm their emotions. Customary beatings, purgations, and torture reflected the fear and horror experienced by most people in the presence of the retarded and the insane. The Napoleonic Code of 1804 merely implemented a generally accepted policy when it stipulated severe punishment of any person who allowed insane individuals to walk unchained in the streets. Even as late as the mid–nineteenth century, many hospitals for the insane in Belgium, France, Germany, England, and the United States restrained mental patients with chains, abused them violently, and deprived them of proper nutrition, medical attention, and suitable work or recreation.

In a few places during the fifteenth century, humane treatment had been introduced, as at the shrine of Saint Dymphna in Gheel, Belgium (in contrast to the typical inhumane practices in

the infamous Bedlam hospital of London). The refuge at Gheel
became a model for several other institutions devoted to sympathetic care of mental patients.

The sixteenth-century Swiss physician Paracelsus, at times
lecturing and practicing medicine in Basel, Strasbourg, and
Salzburg, was one of the most gifted and influential advocates of
humane treatment. Condemning the widespread belief that demons were the causes of insanity, he attributed mental illnesses
to inner psychic forces. These disturbances, he said, could often
be readjusted and healed by nature, but sometimes when the
patient's psychic forces became weak or fatigued they required
special chemical remedies. He subscribed to notions that magnets applied to the body would cure many diseases and that the
planets controlled organs and functions of the human body. He
prescribed metallic elements (such as antimony) as well as cam-
phor and an extract of opium, to which he gave the name lauda-
num. He used mercury in the treatment of syphilis. He also
concluded correctly that some diseases affecting mind and body,
such as syphilis, could be transmitted from the mother to the
fetus by blood circulation during conception and embryonic development. Paracelsus respected Hippocrates but rejected the
theory of unbalanced temperaments (recapitulated by Galen,
whose works he detested) as the cause of personality disorders.

Cornelius Heinrich Agrippa (Agrippa von Nettesheim, 1486–
1535), German soldier, theologian, magician, and physician, a
native of Cologne and a loyal Catholic, was another staunch advocate on behalf of mental patients. He served as secretary to
Maximilian I. Later, having become a public advocate in the
French town of Metz, he denounced the monks for their belief in
demons and defended a woman accused of witchcraft. His agitation against the persecution of mentally abnormal persons, his
appeal for a return to the kindly ideas of the early Church, and
his concept of a threefold spherical universe, contradicting traditional theological ideas about natural phenomena, aroused the
animosity of the Inquisition, but he gained the support of an
increasing number of adherents attracted by his courage and
ability.

One of Agrippa's students, the Belgian physician Johann

Weier, carried on the campaign against the belief in witchcraft and demons that was the main cause of inhumane treatment of the insane. Carefully observing his mental patients over long periods of time, Weier obtained significant information about symptoms and causes of their illnesses. His evidence and conclusions, published in 1563, aroused sympathetic interest on the Continent and justify his reputation as one of the founders of psychiatry.

In 1584 Reginald Scott, a British agriculturist, published a scientifically accurate volume, *Discovery of Witchcraft,* to refute the prevalent belief in witches and demons as supernatural forces responsible for the magical mental and physical powers and evil deeds of their victims. No less an opponent than King James I of England ordered Scott's book to be burned (a means of eliminating literary competition inasmuch as the king had in 1597 published his own volume, *Daemonologie,* demanding extreme repression and punishment of witches). In France, even the political philosopher Jean Bodin (1530–1596), who believed himself to be guided by one good demon and another evil demon, wrote a volume on the demonic work of sorcerers and insisted that suspected witches be burned at the stake.

Much more rational were the views of the French priest Saint Vincent de Paul (1581?–1660), who had been captured by pirates and worked for seven years as a galley slave until he converted his master and with him escaped. It is no wonder that he later sponsored the establishment of a hospital at Marseilles for galley slaves. He became a founder of the Lazarists, building hospital facilities at Saint Lazare to provide humane treatment of mental patients and others. Two centuries later, in many lands the hospitals of the Society of Saint Vincent de Paul (founded in 1853) implemented his conclusions that there is no essential difference between mental and physical diseases and that humane treatment should be provided for all patients alike.

The British neurologist Thomas Sydenham (1624–1689) adhered to the same professional attitude as Saint Vincent de Paul, devoting himself with equal dedication to the diagnosis and treatment of mental and physical illnesses. In 1682 he described the symptoms of the neurological disease Saint Vitus's dance

(Sydenham's chorea), an infectious disease comparable to rheumatic fever. Sydenham himself suffered from gout, and his experience helped him to develop a classic diagnosis and description of that disease. On the basis of numerous careful observations of patients, he agreed with Hippocrates that deep-seated chronic ailments are caused by maladjustments in body fluids, attributable to unhealthful dietary and other lifelong excesses. He concluded that acute ailments are caused by environmental forces, resistance to which creates inflammations and fevers. His rejection of traditional medical dogmas and procedures and his willingness to apply whatever therapy seemed promising justified his posthumous reputation as the British Hippocrates. (It is said that he might, for example, cure a hypochondriac patient who was extremely difficult to treat by sending him on a fool's errand that resulted in shock, anger, and then sudden, full recovery.)

TUKE, CONOLLY, PINEL, ESQUIROL, SEGUIN

In England witchcraft trials and penalties, never so extreme as in other countries, ended early in the eighteenth century. The British Quaker William Tuke (1732–1822) founded a retreat for mental patients at York and instituted a training program for its nurses. This center, under the benevolent management of the Society of Friends, set an example emulated by pioneers in many similar institutions. Tuke's grandson, Samuel Tuke (1784–1857), published a popular volume in 1813 describing the humane treatment used in the York retreat, and also a guidebook in 1815 on the construction and management of similar institutions.

The English physician John Conolly (1794–1866), a graduate in medicine at Edinburgh University, became a professor of medical practice at University College in London in 1828; later wrote a text on the diagnosis of mental illness *(Indications of Insanity)*; and soon thereafter founded with two colleagues a medical society for the improvement of medicine, which eventually became the British Medical Association. From 1839 to 1844, during his professional work as the resident physician in a large mental hospital outside London he carried out William

Tuke's principles of nonrestraint and humane treatment, but on a larger scale, spreading the new gospel throughout England and abroad. During his last decade, he maintained a private hospital where he continued to practice humane methods of therapy.

In 1792 (the year that William Tuke founded the center at York), the eminent Parisian physician Philippe Pinel similarly pioneered in the humane treatment of mental patients. Pinel graduated in medicine at the University of Toulouse in 1773. For many years thereafter he concentrated on translating and later writing medical treatises, inspired at first by work of the Italian physician Giorgio Baglivi, who taught that adverse conditions in the solid tissues and organs of the body cause mental disease. In 1791 Pinel wrote an influential volume concerning the treatment of mental abnormality. In 1792 he was appointed head physician at the Bicêtre mental hospital and in 1794 head physician at the Salpêtrière hospital, both in Paris, where he also continued to lecture and to write authoritative medical texts. He achieved world renown by immediately unchaining the mental patients in the two hospitals; maintaining detailed records and case histories of the inmates; providing them with clean housing, good food, and workshops; and insisting upon thorough training of staff attendants.

Jean Étienne Dominique Esquirol (1772–1840) of Toulouse studied under Pinel during the 1790s, later served as Pinel's assistant at the Salpêtrière hospital, and in 1811 was appointed resident physician, in which capacity he delivered lectures exposing inhumane practices in French mental hospitals. The campaigns of Pinel and Esquirol resulted in a government investigation and in gradual improvement of hospital environments. On the basis of observations and records of numerous patients, Esquirol had associated the disease of general paresis with syphilis, then a common affliction. He described symptoms such as progressive motor deterioration and paralysis, delusions, and loss of identity. (It was not until 1897 that the Austrian psychiatrist Richard von Krafft-Ebing, famed for his investigations of sexual aberrations, proved syphilis the cause of general paresis when he noticed that inoculating paretics with the spirochete *Treponema pallidum* responsible for syphilis produced no additional signs of it, indicating that the paretics already had syphilis.) In 1838 Esquirol published two volumes summarizing the medical, hygienic, and legal aspects of the principal mental illnesses.

The French physician Édouard Seguin (1812–1880) studied under Pinel's associate Itard, the famous teacher of Victor, the "Wild Boy of Aveyron." In 1837 Seguin, commencing a long-term service to retarded children, taught language skills with remarkable success to a mentally retarded boy. He instituted the systematic training of idiots in his own school in 1839, and soon thereafter in Paris hospitals. His program featured physical-education activities and practice in handling materials such as clay figures, scissors, pictures, and compasses to help the child develop coordination, agility, and motor skills. Seguin's methods of manual training were highly successful. In Paris, however, he encountered political difficulties when he advocated utopian socialist ideas. In 1848 he emigrated to the United States, where (in Massachusetts, Pennsylvania, and New York) he continued to promote and implement his system of manual instruction. He persuaded several state governments to establish schools for the feebleminded in which his physiological methods often enabled retarded children to become self-sustaining. He became well known among American teachers for the Seguin form-board performance test, which he constructed to measure the mental abilities of subnormal pupils.

MULLER, CHIARUGI, RUSH, BEERS

The views concerning mental illness of social reformers in England and France spread rapidly to other lands, in some instances reinforcing programs already in progress. In Germany, Anton Muller (1755–1827), employed at a well-known hospital for the insane, gained many supporters of humane treatment in such institutions, while in Italy, Vincenzo Chiarugi (1759–1827) carried on an effective campaign. In 1816 an experimental school for training feebleminded pupils was opened in Salzburg, Austria. Steady progress continued in Germany, and by 1867 special classes were being organized in many schools of German cities for the instruction of mental defectives.

In the United States, the celebrated Philadelphia physician, staunch abolitionist, and signer of the Declaration of Independence Benjamin Rush campaigned for basic reforms in hospital procedures even though he devised and often still used a confining chair to restrain mental patients. He wrote several medical works that advocated a rational, scientific approach to the diagnosis and treatment of mental illnesses. He campaigned for the removal of chains from the insane and for the establishment of specialized hospitals to care for them.

In 1841 the American philanthropist and prison reformer Dorothea Lynde Dix undertook investigations of conditions in Massachusetts poorhouses and asylums, which eventually resulted in the release of mental patients from jail, the condemnation of widespread abuses, and the establishment of numerous special institutions for the rational, humane treatment of the insane. Similar reforms were soon adopted not only in Massachusetts but also in nineteen other states, as well as in Newfoundland, Scotland, England, Austria, Belgium, and Japan. In 1846 the Utica, New York, State Hospital (then called the Utica State Lunatic Asylum) was the meeting place for a new association of administrators of mental hospitals, which later became the American Psychiatric Association, a prestigious and effective professional organization.

A series of events in the early 1900s, initially involving a single individual, gave impetus to practical reforms in the treatment of mental patients. Clifford Whittingham Beers (1876–1943), a Yale University graduate and New York City businessman, began to exhibit symptoms of severe mental disease. He was admitted to a sanatorium in which he received irrational, restrictive, ineffective treatment from incompetent attendants under oppressive conditions. Nevertheless, he recovered fully and in 1907 wrote the volume *A Mind That Found Itself,* published in more than twenty-four editions, exposing the inefficiency still prevailing in mental hospitals. His accurate, detailed, vivid account of his illness, treatment, and recovery brought home to millions of people that they themselves or their loved ones might under stress develop similar illnesses and suffer the same restraints, incompetence, and ordeals experienced by the author.

Beers became the foremost leader in this field and founded the mental-hygiene movement. He organized the Connecticut Society for Mental Hygiene in 1908, the National Committee for Mental Hygiene in 1909, the American Foundation for Mental Hygiene in 1930, and the International Foundation for Mental Hygiene in 1936. (In 1937 a book by an anonymous author entitled *Alcoholics Anonymous* resulted similarly in the formation of a cooperative movement by the same name, enabling alcoholics to obtain successful group psychotherapy.)

Many national and international organizations have been formed to disseminate information on mental health and hygiene, especially the causes and recognition of early symptoms of mental disorders, methods of prevention, and therapeutic programs. In the United States, more than 6 million people annually obtain psychiatric care in public or private hospitals and clinics, while many others consult physicians, psychologists, or psychiatrists in private offices, public or private nursing homes, or public rehabilitation centers. Still others in need of counseling or therapy avoid it owing to unawareness of their real condition, fear of the stigma often attached to mental illness, insufficient funds for private service, or lack of faith in the efficacy of available treatment.

MESMER, BRAID, CHARCOT, LIÉBEAULT, BERNHEIM, JANET

In 1774 the Austrian physician Franz Anton Mesmer successfully treated a patient suffering from hysteria by means of magnets applied to the patient's body, therapy Paracelsus had recommended in the sixteenth century. (Mesmer was a respected physician, an accomplished musician, a close friend of Leopold and Wolfgang Mozart.) Using the magnetic treatment, Mesmer restored to health hundreds of mental patients, including paralytics, and other physicians duplicated the method with the same results. Suddenly, however, Mesmer discovered that he could cure many patients by merely touching them or even by simply waving his hands in a dramatic manner. He concluded that some form of animal magnetism emanating from himself was responsible for his successes. His achievements aroused widespread interest but also skeptical opposition so that mesmerism became a lively controversial issue. Mesmer moved from Vienna to Paris, where for five years he used his method successfully, until in 1784 King Louis XVI ordered an investigation by a commission of eminent scientists, including Benjamin Franklin, then American ambassador to France. The commission reported on the basis of a few limited experiments that they could find no evidence of animal magnetism at work, that the effects sometimes observed must have resulted from the patients' imaginations, and that Mesmer's procedures were useless and possibly harmful.

Meanwhile in 1780, Mesmer's disciple the Marquis de Puységur had observed that during magnetic treatments some patients walked about aimlessly in a trancelike sleep but afterward were unable to recall this experience. Further observations disclosed that the magnetizer's suggestions during the period of artificial sleep could make patients lose the sense of pain, act as if paralyzed, experience hallucinations, answer difficult questions perfectly, or even understand instructions for their future behavior, which they would later carry out precisely when awake although they could not recall having received them. Eventually these reactions became known as phenomena of hypnotism and posthypnotic suggestion.

Mesmer left Paris in 1792, during the French Revolution, and shortly thereafter settled in Switzerland, where he practiced as an obscure physician. In 1812, three years before his death, he was consulted by scientists of the Berlin Academy who wished to honor him for his discovery of magnetic therapy. In 1830 the Parisian physician Alexandre Bertrand attributed magnetic influence to psychological suggestions affecting primarily the minds and indirectly the bodies of hypnotized patients. In 1831 the Academy of Medicine in Paris officially approved magnetic therapy, which then became a fad subject to gross abuses. Consequently, the procedure was again condemned by most of the medical profession. The distinguished British physician John Elliotson resigned from the faculty of London University in 1838 when he was attacked for teaching and practicing Mesmer's theories, but he continued to advocate mesmeric procedures. In 1843 he published a guide to painless surgery through the use of mesmerism. Although the technique remained in vogue for a time, it was later abandoned owing to the discovery of the anesthetics chloroform and ether.

During the 1840s, the Scottish surgeon James Braid reported on his experiments indicating that mesmeric influence is subjective in character and that during magnetic sleep patients are not unconscious but on the contrary are extremely sensitive to suggestions. In 1841 he named the process *neurohypnotism,* later shortened to *hypnotism.* The remarkable successes of Braid and other physicians in ameliorating symptoms of mental illness by means of hypnosis contrasted sharply with customary, largely futile methods of bleeding and purgation, and their accomplishments paved the way for the contributions of the leading French practitioners Charcot, Liébeault, Bernheim, and Janet, and the Austrian pioneer Sigmund Freud.

Jean Martin Charcot, the most influential nineteenth-century French neurologist, who was appointed professor of anatomy at the University of Paris in 1860 and organized the neurological clinic at the Salpêtrière mental hospital in 1862, conducted numerous studies of hysteria. He concluded that hypnosis must be closely related to hysteria because usually only those of his patients could readily be hypnotized who seemed liable to develop symptoms of hysteria, such as numbness or temporary loss of sensation in the skin of specific body areas, temporary blindness, partial paralysis, or inability to speak. He noted that symptoms of hysteria could be produced and also be eliminated in susceptible individuals by suggestion and hypnosis. He theorized that such persons were likely to develop hysteria because of inherited pathological conditions in the nervous system, although he did not altogether rule out secondary psychological factors, which often seemed to precede the manifestations of hysteria. He postulated three distinct stages of hypnosis: light drowsiness; a deeper stage of rigidity; and a final stage of dissociation with involuntary reactions. Despite his astonishing cures of hysterical patients and his great prestige, Charcot's assumption of a hereditary cause cast doubt upon the long-term efficacy of hypnotic therapy, since that procedure deals with symptoms rather than with inherited defects.

Physiologists—for example, R. Heidenhain at the University of Breslau, Germany—related hypnotic reactions to inhibiting effects upon the brain exerted by repetitive, monotonous sensory and motor experiences during hypnosis. More widely accepted were the views of physicians at the Nancy, France, school of psychiatry under the leadership of Ambroise Auguste Liébeault (1823–1904), who had applied hypnosis successfully for two decades to hysterical patients. His protégé Hippolyte-Marie Bernheim (1840–1919), wrote *Concerning Suggestion* (1889), which attributed hypnosis primarily to the power of verbal suggestion. Liébeault and Bernheim held that suggestion in hypnosis is deliberately planned and exaggerated but otherwise similar to ordinary verbal suggestion used as a means of persuasion in everyday living; also that individuals differ considerably in their susceptibility to any type of suggestion. Freud studied their views at Nancy in 1889 and endorsed them as one element later elaborated on in his system of psychoanalysis and psychotherapy.

Pierre Marie Félix Janet, Charcot's successor at the Salpêtrière hospital in Paris, carried on extensive studies of psychoneuroses, concentrating on the use of hypnosis to analyze hysteria. He believed that the disorder arose from a lack of sufficient nervous energy needed to achieve harmony, integration, and control in one's mental operations and experiences. The result was typically dissociation of ideas or personality accompanied by symptoms such as tics and episodic sleepwalking, paralysis, and amnesia. He noted the hysteric's common attitude of *belle indifference,* in which the patient, deeply disturbed by dissociation, seems to take the most severe problems for granted even while protesting that they are insufferable. Extremely neurotic patients are unable to appreciate and adjust to reality. Hysterics, he declared, quickly lose their social sentiments, moral standards, and altruistic tendencies as a consequence of their disorder. Suggestion and hypnosis help the patient to organize mental experiences, whereupon the restoration of integrated personality eliminates neurotic symptoms. According to Janet, the motives of hysterics are mainly unconscious. He assumed contributing physiological causes but was unable to describe the precise mechanisms whereby psychological factors produce the initial characteristic symptoms of neurosis.

Janet applied the procedure of posthypnotic suggestion, which had been described by the Marquis de Puységur. He identified the compulsive reactions of obsessional neurosis, *psychasthenia*, as a form of abulia (marked by defects of recognition and recurring fixed ideas) involving weakness or indecision of will. Such reactions are not modifiable by hypnosis, suggestion, or reasoning. He also identified another type of neurosis, *neurasthenia*, an anxiety reaction characterized by severe tension and fatigue, symptoms popularly referred to as a nervous breakdown. He believed that neuroses develop initially from degeneration in physical structures of the nervous system. This process eventually creates extreme psychological tension in the patient, who can make only weak, inadequate efforts to resolve his inner conflicts. Several decades after Janet's treatise on hysteria was published, the American medical psychologist Morton Prince applied the same ideas about personality dissociation to the diagnosis and treatment of patients exhibiting multiple personalities, a pathological dissociation sometimes revealed during the hypnotic trance.

VON HALLER, GRIESINGER, MEYNERT, MOREL, MAGNAN

The eighteenth-century Swiss anatomist Albrecht von Haller formulated a physiological explanation of mental illnesses. Citing evidence derived from extensive postmortem investigations, he attributed severe mental abnormalities to organic factors such as pathological brain conditions and neurological defects. This theory was restated in 1845 by William Griesinger (1817–1868) in his *Pathology and Therapy of Psychic Disorders*. The physiologist Theodor Hermann Meynert (1833–1892), well known for his studies at the Vienna Psychiatric Clinic on aphasia and other brain disorders, agreed that cortical brain diseases (then called mania and melancholia) affect blood vessels and neural structures, resulting in emotional disturbances accompanied by paranoid delusions and other abnormal reactions. The psychiatrist B. A. Morel (1809–1873) shared Charcot's theory that inherited neural defects cause serious mental abnormalities. In the 1890s, the psychiatrist Valentin Magnan (1835–1916) associated mental diseases such as paranoia with physical causes: for example, alcoholism, syphilitic infections, and childhood trauma. He grouped paranoid delusions (previously described by Griesinger and Meynert) into three stages: (1) the initial stage of acute, episodic delusions; (2) the more advanced stage of persisting persecutory delusions; and (3) the final stage of grandiose delusions and hallucinations. Most neurologists, adhering to organic theories, believed that malfunctions in the brain and nervous system, frequently induced by internal diseases, interfere with passage of neural impulses across synaptic junctions of nerves, thereby producing symptoms such as pain, dissociation, delusions, and abnormal behavior patterns.

KRAEPELIN, BLEULER, WAGNER-JAUREGG

In the late eighteenth century, on the basis of his careful analyses of patients and case histories in the two Parisian hospitals he headed, Pinel grouped mental diseases into three main classes: mania, melancholia, and dementia. (Mania, he said, was characterized by violent emotions and excitement; melancholia by deep depression; while dementia referred to a variety of other serious progressive organic psychoses.) A half-century later, Griesinger included many specific emotional and functional disturbances under the heading of mental illness, as, for example, hysteria. He believed that all forms of mental abnormality are basically similar, though they may differ in origin, development, severity, and consequences. Griesinger and Meynert described paranoia as a distinct mental disease involving emotional disturbances and persistent delusions, and in 1879 Richard von Krafft-Ebing applied the term *paranoia* to various types of delusional psychosis.

Finally, in an authoritative treatise on mental diseases published in 1883, the great German psychiatrist Emil Kraepelin, who followed Pinel's example of analyzing thousands of case histories, formulated a comprehensive classification of organic mental disorders, which he thereafter revised periodically; it was not superseded during his lifetime. He identified and described major psychoses, which he grouped into two divisions: (1) endogenous diseases arising internally (including dementia praecox, or "premature insanity" so called because of the mistaken assumption that its reactions usually begin with dysfunctions of sex glands during adolescence); and (2) exogenous diseases (for example, general paresis) arising from trauma, infections, or other external forces affecting the brain and nervous system as well as circulatory, digestive, and other organs. He delineated the symptoms of catatonia, a schizophrenic psychosis named and discussed by Karl Ludwig Kahlbaum in 1872, characterized especially by the patient's negative, hostile attitudes, mental rigidity, fantastic delusions, and stupor often followed by extended periods of extreme excitability. He elaborated on symptoms of hebephrenia (another form of schizophrenia), such as silly behavior, regression, and perfectionist attitudes along with unclean personal habits, delusions, and hallucinations.

In 1899 in his *Textbook of Psychiatry* (first published in 1893), Kraepelin revised his classifications to identify manic-depressive psychosis as a single mental illness; its symptoms had previously been associated with several forms of mania, melancholia, and circulating or alternating insanity. He believed that internally arising diseases are mainly the results of inherited organic defects and therefore largely incurable, whereas the manic-depressive disorder and other externally arising illnesses such as neuroses can often be ameliorated or even sometimes cured by means of appropriate treatment.

The Swiss psychiatrist Eugen Bleuler, author of *Dementia Praecox,* published in 1911, agreed with Kraepelin that dementia praecox results from functional organic maladjustments (probably dependent upon an internal toxic process). But he asserted that the disease arises long after adolescence, and he therefore changed its name to *schizophrenia,* a combination of two Greek terms for splitting of the mind. He found the main characteristic of this disease to be a lack of coordination and a lack of integration in the patient's feelings and ideas, a split between his intellectual processes and his emotional reactions or attitudes, which makes his ideas illogical and produces emotional outbursts. The patient's associations are fragmented to such an extent that he becomes uncertain or ambivalent about his flow of disconnected ideas and then suddenly abandons them altogether or seems incoherent and totally introverted. Bleuler also analyzed the process of disorientation in alcoholics, describing their familiar symptoms of instability; crude behavior; impulsiveness; and jealous, suspicious, aggressive, fluctuating thoughts, emotions, and attitudes. Noting episodes of withdrawal from reality among children as well as adults, he coined the term *autistic thinking* to denote a form of persistent infantile introversion, fantasy, and daydreaming.

Bleuler adhered to the theory that everything a person does in his thinking, feeling, and acting leaves a permanent trace in memory, subject to recall so that it may become a factor in subsequent association, dissociation, readjustment, or reintegration of thoughts, emotions, and personality. His view resembled in some respects the theory of Freudian psychoanalysts that cumulative dynamic repressed or submerged ideas and experiences stored in the unconscious mind but often capable of being resurrected can become effective factors in the genesis, development, diagnosis, and treatment of mental illness. He was more optimistic than Kraepelin about possible therapeutic measures, noting that quite a few schizophrenic patients improved and some fully recovered.

Bleuler's contemporary, Austrian psychiatrist Julius Wagner-Jauregg (1857–1940), contributed mainly to chemical methods of psychotherapy. In 1917 he treated a few syphilitic victims of general paresis successfully by inoculating them with malaria parasites so as to induce high fevers. For this achievement, later repeated for hundreds of patients, he was awarded the Nobel Prize in 1927. This chemical method and subsequent electrical and mechanical methods of inducing high fever were applied widely during the years before the development of penicillin and other antibiotics during the 1940s. (Wagner-Jauregg had pioneered also during the 1900s in the treatment of cretinism, a congenital condition that causes physical stunting and mental retardation, by administering thyroid extracts to provide the hormone thyroxine.)

The nineteenth-century British physician John Haydon Down was the first to describe Down's syndrome (previously called mongolism). This condition of extreme mental retardation has been associated since the 1950s with a chemical imbalance caused by there being three instead of the normal two chromosomes in pair 21 of each cell. Research during the 1970s indicated that about 20 to 25 percent of Down's syndrome cases are caused by defects in the father's chromosomes transmitted in his sperm.

Mental retardation may result from many causes besides glandular disturbances, as, for example, birth injuries, brain damage, or adverse environmental conditions, factors affecting the neonate's respiratory, motor, and neural systems. Even normal birth sometimes produces excessive nervous tensions in infants following separation from the maternal protective environment.

Bleuler's disagreement with Kraepelin about the inception of dementia praecox during adolescence was justified by subsequent clinical investigations and presaged the drastic changes soon to occur in abnormal psychology. Many new disagreements resulted in confusing attempts by psychiatrists to modify Kraepelin's classification system to take into account new evidence, theories, and therapies. In 1952 the official classification of the American Psychiatric Association grouped mental disorders into two broad divisions:

1. The simple, catatonic, hebephrenic, manic-depressive, and other schizophrenic reactions cited by Kraepelin as well as paranoid reactions were classified as *functional psychotic disorders* of psychogenic origin. These disorders were not attributed to structural changes since they could not be traced to definite impairment of brain tissues. This broad division of mental illnesses included *psychosomatic disorders* affecting organic autonomic and visceral body systems; *psychoneurotic disorders,* such as anxiety reactions; and *personality disorders.*

2. Epilepsy, circulatory disturbances, senile brain disease, central-nervous-system disorders linked to syphilitic or other infec-

tions or to trauma, drugs, poisons, or alcohol intoxication, and mental deficiency were all classified under *organic diseases* caused by brain lesions and the impairment of brain-tissue functions. This classification reflected several decades of accumulation of information about mental illness by Bleuler, Wagner-Jauregg, and many other clinicians; the progress made in diagnosis and therapy; the development of psychosomatic medicine (exploring relationships among mental operations, emotions, and physical ailments); and especially the increasing influence of divergent approaches to the study of normal and abnormal personality and behavior—the views and contributions of biologists, neurologists, and physicians, psychobiologist followers of Adolf Meyer, sociologists and anthropologists, and Freudian and non-Freudian psychoanalysts.

TROTTER, KRETSCHMER, SCHILDER, ALZHEIMER, BENDER

From a biological point of view, the eminent British surgeon Wilfred Trotter (1872–1939) concluded that conflicts between desires or habits of individuals and their basic inherited instincts are at the bottom of psychological tensions, feelings of guilt or resentment, and introverted withdrawal or flight from reality, a complex of factors resulting in the development of deep-seated neurotic disorders. His emphasis on heredity was endorsed by the German-American geneticist and psychiatrist Franz J. Kallmann, whose studies of schizophrenic twins at the New York Psychiatric Institute in the 1940s convinced him that inherited characteristics are more important than environmental conditions in causing schizophrenic and other functional psychotic diseases. The neurologists Warren Tay as long ago as 1881 and Bernard Sachs in 1887 described as hereditary the symptoms of Tay-Sachs disease of the nervous system (formerly called amaurotic family idiocy): progressive deterioration of vision, severe mental retardation and degeneration, and paralysis.

Ernst Kretschmer (elaborating his theory associating body build with mental illnesses) portrayed short-limbed stocky patients (pyknics) as alternatingly hyperactive and depressive manic-depressives; long-limbed thin patients (asthenics) and physically disproportioned patients (dysplastics) as withdrawn, regressive schizophrenics; and muscular patients (athletics) as suspicious, delusional paranoid individuals. The German-American psychiatrist Paul Schilder (1886–1940) delineated symptoms of the hereditary Schilder's disease of the brain—namely, visual abnormalities, spastic paralysis, and gradual mental deterioration. Investigating the presenile mental disorder of Alzheimer's disease, Alois Alzheimer (1864–1915) attributed its symptoms of memory defects, visual and speech difficulties, and convulsions to lesions of the brain cortex, although other investigators blamed not only disintegrative structural changes but also highly disturbing emotional experiences. In the 1930s, the American child psychiatrist Lauretta Bender reported that brain damage caused by infectious encephalitis impairs a child's ability to draw figures of the human body, one of the signs of incipient organic psychosis. Bender attributed schizophrenia to delayed maturation of the embryo, the effects of which become apparent during periods of crisis in life experience. She included among symptoms of childhood schizophrenia autistic reactions of fantasy or daydreaming, maladjustments in physiological functions, extreme introversion, resentment, and other disturbances involving interpersonal relationships.

MEYER

The Swiss-American psychiatrist Adolf Meyer (1866–1950) studied typical intellectual, emotional, and motor reactions of mental patients to their problems and life situations. Thus whereas Kraepelin described manic-depressive psychosis affecting a group of mental patients as a single distinct disease originally caused by inherited organic defects, Meyer concentrated on describing the abnormal responses of such patients, behavior disorders that he called *thermogasis*. When he applied this method of analysis to patients whom Kraepelin had classified as generally incurable victims of dementia praecox or schizophrenia, Meyer concluded that their reactions, which he called *parergasis*, indicated several rather similar schizophrenic diseases that could often be ameliorated. In a report published in 1906, he declared that many schizophrenics could be cured if their illnesses resulted not from the basic organic diseases cited by Kraepelin but from repeated failure to adjust to life situations and resulting cumulative disappointments.

Meyer emigrated from Zürich to the United States in 1892. He taught at Clark University from 1895 to 1902, at Cornell University from 1904 to 1909, and then for forty years at The Johns Hopkins University, where he headed the hospital psychiatric clinic. His theory and methods of analysis and therapy, which he called *psychobiology,* had immense influence among psychologists and psychiatrists during the first half of the twentieth century, and he ranks with Kraepelin and Freud as a pioneer in abnormal psychology.

According to Meyer and his numerous disciples, all behavior can be understood only by evaluating the individual's entire life history and whole personality, including hereditary structures and tendencies; health and physical condition; and, most important, the life situations, problems, human relationships, and environmental stresses encountered in past experience. The individual's previous and present interests, ambitions, attitudes, habits, ideas, abilities, fears and other emotions, inner conflicts, and defense mechanisms must be taken into account. Such information will help identify the causes of abnormal personality traits and mental disorders and will point the way to ameliorate or remedy both physical and mental illnesses. The psychobiologist therapist, he urged, should reassure the patient about the possibility of recovery and should help him (with the aid of hypnosis in some cases) to recall disturbing episodes submerged in his unconscious mind. He recommended that the therapist construct a life chart of the patient's symptoms to illuminate the cumulative factors and personality traits contributing to his disturbances. In psychobiological therapy, the patient is encouraged to discuss his life history freely in order to develop insights into past events, successes, and failures, to understand present problems and situations, and to adopt new attitudes, goals, and behavior patterns.

CAMERON, MALINOWSKI, BENEDICT, FARIS, HORNEY

In the 1930s and 1940s, from a social-psychological point of view, Norman A. Cameron, reporting on his investigations of schizophrenia, senile dementia, and paranoia, concluded that the delusions, inferiority and guilt feelings, and other abnormal reactions involved in these psychoses are not due mainly to physiological factors but arise from repeated failure to share personal feelings and experiences with other people. Such long-term maladjustment in the case of a paranoid, for example, eventually causes him to live in a strange, unreal pseudocommunity, a world of his own imagination.

The renowned Polish anthropologist Bronislaw Kasper Malinowski (1884–1942), author of *Sex and Repression in Savage Society*, attributed neurotic illnesses to cultural influences, especially sexual repressions, insecurity, everyday frustrations, and antagonistic or authoritarian social controls. Comparing spontaneous, relatively tolerant family and social relationships in one primitive society with the very strict, impatient, disciplinary relationships in two nearby communities, he found almost no cases of neurosis in the former but a high incidence of neurosis in the authoritarian societies, even though all three communities were much alike in race, language, and traditions. Similar investigations and conclusions were reported by the sociologists Ruth Benedict and Ellsworth Faris and by the psychoanalyst Karen Horney.

Benedict noted that reactions such as love, jealousy, and aggression vary in intensity with the diverse social and cultural environments of primitive communities, resulting in different types and varying incidences of neuroses and psychoses. Faris reported that psychotic cases could rarely be found in some of the very simple societies of the Congo, a phenomenon he contrasted with high rates of schizophrenia in the dilapidated, socially disorganized neighborhoods of Chicago. He observed that in Chicago some types of psychosis were especially frequent in poverty-stricken areas, other types in more prosperous areas. Horney attributed an extremely high incidence of neurosis in

Western societies to constant frustrations felt by individuals confronted by contradictory, confusing, deceptive social institutions, customs, and practices. (Franz Kallmann estimated that about nine of every thousand persons in the United States have been ill with schizophrenia.) Typical of many research studies investigating cultural influences on mental illness, a study by L. G. Kiloh in 1975 reported that Australian aborigines seldom exhibit neurotic symptoms. Numerous investigators have attempted to trace effects of racial and cultural factors upon the incidence of neuroses and psychoses. However, studies in the 1970s by R. Lorion, J. G. Rabkin, E. L. Struening, and others found no causal relationships between race and severe mental diseases.

ROGERS, THORNE, MORENO, KLEIN, ANNA FREUD

The therapeutic technique of *nondirective counseling* (also called client-centered counseling) was developed by Carl Ransom Rogers of the University of Chicago during the 1940s to help individuals gain self-understanding and self-reliance by recognizing and then eliminating their social tensions, doubts, resentments, and inner conflicts so that they can make a fresh start toward healthful adjustments. In nondirective counseling, the therapist listens attentively, without expressing approval or disapproval, to whatever the individual says about himself, his experiences and feelings. The procedure was designed to relieve the kinds of inner conflicts often cited by Karen Horney.

This approach worked well among many adolescents and intelligent young adults affected by mild neurotic disturbances, but more directive therapeutic methods seemed necessary for persons with serious mental illnesses. Techniques that require the therapist to plan and provide reeducative information, insights, and modes of self-evaluation for such patients were utilized successfully by Frederick C. Thorne in his system of *directive psychotherapy*. Thorne advocated careful advance planning for controlled interviews in which the therapist persuades the patient to change his behavior and encourages him to try again whenever he falters or to persist when he begins to improve. (In 1944 the psychiatrist A. F. Bronner at the Judge Baker Guidance Center in Boston, Massachusetts, stated that elaborate programs of this kind worked effectively for receptive, bright delinquents but not for many described as morons, neurotics, and psychotics.)

In the 1930s at New York University and later at Columbia University, sociologist J. L. Moreno constructed diagrams (sociograms) that graphically showed reciprocal likes and dislikes among members of social groups as well as their interrelationships as leaders, followers, or outcasts. Moreno also developed psychodrama as a form of group therapy in which the therapist observes a neurotic patient act out a role, unrehearsed, before a small audience of peers, relating his past experiences, motives, and emotions, and exploring reasons for his difficulty. The dramatic performance brings repressed experiences and submerged emotions to the surface, revealing significant information to the therapist and helping the patient to understand his own repressed feelings, while sharing disturbing emotions and problems with a sympathetic audience and thus relieving inner tensions and preparing the way for new patterns of behavior.

In Berlin during the 1920s and in London for several decades thereafter, the psychoanalyst Melanie Klein (1882–1960) adhered to Sigmund Freud's early concept that unconscious infantile sexual conflicts, complexes, and guilt feelings are responsible for later adult mental illnesses. Klein applied this concept in play technique for very young emotionally disturbed children. As the child plays, the therapist explains to him in simple language the relationship between his play activities and the unconscious motives behind them, the causes of his aggressive, guilt-laden feelings and, for example, his impulsive habits of biting, spitting, and the like. This technique permits the child to share emotional conflicts with the sympathetic therapist and develops in the child the same improved insight into his own behavior that adults derive from uninhibited expression of inner conflicts, Freud's method of free association.

Klein assumed the prevalence of serious psychological illnesses among infants, which would persist throughout life unless they were eliminated during childhood. But in Vienna during the 1920s and 1930s and in England during four decades thereafter, the psychoanalyst Anna Freud (1895–1982), Sigmund Freud's youngest daughter, accepted her father's later concept that the child gradually learns to control his psychosexual energy as he uses the powers of his conscience or superego. She applied this concept of gradual development to a new, permissive therapy of free play. She maintained that through observation of children's spontaneous play, the mainsprings of thought, feeling, and behavior among both normal and disturbed or retarded children can be identified. This process is to be accompanied not by drastic correction but by patient encouragement, suggestion, and spontaneous play experience, subject to moderate control by adults. Anna Freud noted that children are affected profoundly by fear of losing parental love and by similar potential adversities in family relationships. Children differ widely among themselves and from adults in defense mechanisms and reactions to stresses. Therefore, therapeutic and educational experiences should be adapted to the individual's personality traits and needs.

Although he discounted Sigmund Freud's emphasis on infantile sexual experiences, the Viennese psychiatrist Heinz Kohut (1913–1981) of the University of Chicago agreed that adverse family relationships tend to lessen self-respect and produce neurotic personality traits requiring sympathetic supportive therapy.

WATSON, SKINNER, ROLF, PERLS, BECK

The behaviorists Watson and Skinner, adhering to Pavlov's conditioned-reflex theory and techniques, held that prompt replacement of undesirable behavior by repeated desirable responses to specific stimuli and situations would provide effective therapy for maladjusted individuals. Bad habits could be eliminated and new habits formed, excessive fears and phobias avoided, and even (through biological practice and feedback) automatic body functions controlled and modified—all by conditioning associated with pleasant or unpleasant consequences and anticipations in the patient's mind. Many contemporary psychologists accept this view to some extent but do not believe enough is known about genetic and environmental factors and remedies to justify the behaviorists' extremely high expectations concerning their current therapeutic materials and techniques.

In the 1940s, a unique type of Gestaltist structural integration of personality through physical movements of the body was advocated by the physiologist Ida P. Rolf (1896–1979). In the Rolfist technique, the patient modifies his physical movements as directed and is expected to gain thereby fuller understanding of the self as a mental and physical organism capable of continual change, renewed vigor, enthusiasm, and effective readjustment and self-direction.

The American psychiatrist Frederick Perls, applying Gestalt theory, developed a popular integrative therapy wherein the therapist discusses the patient's thoughts, feelings, and past experiences with him until the patient understands clearly his relationships as an integrated unique person with other people and with the entire physical and social world. Recently, the psychiatrist Aaron T. Beck of the University of Pennsylvania applied a somewhat different method of modifying the patient's world view. In Beck's *cognitive therapy,* the patient is guided to correct his own fixed erroneous ideas and attitudes, exaggerated or unreasonable fears, and impractical goals by discussing with the therapist rational and satisfying explanations and probable solutions. (Similarly, counselors and psychiatrists often bring conflicting family members together for discussions in the hope of restoring harmonious family relationships.)

SIGMUND FREUD

Freud, founder of psychoanalysis, was born in 1856 in Freiburg, Moravia (then an Austrian province). He studied medicine at the University of Vienna, receiving his medical degree in 1881, then joined the faculty as an unsalaried lecturer on neurology in the department of his famous teachers, the anatomists Brücke and Meynert. On leave of absence in 1886, he studied in Paris under Charcot. In 1889 he went to Nancy to study the therapeutic methods of Liébeault and Bernheim. Afterward he taught neurology at the University of Vienna, beginning in 1902 as an instructor, later as assistant professor, and finally as full professor. The Nazi occupation of Vienna forced him to leave in

1938 for London, where he died the following year. Among his important works are *The Interpretation of Dreams* (1900); *The Psychopathology of Everyday Living* (1901); *Introductory Lectures on Psychoanalysis* (1916); *The Ego and the Id* (1923); *Civilization and Its Discontents* (1930); and *Moses and Monotheism* (1939).

Freud classified neuroses into the following types: (1) obsessive compulsive, in which the patient is wholly absorbed by a single impulsive desire or idea; (2) anxiety reaction, or anxiety neurosis, marked by a general state of uncertainty, vague agitation, and fear; (3) conversion hysteria, in which the patient transforms his inner conflicts into symptoms of a physical illness; and (4) neurasthenia, a type of chronic weakness and fatigue attended by physical tensions and discomforts, apathy, and irritability.

Freud's therapeutic methods consisted of the following techniques. (1) In *free association,* the therapist listens with interest and close attention during repeated consultations while the patient talks freely about personal experiences, difficulties, emotions, relationships to other people, dreams, hopes, and desires. Free association provides cues for the therapist concerning causal factors and to some extent relieves the patient of tensions arising from inner conflicts or repressed emotions. (2) In *dream analysis,* the patient describes his dreams (usually in episodic, partial, or distorted versions) to the therapist, who can often gain from them insights into the patient's unconscious impulses, repressed experiences, and feelings of guilt, anxiety, and unfulfilled wishes. The patient's distorted versions of dreams might indicate an unconscious need to conceal socially unacceptable ideas or desires. (3) In *transference,* the patient recalls and describes past experiences while the therapist connects and explains the disconnected events until the patient gradually relates to the therapist as if the latter were his parent. The patient may react to the therapist either with close emotional attachment or with hostility. Eventually, however, he will begin to achieve self-understanding and self-acceptance. He will then cease being disturbed by repressed fears or guilt feelings.

Freud's therapeutic methods (like his basic theories) were en-

dorsed by most psychiatrists during his later years and for several decades thereafter, but too many professionals and laymen
expected psychoanalysis to become a cure-all for severe mental
disorders—an expectation never shared by Freud himself—and
they tended to lose confidence in his psychoanalytical procedures
when this didn't happen. Moreover, Freudian psychoanalysis
demands expertise and patience on the therapist's part during
several years of frequent consultations. The techniques have often become so time-consuming and costly that many hospital
clinics have adopted for outpatients abbreviated psychoanalytic
therapy advocated by the Freudian psychoanalysts Wilhelm Stekel and Sandor Ferenczi. This procedure requires only persua-
sive reeducation in a few brief meetings between a staff therapist
and a patient.

In the 1970s, the American researchers D. H. Malan, E. S.
Heath, H. A. Bacal, and F. H. G. Balfour reported in the *Archives of General Psychiatry* that mental patients often improve
remarkably during a single meeting with a sympathetic psychiatrist, thereby making alternative short-term or long-term psychotherapy seem unnecessary. Also in the 1970s, J. G. Rabkin,
H. J. Steadman, and other investigators, after reviewing numerous research studies on the behavior of former mental patients,
concluded that it is impossible to identify potentially violent persons, that criminal activity by released patients with no record of
previous crime is not more frequent than in the normal population, and that rehousing them in the community is therefore often, though not always, feasible. Research studies indicated that,
although the task is difficult, efforts of physicians and community agencies to diagnose and treat physical illnesses during the
earliest stages help to prevent or ameliorate related psychological
disturbances.

JUNG

Jung developed a type of psychoanalytic therapy based upon
his word-association test and an interpretation of the patient's
spontaneous physical and oral self-expression. The patient states
the very first other word he associates with each given word; this

is a method of uncovering unconscious mental associations, desires, and conflicts. The therapist also may instruct the patient to draw, dance, or otherwise dramatize past images and conversations on the assumption that such active imaginative reactions will illuminate unconscious causes of mental disturbance and have a cathartic effect. Jung referred to two kinds of unconscious activity: submerged, repressed experiences reflected by clues in dreams or conversation; and basic drives or inherited traces of racial instincts and tendencies. He also referred to the individual's intuitive anticipations of future events. These concepts were basic to the school of analytic psychology that he founded. Since, however, Jungian therapy proved time-consuming and costly, his method of stimulating therapeutic self-expression lagged in popularity.

BERGER, MONIZ, FREEMAN, WATTS, POOLE

In the United States, many trained psychiatrists, clinical psychologists, and counselors increasingly resorted to surgical, electrical, and biochemical methods of treatment for millions of neurotics, alcoholics, drug addicts, and other emotionally disturbed patients.

Brain surgery was practiced in ancient times, and Hippocrates, describing symptoms of head injuries, cautioned physicians to be careful about making incisions in the brain that might cause convulsions. Modern brain surgery is said to have begun with the work of the French surgeon and anthropologist Paul Broca, who was appointed professor of surgery at the University of Paris in 1849.

Sophisticated surgical techniques have been developed to diagnose and treat brain injuries and brain tumors. Hans Berger's discovery in 1929 of alpha and beta electric waves generated by brain activity was soon followed by the work of other researchers who identified delta brain waves, having a frequency of three to six waves per second. Electroencephalograms (brain-wave recordings) proved useful for diagnosing grand mal and petit mal epilepsy and encephalitis and for locating brain tumors. (In 1944 the American psychiatrist Paul H. Hoch and psychologists

J. F. Kubis and Fabian L. Rouke reported that abnormal brain waves of schizophrenic patients were eliminated upon recovery from the disease.) Recently, analyses with radioisotopes have been helpful in pinpointing the sites of brain tumors.

In 1936 the Portuguese neuropsychiatrist Egas Moniz originated prefrontal lobotomy, severing some neural connections between the brain's frontal lobes and thalamus with beneficial results in reducing or eliminating pain and various symptoms of psychosis. During the past several decades, improved surgical procedures have been developed for cautious use with psychotic patients, benefiting many individuals unresponsive to other types of therapy.

In the 1940s, the American neurosurgeons Walter Freeman and James W. Watts originated an improved technique of transorbital lobotomy with excellent results, better for senile psychoses, painful brain cancers, and involutional melancholia than for schizophrenia. In topectomy, another variation of prefrontal lobotomy, devised by Lawrence Poole, small areas of the frontal brain cortex are cut away; this procedure came into frequent use during the 1950s at about the same time as the comparable technique of thalamotomy, in which areas of the thalamic processes are excised by electric needles. Ultrasonic sound waves have also been used for the same purpose.

Unfortunately, notwithstanding significant benefits for carefully selected patients, brain surgery has frequently had adverse effects, often mild but sometimes severe, upon attitudes, powers of concentration, judgment, and personality traits. These consequences are attributed by critics at least in part to a scarcity of highly trained, experienced neurosurgeons who are careful not to overuse or misapply surgical therapy.

SAKEL, VON MEDUNA, CERLETTI, BINI

Chemical and electrical therapies came into common use during the 1940s and thereafter. As previously mentioned, at the turn of the century Wagner-Jauregg successfully treated many cases of cretinism with thyroid extracts and later used fever therapy for general paresis. In the 1930s, the Viennese physicians Manfred J. Sakel and H. Wortis developed insulin-shock therapy for morphine addicts and schizophrenics; the American researchers H. H. Merritt and T. J. Putnam reported remarkable effects of Dilantin for control of epileptic seizures; the Hungarian clinician Ladislas J. von Meduna used the drug Metrazol as shock treatment to control convulsions of schizophrenics; and the Italian scientists U. Cerletti and L. Bini originated electric shock treatment, which proved beneficial for cases of severe depression and involutional melancholia.

In the 1940s, the American psychiatrists Paul H. Hoch, K. P. Albert, and H. Waelsch reported that glutamic acid increased the mental efficiency and improved the social adjustment of some mentally retarded patients. Since then, a vast array of pharmacological natural and synthetic substances have been made available by drug manufacturers in Western countries to meet the brisk demand for prescription drugs: sedatives, barbiturates, and tranquilizers; lithium to reduce manic-depressive mood swings; Antabuse to combat alcoholism; amphetamines (often addictive and at times causing psychoses through overuse) to stimulate brain reactions; estrogenic hormones (some possibly carcinogenic) to counteract female endocrinological maladjustments; methadone hydrochloride for heroin addicts; neuroleptic agents such as hydrazines to combat severe depression; Dilantin and methoin to reduce epileptic convulsions; and innumerable other therapeutic chemical substances. Most popular have been the tranquilizers: for example, chlorpromazine, reserpine (which occasionally has the side effect of causing depression), and meprobamate (credited to the Czech-American physician Frank M. Berger in 1954). Tranquilizers seem to counteract some of the psychological, intellectual symptoms of mental illness (those cited by Bleuler) more effectively than they do the typical physiological symptoms of deep-seated mental disorders.

Psychiatrists generally agree that all chemical therapeutic substances should be used with caution, mainly as adjuncts to other means of treatment. Contemporary research methods, however, such as those using new techniques of analyzing radioactivity in brain tissues and photographic computer-assisted tomography and positron emission tomography (to probe brain chemistry and reactions) should eventually result in the utilization of many new, safe, and beneficial therapeutic substances.

12 PSYCHOLOGY IN MODERN SOCIETY

Social psychology is the science that studies relationships and interactions between the individual and the groups with which he has direct or indirect association. Social psychologists investigate the psychological effects of group activities upon individuals, and, conversely, the effects of individual behavior upon social institutions and organizations. The evolutionary theories of Herbert Spencer; the moralist, religious hypotheses of Eduard Spranger; the conative concepts of William McDougall; and the psychoanalytic postulates of Sigmund Freud were important contributions to the early development of social psychology as a scientific discipline.

SPENCER, SPRANGER, McDOUGALL, FREUD

In his *First Principles of Philosophy* (1862), Herbert Spencer asserted that not only the organic structure of human beings but also their social and cultural products, such as language, science, and the industrial and aesthetic arts, change gradually owing to natural causes and evolutionary processes. Thus, as language develops from primitive to advanced stages, words become shorter, compound vowels fuse into single vowels, unnecessary endings disappear, and expressions change in a process of consolidation and integration. The expression *God be with you,* for instance, evolved through contraction into *Good-by.* (Bronislaw Malinowski's firsthand studies of the primitive Tobriand societies in the 1950s suggested an opposite conclusion, for the Tobrianders generally used a single meaningful word to express ideas that Western peoples express in clauses and complex sentences. The linguist Edouard Prokosch of Yale University theorized that cold climates among northern peoples might favor nearly closed lips and mouths and fewer vowels, whereas hot climates might encourage the use of more vowels and more explosive consonants.)

Spencer maintained that, in contrast to the parts of the body which change in order better to serve the functions of the whole organism, individuals act, adjust, and change for the sake of themselves. Society, in fact, exists to serve its parts, the individuals who compete and struggle to satisfy biological and other personal needs. For Spencer, competition is a natural mechanism for the selection and survival of the fittest individuals. He concluded that evolution prolongs the life-span and makes life more enjoyable, bringing happiness to individuals and also to the whole community—provided that individuals become wise enough to respect the needs and pursue the happiness of others as well as of themselves. Altruistic motives are useful for the practical purpose of achieving the happiness of all people. Spencer assumed that acquired personality traits, traditions, and customs are transmitted to succeeding generations just as physical, structural changes are inherited. (Critics have charged that Spencer ignored the danger that evolution and struggle can be destructive, as, for example, if technological development enables men to destroy civilizations and even the species itself.)

The German philosopher Friedrich Wilhelm Nietzsche (1844–1900), who condemned Christianity for its view that the meek will inherit the earth, carried the survival-of-the-fittest doctrine to the extreme. He insisted that might made right, that the superman (the forceful, active, sthenic type contrasted by Kretschmer with the weak, retreating asthenic type) should master the inferior, moralistic multitudes. Implementing the doctrine of rugged individualism, the superman must relentlessly subdue and suppress weaklings who harbor resentment against him, their natural ruler. Supermen can sometimes feel resentment during their own struggles for power, but they ventilate their feelings in the fight for victory, whereas the unfit hordes hide their resentment because they fear to oppose their invincible master. Nietzsche agreed with Darwin that the masses of any species are naturally inferior to those fittest individuals who tend to live apart from the herd. But he added the idea (not accepted by Darwin, who valued contributions of the masses to evolution) that the multitude should be sacrificed if necessary so that the superman will rise up out of the herd to become the all-powerful master of the race.

The British philosophers Thomas Henry Huxley and Leonard Trelawney Hobhouse agreed with Spencer that social institutions evolved but they insisted that ethical ideals and cooperation were much better ways and means than competition to achieve the good society. Pillsbury, however, commenting about experiments on motivation during the 1930s and 1940s, concluded that, at least in American society, competition and working for oneself were usually more effective incentives than cooperation and working for the well-being of the community. Moreover, he maintained that repeated failure to achieve personal advancement and social acceptance tended to weaken an individual's ideals and social goals.

Eduard Spranger, in *Forms of Life* (1914) and *Types of Men* (1928), held that the individual's major life goals determine his personality type and therefore his relationships to others. Spranger declared that the behavior of individuals should be assessed on the basis of their dominant concerns and values. Each person also possesses subordinate interests, but these supplement his principal goals. A person dominated by political ambition, for example, seeks power as his main objective. Others may be dominated by economic, artistic, intellectual, social, or religious aims. Spranger felt that permanence and truth were the criteria for judging which interests and goals most deserved loyalty. On this basis, he designated eternally true religious truths and ideals as the highest values; and temporary, superficial economic desires as the lowest values. Social and political ambitions are worthwhile only if rooted in religion, social ideals, and a lasting community spirit. Education should be designed to inculcate those values so that they will become the individual's dominant motivation and concern.

For William McDougall, what the individual instinctively tends to do in order to satisfy felt innate needs is the central force in all societies. Thus man's instinct of pugnacity has done even more than ethical or moral tendencies to shape modern society. The desire for social approval and the fear of social disapproval, reflecting the force of public opinion, impel men to control their fighting instincts, but pugnacity and rivalry (equally with similar dominant impulses of tenderness and parental love) remain as powerful individual incentives in social relationships.

McDougall held that no person in isolation could develop moral judgments or ideals; they are acquired as the result of common language, traditions, and educative relationships available only in civilized societies. He warned that laws and customs must not become so rigid as to deprive individuals of freedom to make their own moral judgments and choices, since self-direction is necessary for spiritual growth and social development. Society should help each person to advance through four successive stages: (1) the stage of instinctive dominating impulses and actions; (2) the stage of modified instinctive impulses and actions, a development resulting from social influences such as rewards and punishments; (3) the stage of increased self-control and self-expression motivated by the individual's expectations of future social rewards (such as praise) and punishments (such as blame); and (4) the final, highest stage, during which the individual does what he believes to be right regardless of consequences.

Sigmund Freud, in what became orthodox psychoanalytic theory, postulated two innate, instinctive drives as primary forces shaping human social behavior—namely, the life instinct and the death instinct. Like Darwin, Freud believed that man gradually evolved into a species endowed with conscience and with ability to reason, qualities superimposed upon unconscious primitive tendencies shared with lower animals. Social behavior is a form of sublimation of animalistic impulses and appetites often submerged and suppressed in the unconscious mind. (Freud had no faith in religion as a source of truths about human behavior, but he realized its psychological influence. Western religious leaders do not generally condemn his search for facts based upon experiments and scientific observation, and some draw parallels between Freudian ideas of unconscious repressed emotions and biblical references to similar human experiences.) The Freudian view of social interaction states that society makes demands upon the individual, and he, through his ego and superego, reacts by modifying his behavior in accordance with society's moral standards. Freudian psychoanalysis aims at a balance between life and death instincts, thereby enabling the individual to satisfy both his acceptable desires and the moral demands of his community.

DEWEY, MEAD, PARSONS, WEBER, WATSON, SKINNER

John Dewey pointed out the inseparability of thought from emotional, physical, neural, biological, and social experiences. The whole person, the whole society, the whole environment and life situation, and every reaction and interaction are all involved in human nature, learning, growth, and conduct. In modern society, emergent factors, such as scientific advances, industrial innovations, and democratic political systems, require new ideas and modes of behavior. Men must be willing to experiment, to test their ways of thinking and living on the basis of their practical value for solving social problems and achieving social reconstruction. There is no such thing, in Dewey's view, as a fixed law of nature determining the future destiny of mankind, and no justification for Spencer's theory of inevitable, regular changes in man and society from lower to higher levels of civilization. The task of social psychology is to explore objectively the nature, causes, and forces of social change, and the best means and methods of coping with continual change in natural forces, human nature, and social conditions.

The philosopher George Herbert Mead (1863–1931) of the University of Chicago, agreeing with Dewey's view of the individual as part of an integrated, sharing society, and with Wundt's view of mind as a social activity, set forth unique interpretations of socialization.

There is a difference between a person's idea of himself and what he really is and does. Morever, no matter what he does, the final results will be uncertain, largely unpredictable. What a person thinks about his own personality, said Mead, will depend upon what other people think of him. His self-image will be affected by how he appears to them, especially to close associates whom he respects. His self-image, his ego, continually changes in reaction to his social world. Since one cannot count on sure results, he must make the best of what he can accomplish in his uncertain universe.

The sociologist Talcott Parsons, applying Mead's basic ideas to problems of social psychology, delineated four elements of social behavior: (1) the actor; (2) his goal, conscious or unconscious; (3) uncontrollable conditions of his actions; and (4) the means and methods he can control, as for example, studying in order to pass examinations or to become a philosopher. What the actor does merely to fulfill an obligation, said Parsons, may not reveal, and in fact may conceal, his real goal, and he may also rationalize his behavior to justify it in his own mind.

The German jurist and student of social theory Max Weber (1864–1921) believed that social psychology should describe what people do and what they intend to do in society—not what they ought to do, which is a matter for their religious beliefs to determine. Weber set forth his views in several works, including *The Protestant Ethic and the Spirit of Capitalism* (1920), that explored practical effects of Protestant religious and ethical ideas upon modern capitalistic enterprises and the role of economic motives in building the foundations of Protestant religious institutions.

Like Mead, Weber emphasized the element of uncertainty and chance in human affairs, and, like Mead, he adhered to the pragmatic view that everyday accomplishments are the significant factors in human experience. Economic motives and enterprises are decisive influences on both the individual and the social order. Practical achievements, not the drives for power (prized by Nietzsche), should motivate individuals. Economics, politics, and religion are closely interrelated. In large economic, political, and religious organizations, direct fact-to-face contacts are limited and must be supplemented by bureaucracies, regulations, rules, and policies. Leaders, agitators, and functionaries appeal for individual support on the ground that their proposals will enhance the basic aims of their organization's membership.

J. B. Watson and B. F. Skinner agreed with the pragmatic

view that the value of what an individual does depends upon the results of his behavior, contrary to McDougall's conviction that inner purposes and moral inhibitions, often counter to social pressures, should be the first consideration. From another standpoint, the sociologists Robert E. Park and William Graham Sumner attributed more lasting influence on the individual's behavior to the norms, customs, and ideals of the community than to specific stimulus-response mechanisms cited by behaviorist psychologists.

BERNHEIM, LE BON, TARDE, DEWEY, SIDIS, THORNDIKE, PIAGET

In 1910 McDougall summarized with approval the ideas of Hippolyte-Marie Bernheim about the importance of suggestion and suggestibility in the behavior of both normal and abnormal individuals. (McDougall rejected Janet's assumption that all hypnotizable individuals are hysterics, and also the assertion of some psychologists that suggestion operates primarily in the subconscious mind or subliminal self, where it dissociates other mental processes and then rises to dominate the conscious mind.)

Bernheim cited factors that impel a recipient either to accept or to reject a suggestion. If the recipient lacks knowledge about the subject of the suggestion, he may be highly susceptible; but if he knows a great deal about the matter, as well-educated people often do, he may criticize or condemn the suggestion. Any person may vary in suggestibility from time to time: for example, when he is ill, fatigued, or under the influence of drugs. There are natural differences among individuals in suggestibility, some being instinctively inclined to submit to superior authority, others habitually antagonistic to such authority. McDougall agreed with Bernheim that suggestions frequently are autosuggestions, created by individuals in their own minds, sometimes impelling them to irrational conclusions—just as a sick person, after ingesting a placebo, apparently improves only because he assumed the pill to be a real cure.

The celebrated French physician and sociologist Gustave Le

Bon (1841-1931) and the noted French sociologist and criminologist Gabriel Tarde (1843-1904) analyzed suggestion in rational, irrational, and impulsive group behavior. Le Bon and Tarde pioneered in describing the potent effects of suggestion and imitation upon social behavior. Their writings inspired many psychologists and sociologists to investigate these phenomena during the first half of the twentieth century. Le Bon's views, emphasizing the impact of suggestion on unconscious emotions and unconscious motives, and contrasting such processes with conscious, fully rational reactions of the individual and the group, were published long before Freud suggested similar concepts. (As early as 1872, Le Bon had written that much of human behavior is nonrational, impulsive, not dependent upon the intellect.) Social scientists began to describe unconscious and conscious suggestion and imitation as factors in social control, obedience to authority, group activities, persuasion, and propaganda. Le Bon held that imitative behavior is often a dynamic unconscious form of behavior to be differentiated from deliberate, rational behavior.

For John Dewey, *imitation* meant that two people utilize the same means to accomplish their purposes. Each individual's purpose is decisive, and imitation is only an auxiliary factor, a convenient way of doing whatever the imitator intends to do. Trying to explain human behavior as the result of imitation, he contended, is like saying that opium puts men to sleep because it has an evil power of its own, whereas the real cause is the reaction to it of the body. Human behavior in society consists of purposive reactions to whatever other people say or do.

Bernheim, Le Bon, and Tarde, however, insisted that suggestion and imitation, unlike opium in the body, stimulate, reinforce, and modify the individual's purposes and that society would be very different without them. Often the individual may not understand clearly what he is imitating or, as in a crowd situation, may not even stop to think about it. In hypnosis the subject does not reason about alternative ways and means but promptly does what he is asked to do. Suggestion during hypnosis is less drastic but otherwise rather similar to imitation in the conscious state.

The Russian psychopathologist Boris Sidis (1867–1923) agreed with Le Bon that suggestion is a powerful direct influence on social behavior. He defined autosuggestion as suggestion coming from within the individual to himself, and he declared that anyone could counteract excessive fears by suggesting to himself that such fears are instinctive reactions to imaginary dangers. He advised insomniacs to suggest to themselves that sleeplessness is nothing to worry about and becomes harmful only if they do worry about it. Autosuggestions about the advantage of simply resting in bed will help to remedy the most severe cases of insomnia.

Thorndike stated that imitative tendencies can be inborn potent forces in motivating behavior. He pointed out that imitative behavior is similar to but not actually identical with the behavior being imitated and that susceptibility to suggestion as well as habits of quick imitation of others vary widely among individuals.

In his *Psychology of Intelligence* (1947), Piaget, analyzing the processes of intellectual growth, attached great importance to an early developmental stage of immediate imitation. He said that at a later stage imitation is delayed because the child takes time to comprehend and assimilate actions he is about to imitate. Piaget held that speech is learned through imitation of ready-made signs or symbols of meanings. Young children tend to emulate without hesitation the habits, mannerisms, moral standards, and behavior of their parents. Often children, eager to be respected, imitate unworthy adults repeatedly, and readily acquire adult habits of lying, cheating, stealing, and the like, doing under the influence of this kind of social pressure things they would not otherwise want to do. Eventually, through habitual imitation, they change in personality, for, as the saying goes, "Monkey is as monkey does." An adult advised by a friend to give up smoking may often ignore the suggestion, but if the suggestion is offered by physicians, he may perhaps reluctantly accept their advice. Similarly, a child who wishes to stay up late but also wishes to please his mother may resolve the issue under social pressure by going promptly to bed. His decision may be rational or it may be merely an impulsive reaction to suggestion.

BEKHTEREV, COOLEY, SIMMEL, DURKHEIM, LEWIN, RIESMAN

For the pioneering Russian behaviorist Vladimir M. Bekhterev, social behavior depends upon two kinds of conditioned reflexes: (1) instinctive, automatic reactions centered in egoistic, physiological motives and processes; and (2) purposive reactions based upon the individual's past experiences in association with other people, reactions reflecting acquired positive or negative, desirable or undesirable, social attitudes. Applying his conditioning theory to the analysis of individual behavior in groups and societies, Bekhterev concluded that all such relationships and reciprocal activity are determined by intellectual functions of the brain and nervous system. The way each person feels and acts toward others depends upon what he has felt and thought about them in the past as well as his immediate awareness and evaluation of their present actions. The accumulated effects of conditioned reflexes in innumerable social situations are extremely complex, and often virtually impossible to identify, accounting for the infinite variations and differences in the personality and character of individuals.

The American sociologist Charles H. Cooley analyzed social relationships, the effects of social contacts upon children and adults, and the psychology of collective behavior. Cooley differentiated between primary and secondary social groups.

Primary groups are those with relatively close, face-to-face, intimate, sympathetic, friendly, informal personal contacts between individual members. Such groups are characterized by shared experiences, goals, and ideals; mutual understanding; lasting relationships; and cooperative efforts. Cooley noted, however, that social relationships in primary groups sometimes deteriorate as a result of hate, envy, and jealousy. The family, neighborhood, clubs, and play groups are examples of the primary type of groups. The family is the most effective primary group for training children, whose attitudes and habits are profoundly affected by the examples of parents and others in the household.

Secondary groups, which include the business establishment,

church, state, and nation, are relatively impersonal, distant, formal, and controlled by regulations, laws, and schedules. The behavior of an individual in a primary group is different from his behavior in secondary groups. In primary groups, the members possess very similar, though not identical, aims and purposes, and tend to work informally for the welfare of the group. In secondary groups, the members work mainly for common, often special-interest, benefits and services.

The German philosopher and sociologist Georg Simmel (1858–1918) regarded the ideals and moral standards of individuals as far more important than their immediate activities or experiences. Nevertheless, he explored the effects of size and other physical factors upon social groups and their members. According to Simmel, the smaller the group, the more intimate its members tend to be in their relationships, whereas in larger groups, each member is less important, and warm sentiments among members are less common. The behavior of a couple living together will be greatly affected if joined by a third person since the size and average contacts within the group will have been increased by 50 percent. The addition of a fourth and fifth person to the group of three will have somewhat less impact on its social relationships. Confined inadequate quarters tend to disturb relationships, stimulating antagonisms and resentments. In large groups, individuals find it difficult to develop shared interests and rapport; misunderstandings, suspicions, and subterfuges frequently develop. Attempts are made to resolve conflicting views by persuasion, democratic adjustments and decisions, compromises, and rules and regulations. Within every group, some members may acquire a status of superiority and authority through achievements, shrewdness, or driving ambitions.

Evolutionary theories formulated by Herbert Spencer, Edward Burnett Tylor, and Benjamin Kidd assumed that, in the history of civilization, social institutions changed and progressed from very primitive to savage, then to barbaric, and eventually to advanced stages, and that in the modern era religious faith and ethical ideals represent the highest stage of mental evolution yet achieved.

Émile Durkheim (1858–1917) rejected the idealist concept of

continuous social progress toward philosophical or religious truth. Durkheim believed that, although it is a composite of individuals, society also has its own collective mental qualities, moral ideals, and aesthetic values, all of which vary widely among different communities. Each community has its own goals and values. To achieve them, its members (organized in diverse groups) divide among themselves the work needed for their common purposes and obey customs and rules that they have accepted. Durkheim held that scientific studies of human behavior should be designed to explore the psychological influences of the entire society, including its integrated mental and moral forces as well as its institutions, upon the individual's personality and social relationships. Thus, on the basis of his research studies, he attributed suicides to excessive social pressures on the individual; the failure of the community adequately to guide and assist the potential victim; and rapid, contradictory, and confusing changes in social conditions and practices.

Kurt Lewin, applying quantitative, topological appraisals to social demands and barriers, evaluated social pressures on three groups of boys participating in club activities under authoritarian, laissez-fare, and democratic conditions, respectively. Authoritarian procedures encouraged extremist attitudes of either aggression or lack of interest and increased inner tensions, which exploded immediately upon temporary absence of authoritative discipline. The laissez-faire policy resulted in irregular work and minimal accomplishment as well as numerous disciplinary problems. The democratic methods stimulated cooperation, enthusiasm, and consistently superior achievements. Lewin concluded that the amount of self-direction built into the structure of a group or society influences profoundly the attitudes and efficiency of its members. The precise effects of authoritarian, laissez-faire, and democratic social arrangements depend also upon established traditions and customs of the society. Individuals reared in a community traditionally autocratic may find it difficult to cope with sudden demands made upon them by a new laissez-faire or democratic regime, while persons accustomed to democratic arrangements may be confused or demoralized by new laissez-faire or autocratic conditions.

David Riesman, in his writings on civil liberties and in *The Lonely Crowd* (1950), portrayed the middle-class American as a self-conscious, separated, alienated person coping with an impersonal industrialized society. A feeling of separation or loneliness in a huge mixed society disturbs his equanimity, stability, and attitudes toward the community. In childhood and youth, he learns to conform to established customs as a matter of course, never doubting that he is doing so freely. His feelings and judgments about freedom, laws, justice, equity, and other concepts do not necessarily agree with the facts, but he seldom considers changing his views unless he is impelled to do so by adverse experience or conflict with authority. Relatively successful middle-class persons tend to understand and respect one another, developing good rapport and mutually supportive social relationships, the results of their similar class status and interests. Their group experiences tend to undermine rugged individualism and strengthen habits of conformity.

BLUMER, BOAS, BENEDICT, MEAD, KLINEBERG, CLARK, ET AL.

In his analysis of elementary collective behavior, the sociologist Herbert Blumer, who was for many years a colleague of Robert E. Park at the University of Chicago and later professor of sociology at the University of California, described the process of circular reaction whereby one person intensifies the feelings of others in his group, a process of reciprocal imitation causing fear and excitement just as in the case of cattle caught up in a stampede. Blumer held that circular reactions caused insecurity and uncertainty, resulting in social change, possibly new social movements, and even a new social order.

Simultaneously, several anthropologists investigated the social relationships and behavior patterns of individuals in primitive societies. Among their numerous research studies were those of E. S. Evans-Pritchard with the Azandes of the Nile Valley, on their use of witchcraft, oracles, and magic to settle personal quarrels; Franz Boas with the Kwakiutl Indians in Canada on their custom of giving away personal possessions to outshine their neighbors, make them envious, or end a controversy; Ruth Benedict with the Eskimos on their beliefs in good-luck tokens and longevity symbols, and with the pious Pueblo Indians on the Zuñi reservation of New Mexico who despise ambitious individuals and treat them as outcasts; Margaret Mead with North American Indians undergoing drastic social changes and disorganization; and Ralph Linton with the Tanala societies of Madagascar on their custom of consulting the dead about managing community affairs and dealing with severe individual and social problems.

In twentieth-century American society, pervasive effects of social arrangements and relationships upon the attitudes and personalities of individuals were dramatized by the history of racial prejudice. Discrimination against minorities was investigated by psychologists, sociologists, psychiatrists, criminologists, jurists, and political scientists, illuminating the consequences of segregation; desegregation; inequality in economic and social opportunities, rights, and privileges; intermarriage; poor housing; disadvantages in arts, sciences, and education; and conflicts and violence, such as race riots. These investigations preceded nationwide efforts to foster new attitudes and behavior patterns among individuals and groups.

Stereotypes and myths began to give way in the face of scientific evidence. Prominent social psychologists, such as Otto Klineberg at Columbia University, conducted tests that showed no evidence of innate differences in intelligence among black and white children but definite indications of the influence on test scores of social and cultural factors. (Researches of this kind continued for decades; in the 1970s, scientific studies by J. C. Loehlin, G. Lindzey, and others similarly found no evidence of racial differences in native intelligence.) Psychologists Kenneth B. Clark and Gordon W. Allport and sociologists E. Franklin Frazier and Talcott Parsons reported that racial prejudice permeated economic and social institutions, having deleterious effects upon majorities and minorities alike. In individuals, these effects were manifested in superiority or inferiority complexes, defense mechanisms, aggressive attitudes, and emotional and mental disturbances.

In the 1970s, studies of the attractiveness of racial physical features by N. H. Hamm, M. R. Baum, C. Hendrick, and others proved that judgments about beauty vary greatly among individuals and groups and depend upon past experiences. Biases and stereotypes are acquired from the individual's lifelong associations in primary and secondary social groups. A new confident self-image of black women was expressed in their popular expression "Black is beautiful." (A study by V. E. O'Leary in 1974 showed that special training to increase the efficiency of black women employees raised their aspirations to such a degree that most of them gave up their current jobs to seek more interesting and more remunerative employment.) Studies of sex discrimination have revealed its origins in traditions and assumptions inculcated by suggestion, imitation, and traditional practices in the family and other social organizations.

Federal and state laws forbidding discrimination in public enterprises were given impetus by the unprecedented Supreme Court decision of 1954 prohibiting public-school racial segregation. These legal requirements stimulated new attitudes among the population regarding equity and desirable social relations in education, employment, housing, and other community activities even though changes were only gradual, sometimes merely episodic, and created new social problems. Special efforts to compensate disadvantaged minorities for past deliberate social discrimination (affirmative action) risked the charge of reverse discrimination from those who felt that extra training or opportunities and dispensations for a minority group placed the majority at a competitive disadvantage.*

DOOB, THURSTONE, MILLER, A. M. LEE, E. B. LEE

Significant social and psychological analyses of suggestion and persuasion were published during nearly a century of research

*In the Bakke case of 1978, the United States Supreme Court ruled five to four that a California medical school's quota system was unconstitutional because it resulted in the selection of black applicants for admission who earned lower scores on entrance examinations than a rejected white applicant and therefore discriminated against the white person by depriving him of an equal educational opportunity. The majority of justices held, however, that race might be considered along with other factors in the selection of applicants.

subsequent to Le Bon's works of the 1890s. Studies by Leonard W. Doob of Yale University, Edward A. Ross of the University of Wisconsin, Louis L. Thurstone of the University of Chicago, Clyde R. Miller of Columbia University, and Alfred McClung Lee of Brooklyn College were widely disseminated from the 1930s into the 1960s among students of psychology, social psychology, sociology, and education in American universities.

In the 1920s, President Abbott Lawrence Lowell of Harvard University, in *Public Opinion in War and Peace,* described the way in which social issues arise, are debated, and then are settled so that the solutions become part of the established system and organization of the society.* However, critical political and economic events—including international wars; the rise of communism, nazism, and fascism; the worldwide depression of the 1930s; governmental intervention on a large scale in the private lives of individuals; explosive reform movements for civil rights and economic opportunities; and abrupt shifts in public opinion—upset long-established traditions and institutions. Psychologists called for scientific, rational investigation of the forces and techniques of highly sophisticated mass communication and propaganda, which had often affected public opinion and had in their view facilitated impractical or unwise social policies. Psychological warfare had become a worldwide technique of public policy in peace as in war.

Doob's volume *Propaganda* (1935) was one of the earliest significant attempts to describe objectively the role and principles of suggestion and persuasion in modern Western societies. His analyses aptly supplemented views of the great sociologist William Graham Sumner, whose classical *Folkways* (1906) emphasized the importance of social customs and moral standards in molding individual and group behavior; also the views of Le Bon, Max Weber, and Robert E. Park concerning the impact of

* Lowell himself used propaganda techniques in his campaign against the appointment to the Supreme Court of the labor-union lawyer and reformer Louis Dembitz Brandeis and also in his successful attempts to sway public opinion in favor of the execution by the state of Massachusetts of the anarchists Sacco and Vanzetti, who in the opinion of many had been unfairly tried and convicted. Brandeis, too, was a master propagandist who, in his Supreme Court opinions from 1916 to 1939, aroused widespread opposition to traditional, conservative, probusiness, antilabor views.

reciprocal social relationships, economic forces, and the urban physical environment on individuals and communities.

Doob held that propaganda is a form of suggestion intended to modify or control group attitudes and actions based upon those attitudes, to induce people to accept ideas that they might have good reasons to oppose, and to do so by one-sided deceitful or irrational means instead of citing the whole truth or scientific evidence. Education, said Doob, altogether different from propaganda, makes available to individuals and groups whatever proven facts and logical explanations have been discovered on all sides of an issue and enables them to arrive at conclusions through critical thinking. The conclusions thus arrived at are always subject to change or reinforcement whenever additional facts come to light. Doob maintained that, in contrast to the educator, the propagandist endeavors to arouse in social groups illogical impulses and emotions, feelings and attitudes of envy, fear, hatred, uncertainty, and superiority or inferiority, which often induce them to adopt irrational, fallacious, or unjustifiable concepts and decisions desired by the propagandist. From Doob's point of view, even in a worthy cause, deceitful appeals of propaganda are reprehensible, whereas the use of genuinely educational appeals to facts and rational judgment are socially beneficial and lasting.

In order to judge accurately the impact of suggestion and propaganda upon individuals and societies as they seek to achieve their goals, it is necessary to evaluate scientifically their previous and new attitudes and opinions. L. L. Thurstone (1887–1955) at the University of Chicago (using a quantitative approach comparable to the job-analysis methods of the educators E. L. Thorndike and W. W. Charters) constructed an opinion scale to measure personal opinions by rating each opinion within a range from very unfavorable to highly favorable reactions. Test results indicated that individuals form and maintain relatively rigid emotionally colored or stereotyped attitudes and prejudices on controversial public issues. Similarly, H. M. Bell of Stanford University devised the Bell Adjustment Inventory to measure the attitudes of pupils toward their school, teachers, and other pupils.

Tests like Thurstone's were developed by H. H. Remmers at Purdue University and Ross Stagner at Illinois State University. These were followed by numerous scales to measure personal beliefs about religion, civil rights, birth control, communism, and other highly controversial matters. Thurstone, Donald Young (author of *American Minority Peoples*), and other investigators found prejudices of whites against blacks, for example, to be persistent, usually reinforced by cultural backgrounds, traditional stereotypes, and propaganda. Soon a steady stream of public-opinion polls became a feature of American political affairs, facilitating efforts of politicians to gain emotional or irrational support from wavering or uninterested voters.

Clyde R. Miller, a conservative-minded reporter on the Cleveland, Ohio, *Plain Dealer* and an enthusiastic supporter of American participation in the First World War, propagandized for the prosecution of agitators and suspected spies by the government. He attended an antiwar meeting at which the famous socialist candidate for president Eugene Victor Debs was the principal speaker. Miller appealed to government authorities to prosecute Debs for violation of the Espionage Act and was summoned as the chief witness against the socialist leader, who was promptly convicted and sentenced to ten years imprisonment. Debs, however, respected Miller and predicted he would change his mind about the origins and causes of the war. While in France, Miller consulted leading statesmen, concluded that Debs had been right, and attempted in vain to obtain his release by President Woodrow Wilson. In 1920, however, Warren G. Harding, Republican nominee for president, agreed with Miller and promised to release Debs, as he quietly did in his capacity as president on Christmas Day, 1921.

These experiences changed Miller's attitude toward public issues and he became a liberal social reformer. He felt that the American people had been deceived by Wilson's propaganda for a war to "make the world safe for democracy." At Columbia University, he established courses in the analysis of propaganda, originated the Springfield Plan of civic education (in Springfield, Massachusetts) for the prevention and eradication of racial and religious prejudice, and founded with associates in 1937 (aided by the wealthy philanthropist Edward A. Filene) the Institute for Propaganda Analysis, for which he was executive secretary.* He also served for some years as professor of education at Teachers College, Columbia University.

The Institute for Propaganda Analysis published and distributed widely its analyses of propaganda devices until early in the 1940s it decided to suspend operations rather than become a propaganda agency for the government during the Second World War. It was reactivated after the war and operated several years under the direction of Alfred McClung Lee and Elizabeth Briant Lee, coauthors of *The Fine Art of Propaganda,* published in 1939 and republished in 1979. In the 1940s, Miller, with the aid of the philanthropist Lewis K. Rosenstiel, founded the League for Fair Play to expose and combat racist, anti-Semitic, and communist or other totalitarian propaganda.

In *The Process of Persuasion* (1946), Miller described the most common devices of propaganda as follows: (1) *card-stacking,* trapping the propagandist's victim by inducing him to approve and reaffirm innocuous plausible assertions and then persuading him that invalid conclusions follow logically from those simple assertions and must therefore be accepted as valid and irrefutable; (2) *name-calling,* impelling the victim to reject a valid proposition by attaching a contemptuous label to it; (3) *glittering generalities,* making broad statements and assumptions repeatedly without factual evidence in order to induce uncritical acceptance; (4) *transfer,* persuading people to accept propaganda by associating it with respected institutions, traditions, or reputable persons; (5) *testimonials,* inducing people to accept untrue or one-sided ideas because respected authorities have done so; (6) *plain folks,* urging individuals to approve views or proposals because they would thereby be following traditions and customs of their group or class; (7) *bandwagon,* appealing for the acceptance of propaganda to help defeat opposing ideas and become a member of the winning team.

---

* The Springfield Plan consisted of readings, discussions, excursions, and everyday activities whereby schoolchildren from diverse ethnic, social, and cultural backgrounds learned mutual respect and democratic citizenship. The program was widely acclaimed as a community's total war against prejudice.

Quoting a phrase coined by the great sociologist Edward A. Ross, Herbert Blumer referred to an extreme form of the bandwagon appeal as "crowd-mindedness," manifested at times in patriotic hysteria. Blumer, Alfred McClung Lee, and Elizabeth Briant Lee noted the resistance of established institutions to change and the attempts of special-interest groups to control and manipulate instruments of mass communication and propaganda, such as newspapers, periodicals, radio and television programs, films, and books; also the use of repetitive advertising, concealment or distortion of information, slogans, catchwords, partial truths, public meetings, strikes, demonstrations, and the like to sway and control public opinion and the direction of social change. From the point of view of contemporary social psychologists, however, root causes and basic mechanisms that make people susceptible to propaganda remain to be scientifically investigated.

TAYLOR, MAYO, MÜNSTERBERG, BURTT, DICHTER

At the turn of the century, the American economist Thorstein Bunde Veblen (1857–1929) condemned the wasteful, ostentatious behavior patterns of the rich in modern Western society and the tendency of the masses to envy and emulate them. Veblen advocated scientific analysis of and control over economic enterprises to eliminate wasteful, unnecessary, useless or harmful products and distorted modes of living. At about the same time, the practical Pennsylvania inventor and engineer Frederick W. Taylor was advocating scientific industrial methods based upon time, distance, and motion studies of work being performed in shops and factories. His system of evaluation (demonstrated initially at the Midvale Steel Works and at the Bethlehem Steel Company) improved the selection and training of employees, increased the efficiency of labor, and revolutionized incentives and management-labor relationships.

Despite opposition by labor groups and managers, Taylor's system of determining the most efficient work loads and motions, time allotments, rest periods, and hand-brain machine operations speeded production and was widely adopted by industry.

His approach made work more monotonous because of the repetitive, machinelike labor required, but in the final analysis resulted in improved skills of workers, more production and profits, higher wages, and higher standards of living for the majority.
Time studies and the stopwatch became familiar features in
business and industry throughout the Western world. Taylor
predicted that in the long run workers and owners would in
most cases develop mutual respect, friendly or at least tolerant
relationships, and mutual understanding, and would voluntarily
coordinate their efforts to achieve benefits for all participants in
economic enterprises.

Applying a similar scientific approach to industrial relationships, Elton Mayo and his colleagues at Harvard University
studied the motivation and work habits of employees in the
Western Electric Company, a manufacturing unit of the American Telephone and Telegraph Company. They reported that social relationships among the employees had much greater influence than their working conditions upon the rate and quality of
work. Friendly rapport, cooperative attitudes, and respect for
fellow employees enhanced the individual's self-respect, self-
confidence, enthusiasm, and efficiency. Many workers were determined to restrict the rate of work to what the group as a
whole felt to be fair and reasonable for the rank and file. Motivated by this loyalty to the group, they did not respond favorably
to tempting offers of extra pay for faster work, or to appeals on
behalf of company profits and future prosperity. For them, loyalty to the interests, welfare, and decisions of the group became
a decisive motive for an attitude of in-group conformity and even
self-sacrifice. Similar attitudes in an extreme form are often seen
among soldiers, policemen, and firemen who protect and risk
their lives on behalf of their associates.

Differences among individuals in attitudes and behavior patterns of everyday life were investigated by the German-American experimental psychologist Hugo Münsterberg (1863–1916),
who pioneered in this field both at the ancient Freiburg University (founded in 1453) in the 1890s and later from 1897 to 1916
at Harvard University, where he directed work on a new psychological laboratory. Münsterberg believed that human rela-

tionships should be evaluated on the basis of each individual's moral will and dominant lifelong beliefs and motives. Ideals and lifetime purposes endure, he said, but factual information and judgment are transient or often inaccurate. Münsterberg's experiments demonstrated the fallibility and unreliability of the observations and judgments of witnesses in legal trials and the adverse effects of fatigue upon workers' reliability and work performance despite maximum incentives and rewards.

The American psychologist Harold E. Burtt, specializing in animal and applied psychology, elaborated on the conclusions of Münsterberg and of Kraepelin (see p.136), citing experimental evidence, for instance, that inattention, emotional disturbances, physical defects, lack of training, confusing distractions or suggestions, and faulty recollection of events often distort the reports of well-intentioned and intelligent witnesses in legal trials.

In his *Psychology of Everyday Living* (1947), Ernest Dichter (who had studied under the noted specialist in communication Paul Lazarsfeld in Vienna) described his motivation-research techniques that were designed to advertise goods more effectively and adapt products to the desires, emotions, and needs of consumers. Dichter organized a panel of representative American families and conducted interviews with them not only to discover their preferences for a particular brand of product but also to explore the sociological, psychological, aesthetic, and practical reasons for their preferences. Among the factors he considered were personal ideals, self-images, suggestibility, prejudices, conscious or unconscious inhibitions or frustrations, physical or mental difficulties, family situations, personal attitudes, and habits—in brief, all the basic motives and circumstances that influence the preference of consumers for available or potentially available products and services.

Dichter's depth psychology methods in motivation research were remarkably successful in increasing sales and adapting or redesigning products for that purpose. If the majority of consumers prefer heavy white soap bars because they seem to be pure, solid, and dependable, or soap that easily produces a rich lather that will caress the skin pleasantly, such revelations can provide psychological cues for manufacturers who wish to please the public taste and for advertisers who attempt to associate their arguments and appeals with the emotions and desires of the greatest possible number of potential customers.

Critics blamed Dichter for the misuse of his methods by corporations that captured markets from competitors by associating, not really superior or even equally good, but inferior, defective, or harmful merchandise with the intimate desires and personality traits of consumers. In a highly competitive society, moreover, even providers of good products may be tempted to exaggerate or to make dubious appeals for the sake of short-term advantages instead of depending upon eventual long-term demand for superior merchandise. On the other hand, Dichter's research method could also be used by business managers farsighted enough to tell the whole truth about their products and services.

It should be noted, nevertheless, that information reported by any sampling of individuals and families can sometimes be superficial, incomplete, or inaccurate, and some of the truly significant biological, environmental, historical, economic, social, psychological, and other forces affecting human behavior may remain unexplored, unknown, or unpredictable. Even in the case of a single group or society, sociologists and anthropologists differ about facts, causes, and interpretations involved in observed or reported evidence. Despite years of observing one individual, psychologists and psychiatrists may fail to discover the true cause-effect relationships and decisive factors affecting his behavior. But Dichter's motivation researches represented a potentially useful application of depth psychology to the study of group behavior and commercial pursuits of everyday living.

PARK, McKENZIE, BARKER, ET AL.

In recent decades, still another field of applied psychology, that of environmental psychology, developed as a significant area of scientific research. Leading sociologists, especially Robert E. Park, R. D. McKenzie, Louis Wirth, Harvey Zorbaugh, Frederic M. Thrasher, and W. F. Whyte, all formerly at the University of Chicago, analyzed the spatial distribution of population in the physical environment and consequent effects on modes of living and human relationships in urban areas, slums, business districts, suburbs, and rural areas. In the 1960s and 1970s, R. G. Barker, J. R. Aiello, I. Altman, and many other researchers conducted comparable studies from a social psychological point of view. Barker commented that information derived about the environment was generally highly complex and that the conclusions were extremely controversial. Experienced investigators often disagreed, for example, about the prevalence, causes, and effects of air pollution. For decades, school administrators debated the educational advantages of large versus small schools. Nevertheless, some new findings were widely accepted—as, for example, a study by E. P. Williams which indicated that students enrolled in small schools tended to develop a greater sense of self-importance and self-esteem than students in larger schools.

In 1974 the psychologist William N. Dember, formerly at the University of Michigan, characterized the continuing environmental researches as a cognitive revolution in psychology. In the 1970s, the American Psychological Association organized a division for research on population and environmental psychology to investigate the relationships between the environment and human behavior and to ascertain and analyze the specific reactions of people to environmental conditions. Environmental problems reached far beyond particular individuals, organizations, and local communities, involving states, nations, and world regions—as, for example, in studies of pollution of air, water, food, and other resources.

Of special interest in the 1970s were the preliminary researches of Aiello, Altman, and others on the way people perceive and react to residential crowding, posing questions such as the following: Does it bring people into closer social relationship? How does it change their attitudes, stresses, and personality? How do they cope with it? What kinds of environments do most people willingly accept or tolerate? What psychological factors impel them to act or to remain passive about adverse environmental conditions? The individual's perceptions of space, geographic area, and objects and features of the environment, and his feelings and overt reactions to those perceptions, were

being explored by many investigators. In 1981, to cite one illus-
tration, prison wardens reported that crowding of prisoners in
inadequate cells and outdated buildings created resentments,
frustrations, and violent explosions among inmates, engendering
fear and hostility instead of motives for rehabilitation. Recently,
reactions to environmental situations were analyzed in hundreds
of research studies, attempting, for example, to determine why
some people accept buses or prefer some other form of transpor-
tation, or what are the psychological effects of nearness of people
to one another, or of intimacy. Clearly the field of environmental
psychology is in its infancy and, as in many other special fields
of psychology, the basic problems have yet to be fully delineated
and properly integrated into the fabric of general psychology.

INDEX

Abnormal behavior, 240-71
Abraham, Karl, 236
Abstract thinking and personality, 234
Abulia, 254
Achievement tests, 128-31
Achillini, Alessandro, 9
Action, 133-51
Adjustment, types, 133-51, 171-72
Adler, Alfred, 92, 145, 170, 199, 236
Adolescence, 82, 85, 89, 90, 92, 93,
    146, 242
Adrenal glands, 137, 160
Adrian, Edgar Douglas, 16
Adult learning, 86-87, 96
Advertising, 293-94
Aesclepiades, 241
Aesthetics, 154
Afterimages, 34, 174, 188
Agassiz, Jean Louis Rodolphe, 83
Age, and learning, 86-87, 96
    and memory, 189
Agrippa, Cornelius Heinrich, 244
Aiello, J. R., 295
Alcohol addiction, 69, 242, 257
Alcoholics Anonymous, 250
Alcuin, 100-101
Alexander, Franz, 162
Alexander of Tralles, 242
All or None Law, 16
Allport, Floyd H., 143
Allport, Gordon Willard, 90, 91, 123,
    137, 232, 285
Altman, I., 295
Alzheimer's disease, 260
Ambiverts, 230, 236
American College Testing
    Examinations (ACT), 121
American Psychiatric Association, 249
Ames, Adelbert, Jr., 48
Ames, Louise B., 97
Amphetamines, 271
Analytical psychology, 268
Angell, James Rowland, 40, 185

Anger, 156, 157, 159
Animal learning, 208, 212, 213, 217
Anna O., 169
Antabuse, 271
Anxiety, 92, 267
Aphasia, 18
Apperceptive base, 48, 180, 184
Applied psychology, 272-96
Aptitude tests, 119-22
Aquinas, Saint Thomas, 175, 203, 223
Arai, Tsuru, 135, 209
Arber, Werner, 64
Aretaeus, 6-7, 241-42
Aristotle, on character, 221-22
    on emotions, 152
    on heredity, 54-55
    on human growth, 79
    on imagination and dreams, 174-75
    on individual differences, 100
    on learning and reasoning, 201-2
    on mental disorders, 241
    on perception, 28, 36
    on physical structure, 4-5, 14
Army Alpha Examination, 112, 113
Army Beta Examination, 112-13
Arthur, Mary G., 109
Ascham, Roger, 204
Association of ideas, 36, 174, 175-79,
    180
Associative shifting, 212
Asthenics, 230, 259
Athletics, 230, 260
Attention, 42, 44, 46, 47, 48
Attitude-interest test, 107
Augustine, Saint, 3, 28, 175, 203, 223
Authoritarian policies, 148, 262, 283
Autistic reactions, 257, 260
Autoinstruction, 214-15
Averrhoes, 242
Avicenna, 242

Bacon, Francis, 179-80, 205, 223-24
Baer, Karl Ernst von, 58, 83

297

Bain, Alexander, 17, 178–79, 227
Bakke case, the, 286n
Baldwin, Bird T., 96
Ballard, Philip B., 117, 197
Baltes, P. B., 98
Barbiturates, 271
Bard, Philip, 159
Barker, R. G., 295
Bartlett, Frederic C., 196
Basilar membrane, 35, 36
Beck, Aaron T., 266
Bedlam hospital, 244
Beers, Clifford Wittingham, 249–50
Behaviorism, 88–89
Behaviorists, 23–24
Beilin, H., 219
Bekhterev, Vladimir Mikhailovich, 192–93, 281
Bell, Sir Charles, 12
Bell Adjustment Inventory, 124
Belle indifference, 253
Bender, Lauretta, 260
Benedict, Ruth, 262, 285
Beneke, Friedrich Eduard, 229
Bennett, George K., 119
Berger, Frank M., 271
Berger, Hans, 269
Berenger di Carpi, 10
Bergson, Henri, 20
Berkeley, George, 36, 176
Bernard, Claude, 20
Bernheim, Hippolyte-Marie, 253, 278, 279
Bernreuter, Robert G., 123–24
Binet, Alfred, 37, 82, 104–6
Binocular vision, 34, 35
Biologists, 47–60
Birth trauma, 90, 170
Black women, self-image of, 286
Bleuler, Eugen, 68, 256–57
Blumer, Herbert, 284, 291
Boas, Franz, 284–85
Boredom in learning, 209–10
Boring, Edward G., 150–51
Bouchard, Thomas J., Jr., 69
Braid, James, 168, 252
Brain cortex, 17, 24, 25, 46, 192, 197
Brain injuries, 18, 242
Brain surgery, 270
Brain waves, 162, 269
Brandeis, Louis Dembitz, 287n
Bray, Charles W., 36
Breese, Burtis Burr, 35
Breuer, Joseph, 169, 170
Bridges, Katherine M. B., 98, 167
Broca, Paul, 269
Bronner, A. F., 263
Brown, Thomas, 177–78

Brown, Warner, 197
Bruner, Jerome S., 53, 77
B-type images, 231, 232
Buffon, Georges Leclerc, 57
Bühler, Karl Ludwig, 81
Burdon-Sanderson, Sir John Scott, 43
Burks, Barbara S., 74

Cameron, Norman A., 262
Cannon, Walter Bradford, 20, 147–48, 159–60, 162, 334
Carlson, Julius, 160, 161
Carr, Harvey A., 49, 50, 165
Carus, Carl Gustav, 229
Catatonia, 256
Catharsis, 169
Cattell, James McKeen, 38, 39, 103
Cattell, Raymond B., 116, 117, 124
CAVD tests, 116
Celsus, Aulis Cornelius, 6, 241
Cerebral injuries, 18
Cerebral localization, 17, 18
Character, 42, 220–39
Charcot, Jean Martin, 168, 252–53
Chiarugi, Vincenzo, 248
Children's Apperception Test, 127
Chromosomes, 59
Cicero, Marcus Tullius, 100, 202
Circular reaction, 284
Claparède, Edouard, 26, 109
Clark, Kenneth B., 285
Classification of mental disorders, 256, 258–59
Claudy, John C., 85
Client-centered counseling, 74
Closure, principle of, 52
Coghill, George E., 24
Cognitive processes, 215, 216, 218, 219
Cognitive psychology, 53, 77
Cognitive self-concepts, 231
Cognitive therapy, 266
Colet, John, 204
Collective behavior, 281–84
College Entrance Examination Board achievement tests, 131
College Entrance Examination Board Scholastic Aptitude Test (SAT), 121
Color perception, 32–35
Comenius, John Amos, 81, 205
Compensation, 145, 146, 150, 171
Competition, 148, 273
Conant, James Bryant, 126n
Conditioned reflex, 22–23, 281
Conditioning, 88–89, 212–14
Configuration, 51, 52, 218
Conolly, John, 246–47
Conservation of energy, 31, 32

Consolidation in memory, 183
Contiguity, law of, 174
Continuity, principle of, 52
Contrast, law of, 174
Conversion hysteria, 267
Cooley, Charles H., 80, 281–82
Cooperation, 48
Correlation, 60, 61
Corti, Alfonso, 35
Co-twin control, 66
Creative imagination, 217
Cretinism, 257–58
Crick, Francis C. H., 63
Crile, George Washington, 160–61
Criminality, 70, 75–76
Crowder, Norman A., 215
Culture epochs, 84
Culture Fair Intelligence Test, 117
Cuvier, Georges Léopold Chrétien
    Frédéric Dagobert, 5
Cystothymes, 230

Dana, Charles, 159
Dancing mania, 243
Darwin, Charles Robert, 5, 57, 155
Dashiell, John F., 151
Davis, Kingsley, 71–72, 92
Daydreaming, 147
Debs, Eugene Victor, 289
Deduction, logical, 202
Defense mechanisms, 145, 146, 147,
    150
Delinquency, 75–76
Delusions, 241
Dember, William N., 295
Dement, W. C., 199
Dementia praecox, 68, 256
Democratic methods, 283
Democritus of Abdera, 2, 4, 79
Demonology, 243, 245
Depression and electric shock
    treatment, 271
Depth psychology, 293–94
Descartes, René, 152
Developmental stages, 81, 90–99
De Vries, Hugo, 59
Dewey, John, functionalist views of,
    19, 24, 35
    on growth and development, 87, 88,
        98
    on ideas and emotions, 153, 165
    on learning, 216–17
    on memory, 185
    on mind and reality, 38, 40
    on motivation and adjustment, 143–
        45
    on personality development, 234
    on social psychology, 276

Dichter, Ernest, 293–94
Dilantin, 271
Dioscorides, Pedacius, 6, 7
Dissociation, 168, 253, 254
Distributed practice, 182, 183
Dix, Dorothea Lynde, 249
DNA molecule, 63, 64
Doll, Edgar A., 124
Doob, Leonard W., 287, 288
Down, John Haydon, 258
Downey, June E., 123
Downs, R. M., 78
Drawings as tests, 109–10
Dreams, 14, 23, 174, 189, 198–200,
    241, 267
Drives, 143, 146, 147, 171
Drugs and emotions, 172
Dugdale, Richard Louis, 61
Dunbar, Helen Flanders, 162
Durkheim, Émile, 282–83
Dysplastics, 230, 260

Ear, basilar membrane of, 35, 36
Ebbinghaus, Hermann, 38, 104, 129,
    179–82, 183
Ectomorphy, 231
Effect, law of, 193, 211
Ego, 145, 276
Eidetic imagery, 189, 231–32
Electra complex, 145, 235
Electroconvulsive shock treatment, 183,
    271
Electroencephalograms (EEGs), 161,
    199, 269
Elliotson, John, 251–52
Emotions, 152–72
Empedocles of Agrigentum, 20, 54
Endler, N. S., 239
Endomorphy, 231
English, O. Spurgeon, 162
Environmental psychology, 294–96
Environmental studies and heredity,
    69–78
Environment and heredity, 54–78
Epigenetic theory, 57
Epilepsy, 269
Erasistratus, 6
Erasmus, Desiderius, 101, 204
Erikson, Erik H., 90, 91, 170
Eros, 145, 221, 235, 241
Esquirol, Jean Etienne Dominique,
    247
Estrogenic hormones, 271
Eugenics, 62
Evolution and emotions, 156
Exercise, law of, 187, 211
Existentialists, 236–37
Expectancy, 194

Extrasensory perception, 19
Extrovert, 140, 230, 236

Fabricius, Hieronymus, 10
Factor analysis, 115, 116, 117, 118
Faculty psychology, 82, 154
Family relationships, 265, 266
Family studies, 92
Faris, Ellsworth, 262
Farrand, Livingston, 103-4
Fatigue, 47, 48, 135, 137, 210
Fechner, Gustav Theodor, 28, 29-30, 154
Feeling, 43, 46
Feldman, M., 162
Fenichel, Otto, 236
Ferenczi, Sandor, 268
Ferrier, Sir David, 18
Filelfo, Francesco, 204
Flourens, Pierre Marie, 12, 17
Forgetting, 180-81, 182, 192, 198
Foster children, 74-75
Fouillée, Alfred Jules Émile, 226
Fourier, Charles, 149, 225
Franz, Shepherd Irving, 25
Free association, technique of, 267
Freeman, Frank N., 66-67, 74
Freeman, Walter, 270
French, Thomas M., 162
Freud, Anna, 264-65
Freud, Sigmund, on emotions, 169, 170
    on forces and levels of consciousness, 20, 26
    on mental illnesses, 266-68
    on motivation and adjustment, 145
    on personality, 74, 90, 235-36
    on sleep and dreams, 198-99, 200
    on social psychology, 275-76
Fritsch, G., 18
Froebel, Friedrich Wilhelm August, 80, 206
Fromm, Erich, 170, 236
Functionalist psychology, 24, 26, 40, 49-50, 139

Galen, Claudius, 1, 6, 7-9, 221, 242
Gall, Franz Joseph, 17
Galton, Sir Francis, 60, 61, 62, 101, 122
Galvani, Luigi, 12
Galvanic skin reflexes, 161
Garrett, Henry E., 151
Gelman, R., 219
General Educational Development Tests, 131
Generalization, 188

Genes, 59, 62, 63, 64, 65
Genetics, 59, 60, 101, 172
Gesell, Arnold Lucius, 66, 93-95
Gestalt psychology, 40, 50, 88, 154, 194, 217
Gheel, 243
Gifted children, 72-73
Glucksberg, S., 219
Glueck, Eleanor Touroff, 75-76
Glueck, Sheldon, 75-76
Glutamic acid for retarded, 271
Goddard, Henry Herbert, 61-62, 106
Goldstein, Kurt, 127, 233-234
Goodenough, Florence L., 110
Gorgias of Leontini, 2
Graaf, Regnier de, 56, 57
Granit, Ragnar, 21
Griesinger, William, 254
Growth, 79-99
Guarino da Verona, 101, 204
Guthrie, Edwin Ray, 25, 88, 89, 167, 192, 214

Habits, 138, 139, 140, 143, 154, 234
Haeckel, Ernst Heinrich, 83
Hall, Granville Stanley, 39, 82-85, 156
Hall, Marshall, 12-13
Haller, Albrecht von, 11, 254
Hallucinations, 241
Hamilton, Sir William, 178
Handwriting scales, 129
Hartley, David, 36, 177
Hartshorne, Hugh, 97, 123, 238
Harvey, William, 10, 56
Hathaway, S. R., 124
Havighurst, Robert J., 98, 99
Hayakawa, Sam I., 77
Hearing, 30, 35-36
Hebephrenia, 256
Hebrew view of mental illness, 240
Hecht, Selig, 21, 34
Heidegger, Martin, 237
Heidenhain, Rudolf Peter Heinrich, 253
Heilbroner, R., 148
Helmholtz, Herman Ludwig Ferdinand, 31-37
Henle, Friedrich Gustav Jacob, 11, 154, 226
Herbart, Johann Friedrich, 82, 153, 180, 206-7
Heredity and environment, 54-78
Hering, Ewald, 14, 33, 34-35, 187
Herophilus, 5-6
Hildreth, Gertrude, H., 109
Hilgard, Ernest R., 215-16

Hillegas English composition scale, 129
Hippocrates, 1-4, 161, 220, 240-41
Hitzig, E., 18
Hobbes, Thomas, 36, 152, 176
Hoch, Paul H., 269, 271
Hollingworth, Harry Levi, 84
Holt, Edwin Bissell, 115
Holzinger, Karl J., 67
Homeostasis, 20, 147
Homogeneous classes, 104
Homosexuality, 90
Honig, Barry, 35
Hooke, Robert, 11
Hooton, Earnest Albert, 70
Hormic school of psychology, 141
Hormones, 98
Horne, Herman Harrel, 217
Horney, Karen, 92-93, 236, 262, 263
Hubel, David H., 21, 197
Humanists, 204
Hume, David, 36, 177
Humors, doctrine of, 2, 152
Hunter, Walter Samuel, 88
Hutton, James, 57
Huxley, Thomas Henry, 274
Hypnosis, 142, 169, 192, 251-54, 261, 279
Hysteria, 168, 169, 253, 254

Id, 90, 145
Ideas, Platonic, 173
Identical elements, 187-88, 210
Ilg, Frances L., 97
Illusions, 37, 41-42
Imageless thoughts, 45
Imagery, types of, 188-89
Imagination, 173, 176, 179, 191
Imitation, 279, 280
Individual differences, 100-132, 222
Individuation, 167
Inductive reasoning, 202, 216
Inertia, principle of, 137
Inferiority complex, 145-46, 285
Inhibition and memory, 183, 192
Inkblot Test, 126
Inner conflicts, 93
Insane persons, humane treatment of, 243, 244, 245, 246, 247, 248-50
Insight, 51, 213, 216, 218, 237
Insomnia and autosuggestion, 280
Instincts, 66, 86-88, 140-44, 149, 157
Insulin shock treatment, 270-71
Integration, neural, 24, 25
Intelligence, 81-82, 104, 105, 116
Intelligence tests, 73, 104-18
Intelligence test scores, 74

Interviews, 238
Introspection, 38, 39, 45, 51, 163, 203
Introvert, 142, 230, 236
Involutional melancholia, 271
Isolated children, 71-72
Itard, Jean Marc Gaspard, 70, 109
Ittelson, W. H., 78

Jackson, Douglas N., 125
Jaensch, Erich Rudolf, 231-32
James, William, on education, 208
  on emotions, 157-59
  on memory, 184-85
  on motivation and adjustment, 138-41
  on personality, 228-29, 234
  on physical structure, 4, 19
  on sensation, 45
Janet, Pierre Marie Félix, 168, 253
Jensen Educational Aptitude Test, 121
Jersild, Arthur T., 95-96
Jesuit schools, 204-5
Jewish children, 72, 73
Johannsen, Wilhelm, 59
John, E. Roy, 197
Johnson, Wendell, 77
Jones, Mary C., 167
Jost, Adolph, 182
Judd, Charles H., 39, 89-90, 188, 207
Juke family, 61
Jung, Carl Gustav, 122, 149, 171, 230, 236, 268-69
Juvenile delinquency, 75-76

Kahlbaum, Karl Ludwig, 256
Kallikak family, 61-62
Kallmann, Franz J., 68, 259, 263
Kant, Immanuel, 82, 152
Kelley, Truman L., 116
Kent-Rosanoff word-association test, 102, 122-23
Khachaturian, Z. S., 197
Kierkegaard, Sören, 236-37
Klein, Melanie, 264
Kleinman, D., 197
Kleitman, N., 199
Klineberg, Otto, 285
Kluckhohn, Clyde K. M., 92
Knowledge and character, 221
Koffka, Kurt, 40, 50-52, 88, 195, 217
Köhler, Wolfgang, 24, 40, 51, 88, 194, 195, 217
Kohut, Heinz, 265
Korte's law, 42
Korzybski, Count Alfred Habdank Skarbek, 53, 77
Kraepelin, Emil, 39, 68, 122, 136-38, 255, 293

Krafft-Ebing, Richard von, 247, 255
Krauskopf, C. J., 239
Kretschmer, Ernst, 230, 259
Kuder, George Frederic, 119
Kuelpe, Oswald, 39, 49, 134
Kuhlmann, Frederick, 108
Kuhlmann-Anderson Intelligence
    Tests, 108

Laboratory experiments, 133, 135,
    136, 138
Ladd-Franklin, Christine, 34–35
Laissez-faire policies, 281
Lamarck, Jean Baptiste Pierre de
    Monet, 57, 58
Lange, Karl Georg, 4, 157–59
Language, evolution of, 272–73
Lashley, Karl Spencer, 24, 115, 126n
Learning and reasoning, 201–19
Learning curves, 209
Le Bon, Gustave, 278–79
Lee, Alfred McClung, 287, 290, 291
Lee, Elizabeth Briant, 290, 291
Leonardo da Vinci, 34
Lewin, Kurt, 77, 88, 145, 196, 281
Libido, 20, 149, 185, 235
Liébeault, Ambroise Auguste, 253
Life space, 147
Limen, 30
Lindquist, Everet F., 130
Lindsley, Donald B., 162, 178
Linton, Ralph, 285
Lithium, 271
Lobotomy, 270
Locke, John, 36, 176, 205, 224
Loehlin, J. C., 67
Lombroso, Cesare, 75, 229–30
Lowell, Abbott Lawrence, 287, 287n
Loyola, Ignatius, 204–5
Lucas, Keith, 16
Lucretius, 55–56, 203
Lyell, Charles, 57

McCall-Thorndike Reading Scale, 130
McDougall, William, on character and
    personality, 42, 227
  on emotions, 157
  on heredity, 70, 76n
  on instincts, 19
  on learning, 208
  on motivation, 141–43
  on social nature of mind, 38
  on social psychology, 272, 274
McGeoch, John A., 183–84
McGraw, Myrtle B., 96
Mach, Ernst, 41
Machover, Karen, 110
McKenzie, R. D., 294

McKinley, J. J., 124
Magendie, François, 72
Magnan, Valentin, 255
Magnusson, D., 239
Maier, Norman R. F., 172
Maimonides, 175, 223
Make-a-Picture-Story Test, 128
Malinowski, Bronislaw Kasper, 262,
    272
Maller, Julius B., 148
Malpighi, Marcello, 11
Malthus, Thomas Robert, 58
Manic-depressive psychosis, 256, 260
Manifest Anxiety Scale, 128
Marie Three-Paper Test, 111
Masserman, Jules, 172
Maturation, 94–99, 235
May, Mark A., 97, 123, 238
May, Rollo, 200
Mayo, Elton, 292
Mead, George Herbert, 38, 276–77
Mead, Margaret, 285
Medical aptitude tests, 121
Meduna, Ladislas J. von, 271
Mehrabian, A., 124
Meier, Norman C., 119, 120
Memory, 140, 173–200
Memory-for-Designs Test, 111
Memory images, eidetic, 231
Mendel, Father Gregor Johann, 59–60
Menopause, 242
Mental abilities, 116
Mental age, 106
Mental faculties doctrine, 140
Mental heredity of twins, 65–69
Mental illness, 240–71
Mental set, 21, 47, 49
Meprobamate, 271
Merrill, Maude A., 73, 106, 107
Merritt, H. H., 271
Mesmer, Franz Anton, 168, 250–51
Mesomorphy, 231
Methadone hydrochloride, 271
Metrazol, 271
Metropolitan Achievement Test Series,
    131
Meumann, Ernst, 38, 42–43, 226
Meyer, Adolf, 260–61
Meynert, Theodor Hermann, 254
Miles, Catharine Cox, 107, 124
Mill, James, 36, 37, 178
Mill, John Stuart, 38, 178, 226
Miller, Clyde R., 287, 289–90
Miller, George A., 53, 77, 182
Milton, John, 205
Minnesota Multiphasic Personality
    Inventory, 124
Mittelmann, Béla, 162

Mondino de' Luzzi, 9
Mongolism, 258
Moniz, Egas, 270
Montessori, Maria, 109
Moos, R. H., 78
More, Sir Thomas, 204
Morel, B. A., 255
Moreno, Jacob L., 264
Morgan, Christiana D., 126
Morgan, Thomas Hunt, 63
Morrison, S., 162
Motivation, 133–51, 209–10, 211–12,
    213–15, 221–22, 232
Motivation research, 293–94
Motor development, 95
Motor learning, 48
Motor processes, 48
Movement, perception of, 42
Mowrer, Orval H., 92
Mulcaster, Richard, 205
Muller, Anton, 248
Müller, Fritz, 83
Müller, Georg Elias, 33, 182–83
Müller, Johannes Peter, 1, 11, 13–15,
    63, 226
Münsterberg, Hugo, 39, 209–10, 292
Murphy, Gardner, 151, 229
Murray, Henry Alexander, 77, 126

Nakanishi, Koji, 35
National Achievement Tests, 131
National Teacher Examinations, 121
Nelson, A. K., 167
Nerve impulses, 16, 30, 187
Nerves, sensory and motor, 12
Nervous system, 159–60, 165, 166
Nervous system and memory, 183–88,
    192
Neugarten, B. L., 99
Neurasthenia, 254, 267
Neurobiotaxis, 115
Neuron theory, 15
Neuroses, 113, 169, 172, 254, 256,
    262, 267
Newman, Horatio Hackett, 66–67
Nichols, R. C., 67
Nietzsche, Friedrich Wilhelm, 273
Normal distribution curve, 101, 103

Oblivescence, 178
Obsessive compulsive neurosis, 267
Oedipus complex, 145, 235
Ohio State University Psychological
    Test, 121
Operant conditioning, 194, 214
Optical illusions, 41, 42, 48, 51
Orbell, J. M., 148
Osgood, Charles E., 95

Otis, Arthur S., 113
Overlearning, 181, 184
Owen, Robert, 225

Pangenesis, 58
Paracelsus, Theophrastus, 9, 244, 250
Paranoia, 254, 255, 262
Paresis, 247, 256, 257
Park, Robert E., 77, 278, 294
Parsons, Talcott, 277
Paunonen, Sampo V., 125
Pavlov, Ivan Petrovich, 1, 4, 22–26,
    191–92, 212–13
Pearson Karl, 60–61, 75, 102, 103,
    104
Peck, R. F., 98
Peirce, Charles Sanders, 139–40
Perception, 28–53
Pérez, Bernard, 234
Perls, Frederick, 266
Perseveration, 183
Personality and character, 220–39
Personality development, 90–93, 95,
    97, 98–99, 122–28, 236
Personality disorders, 258
Personality tests, 238
Personality traits, 60, 222, 223, 226,
    227, 230, 232
Pestalozzi, Johann Heinrich, 206
Peter of Albano, 5, 9
Petrarch, 204
Phrenologists, 17
Physical education aptitude tests, 121
Physical structure, 1–27
Piaget, Jean, 76, 81, 93, 195, 218, 280
Picture-Frustration Test, 128
Pillsbury, Walter Bowers, 46–49, 150,
    157, 171, 188, 237
Pilzecker, Alfons, 182–83
Pinel, Philippe, 70, 71, 247, 253
Pintner, Rudolf, 108–9, 114
Pintner-Paterson Performance Tests,
    108, 109
Plateaus in learning, 209
Plato, 4, 28, 100, 173, 201, 221, 241
Play activities, 97
Poole, Lawrence, 270
Porteus, Stanley D., 110–11
Positron emission tomography (PET),
    172, 271
Practice and memory, 180–81, 184
Pratt, K. C., 167
Prefrontal lobotomy, 270
Pressey, S. L., 214–15
Pressure sensations, 30
Preyer, Wilhelm Thierry, 80
Problem-solving, steps in, 216–17
Programmed learning materials, 214

Progressive education movement, 217
Projective tests, 126–28
Propaganda, 287–91
Proshansky, H. M., 78
Proximity, principle of, 52
Psychasthenia, 254
Psychoanalysis, 266
Psychoanalytical theory, 20
Psychobiology, 261
Psychodrama, 264
Psychoneurotic disorders, 258
Psychoses, 256, 258, 262
Psychosexual personality, 90
Psychosomatic ailments, 161–63, 258
Psychosomatic Medicine, 162
Public opinion, 287
Purkinje, Johannes Evangelista, 12, 33
Putnam, T. J., 27
Pyknics, 230, 259
Pythagoras, 240

Questionnaires, 123, 124, 125, 237
Quintilian, Marcus Fabius, 100, 175, 203

Race prejudice, 285–86, 289, 290n
Racial inheritance and emotions, 171
Radosavljevich, Paul R., 38
Ramón y Cajal, 15
Rank, Otto, 90–91, 170, 236
Rating scales, 238
Rationalization, 147, 150
Ratke, Wolfgang, 205
Reaction levels, 142
Reaction times, 49, 133–34, 135
Readiness, law of, 187, 211
Reasoning and learning, 201–19
Recall, 182, 184–92
Recapitulation theory, 83, 84
Rechtschaffen, A., 200
Recognition, 182, 189–90
Reconditioning, 168
Reflex arc, 50
Reflexes, 13, 86, 134, 136, 166
Reik, Theodor, 36
Rein, Wilhelm, 84
Reinforcement, 193, 194, 214
Relearning method, 180–81
Religious ideals, 141, 272, 274
Remmers, H. H., 119, 120
REM (rapid eye movements), 199
Repetition, 180–82, 184
Repression, 145, 150, 156, 157
Respondent conditioning, 194
Retardation, 248, 258, 271
Retention, 176, 181, 183–87, 188, 190, 193

Retroactive inhibition, 183
Ribot, Théodule Armand, 47, 48, 155
Rice, Joseph Meyer, 129
Riesman, David, 284
RNA molecules, 64
Rogers, Carl Ransom, 74–75, 263
Rohrer, J. H., 74
Rolf, Ida P., 266
Rorschach, Hermann, 126, 238
Rosenzweig, Saul, 128
Ross, Edward Alsworth, 287, 291
Rouke, Fabian L., 270
Rousseau, Jean Jacques, 81, 152, 206, 224
Royce, J. R., 172
Rubin, Edgar J., 41
Rufus of Ephesus, 6, 7
Rush, Benjamin, 249
Russell, Bertrand, 82
Rutherford, B., 148

Saint Vitus's dance, 243
Sakel, Manfred J., 270
Sallenger, R. T., 98
Sapir, Edward, 53, 77, 219
Sartre, Jean-Paul, 200, 237
Savings method, 180–82
Scarpa, Antonio, 11
Scheerer, M., 127
Scheler, Max, 228
Schilder, Paul, 260
Schiller, Friedrich von, 162
Schizophrenia, 68, 256, 260, 262, 263, 271
Schizothymes, 230
Schleiden, Matthias Jacob, 12
Schneidman, E. S., 128
Schools of psychological thought, 26–27
Schopler, J., 78
Schultze, Max Johann Sigismund, 12
Schwann, Theodor, 11, 12
Scientists, 9–13, 56, 62–65
Scott, Reginald, 245
Seashore, Carl Emil, 120, 186
Seguin, Édouard, 109, 248
Self-image, 276–77
Selye, Hans, 162
Semantic movement, 77
Senile dementia, 262
Senile psychoses, 270
Sensation, 28–53
Sensory-motor circuit, 50
Sentence-completion test, 104, 129
Shatz, M., 219
Sheldon, William H., 230–31

Sherrington, Sir Charles, 1, 15–17, 159
Shields, James, 67
Shinn, Millicent, 80
Shirley, Mary M., 95
Sidis, Boris, 280
Similarity law of Aristotle, 52
Similarity principle in Gestalt psychology, 174
Simmel, Georg, 282
Simon, Théodore, 105, 106
Skinner, Burrhus Frederic, 23, 88, 167, 194, 213, 215, 265, 277
Sleep, 23, 44, 192, 198, 199, 200
Smith, Madorah E., 95, 182
Smith, R. H., 172
Smith, Samuel, 131
Social interaction, 276
Socialization process, 275
Social psychology, 272–96
Socrates, 201
Somatotype, 231
Sömmering, Samuel Thomas von, 11
Space perception, 40, 41
Spearman, Charles Edward, 25n, 76, 115–16, 117
Specific Nerve Energies, doctrine of, 13–14
Speer, Robert K., 131
Spencer, Herbert, 58, 84, 154–55, 156, 178, 272
Sperry, Roger, 21
Spinoza, Baruch de, 152, 176
Spranger, Eduard, 232, 272, 274
Spurzheim, Johann Kaspar, 17
Standardized tests, criticisms of, 131–32
Stanford Achievement Test Series, 130
Stekel, Wilhelm, 268
Stenquist, John L., 119
Stern, William, 227–28
Stetcher, Lorle I., 96
Stimulus-response (S-R bond) theory, 187
Stoddard, George D., 73
Stokols, D., 78
Strayer, L. C., 66
Structural psychology, 37, 38, 39, 43, 50
Sturm, Johannes, 204, 205
Sublimation, 145, 150, 156
Suggestion, 252, 253, 254, 279, 280
Suicides, 283
Sullivan, Harry Stack, 93, 236
Sumner, William Graham, 278, 287
Sundstrom, E., 78
Superego, 145, 276

Superiority complex, 145–46, 285
Sydenham's chorea, 246
Synapse, 16
Syphilis, 244, 247
Szondi Test, 127–128

Tarde, Gabriel, 279
Taylor, Frederick W., 291–92
Taylor, J. A., 128
Tay-Sachs disease, 259
Teaching machines, 214–15
Telling method, 181–82
Temperament, 2, 42–43, 152, 220–21
Terman, Lewis Madison, 72–74, 106, 107, 113–14
Tests, criticisms of, 131–32
Tests and measurements, 100–132
Thematic Apperception Test, 126–27
Theophrastus, 55–56, 79, 221
Thorndike, Edward Lee, on growth and development, 85–87, 96
    on heredity, 65–66
    on imitation and suggestion, 280
    on laws of learning, 208–12, 213
    on memory and learning, 187, 193, 194, 197
    on mental states, 49
    on motivation and adjustment, 135
    on S-R bond connection, 21
    on types of intelligence, 116
Thorne, Frederick C., 263
Thurstone, Louis Leon, 97, 118, 287, 288
Thurstone, Thelma G., 118
Time, perception of, 40–41
Titchener, Edward Bradford, 39, 43–46, 65, 134, 164, 190
Tolman, Eugene Chace, 77, 148, 215
Tomography, 271
Topectomy, 270
Topological method, 146–47
Touch, 29
Trabasso, T., 219
Training and maturation, 96
Tranquilizers, 271
Transference, 267
Transfer in learning, 210
Trial-and-error learning, 194, 208
Trotter, Wilfred, 259
T-type images, 231, 232
Tuke, William, 246
Tumors, brain, 270
Twins, 60, 65–69, 96

Unconscious, 37, 44, 49, 85, 145, 149, 153, 155, 171, 275

Validity of tests, 125
Values and personality types, 232
Varoli, Costanzo, 10
Veblen, Thorstein Bunde, 291
Vesalius, Andreas, 10
Victor, "The Wild Boy of Aveyron," 70–71, 109
Vincent de Paul, Saint, 245
Vineland Social Maturity Scale, 124
Vision, 32–35
Vittorino da Feltre, 101, 204
Vocational aptitude tests, 119–22
Volta, Count Alessandro, 12
Voluntary action, 134, 135, 139, 140

Wagner-Jauregg, Julius, 257, 270
Waldeyer, Wilhelm von, 15, 59
Wallace, Alfred Russel, 58
Warden, Carl J., 148
Washburn, Margaret F., 45
Watson, James D., 63
Watson, John Broadus, 4, 23, 52, 88, 166, 193, 213, 265, 277
Watts, James W., 270
Weber, Ernst Heinrich, 28, 29
Weber, Max, 277
Weber-Fechner law, 30
Wechsler, David, 111–12
Weier, Johann, 245
Weismann, August, 58–59
Wellman, Beth L., 73

Wertheimer, Max, 39, 42, 88, 195, 217
Wever, Ernest G., 36
Wheatstone, Sir Charles, 34
Whorf, Benjamin L., 53, 77, 219
Wiesel, N. W., 197
Wiesel, Torsten N., 21
Willis, Thomas, 10, 17
Willoughby Emotional Maturity Scale, 123
Wilson, Woodrow, 289
Wingfield, A. H., 67
Wirth, Louis, 294
Witchcraft, 243, 244, 245, 246
Wolff, Christian von, 82
Wolff, Kaspar Friedrich, 56, 57
Wolpe, Joseph, 150
Woodrow, Herbert H., 185–86
Woodworth, Robert Sessions, 21, 45, 137, 143, 164, 187, 188
Word-association tests, 101, 122, 238
Wundt, Wilhelm, 37–43, 133, 163, 207

Yerkes, Robert M., 113, 114, 148
Young, Thomas, 11, 32, 33

Zeigarnik, Bluma, 405
Ziller, Tuiskon, 84
Zorbaugh, Harvey, 294
Zyve Scientific Aptitude Test, 121